JOURNEY OF FAITH
IN A HOSTILE WORLD

JOURNEY OF FAITH IN A HOSTILE WORLD

MEMOIRS OF HERMAN JANTZEN

Missionary to Turkestan, Caucasus and Bulgaria
Refugee from Bolshevik Russia

Herman Jantzen

iUniverse, Inc.
New York Bloomington Shanghai

JOURNEY OF FAITH IN A HOSTILE WORLD
MEMOIRS OF HERMAN JANTZEN

iUniverse books may be ordered through booksellers or by contacting:

iUniverse
1663 Liberty Drive
Bloomington, IN 47403
www.iuniverse.com
1-800-Authors (1-800-288-4677)

Because of the dynamic nature of the Internet, any Web addresses or links contained in this book may have changed since publication and may no longer be valid.

The views expressed in this work are solely those of the author and do not necessarily reflect the views of the publisher, and the publisher hereby disclaims any responsibility for them.

ISBN: 978-0-595-47658-9 (pbk)
ISBN: 978-0-595-91921-5 (ebk)

Printed in the United States of America

CONTENTS

FOREWORD

This is a translation of the Memoirs of Hermann Jantzen, 1866–1959, a self-styled missionary to Turkestan, the Caucasus and Bulgaria, from a typed German manuscript, transcribed by Ernest Kuhlman from the original hand-written copy.

The autobiography begins with the migration of several Russian Mennonite families from southern Russia to Turkestan in 1880, where several villages were established. Jantzen fled from the Bolshevik oppressors to Germany in 1923 and then lived for more than 35 years in The Netherlands until his death.

The translation from Kuhlman's German manuscript to English was done by Joseph A. Kleinsasser under the sponsorship of the late John H. Wiebe and Edwin J. Janzen. Some of the foreign words, principally Turkish and Dutch, were retained as in the manuscript unless English equivalents were available. Funk and Wagnalls College Dictionary was used as authority, while Cassells New German Dictionary was used in the translation.

The source of information in the Addendum is the *Mennonitische Rundschau*, Vol. 83, No. 22, and a letter to Ernest Kuhlman dated April 14, 1975, from Mrs. Hermann Jantzen, who lives in Hilversum, The Netherlands.

ACKNOWLEDGMENTS

*To those responsible for the translation of Herman Jantzen's Memoirs, for giving us permission to go ahead and get it printed!

*To Fred Plastow, who years ago read our mimeographed copy of this book, and ever since, has urged us to get its message out to others!

To Deloris, his wife, who did all the typing, etc. etc. etc.!

To Mark Jantzen, who supplied the pictures his father brought back from Holland!

To Henry A. Wiebe, who gave us the where-with-all to get started!

To the friends at Avant, who told us about iUniverse!

And to all who have encouraged us to get it done!

A big thank you!

—Peter Z. & Wilma Friesen

CHAPTER 1

▼

FROM YOUTH TO MIGRATION

I was born in the village of Hahnsau, in Trakt, in Samara Province, Russia on May 28, 1866, where I lived with my parents until I reached the age of 14. My father was Hermannn Jantzen and my mother Cornelia Jantzen, nee Horn. There were two sisters and four brothers. Of the boys, I was the oldest. My sister Marie was three years older than I and my sister Cornelia was the youngest child. In my opinion my mother was the very best woman on earth. I never saw her angry. With the help of two servant girls she was always busily engaged in managing the household. She had a beautiful soft voice and sang much. What Father's strictness could not always accomplish with us rather naughty boys, mother succeeded with her tender love.

Financially we were well off. Father owned about 180 *hektar* or about 450 acres of land. This was also considered three full estates or *Vollwirtschaften*. Farming in those days was big business. On our farm there was a large mill for grinding grain, which was always busy. The mill was managed by a fully trained miller from Prussia, for whom my Father provided a small house and also placed one *hektar* of land at his disposal.

The buildings of a well-to-do farmer were built of dried brick with the exception of the granary. Behind the house was a large garden and behind that was a forest of native trees, which ended at the Creek Tarlich. The village Hahnsau was located in a valley, which protected it from the great blizzards of the winter.

In our household there were three hired men, Russians from Pensa. The main reason for having them was that we would all learn the Russian language well. This was of great advantage to my father as well as for the children. Then, too, children learn a foreign language much more easily than do adults.

As far back as I can remember, my father was always the assistant chairman of our *Wollostj* or district, which was made up of the ten Mennonite villages of the area. Besides that, Father was treasurer of the district and chairman of the school board. As a result of his manifold official positions, he was away from home much of the time, spending it in the colonial courthouse in Koeppenthal, which lay about two kilometers from Hahnsau.

Beginning at age six all children walked daily to school. One teacher was Hermann Bartsch. From age eleven to fourteen I attended the district school at Koeppenthal. Then came a great change in all our lives.

Originally the Mennonites were invited by the Russian government to move from Prussia and settle in Russia with the assurance of freedom from military service and also freedom of religion. These promises were kept for many years. But suddenly a new law was passed which required military service of all the men in Russia, including the Mennonites. The law was passed in 1874 but did not go into effect until 1880.

During the intervening six years, all Mennonites in Russia sent delegations to Petersburg to see the highest officials and to try and regain their freedom from military service. My father also served twice as a delegate to Petersburg. However, their efforts were largely fruitless. The Mennonites did gain freedom from military service in exchange for entry into the forest service instead.

A large majority of our group agreed to this arrangement. But there were those who said that by entering the forest service they would free a Russian for military service in their stead, who would, in the event of war, kill other people. By this means they would, in an indirect way, become murderers and this their conscience did not allow.

My father and many of our relatives belonged to this group. But what was to be done? At this critical time my father was again sent as a delegate to Petersburg where he became acquainted with the then Governor of Turkestan, Baron von Kaufmann. After this man had carefully checked many of the details of our situation, he made our representatives the proposal to have them migrate to Turkestan where he had authority to grant settlers freedom from military service as well as exemption from taxes for 25 years.

This offer was presented to our congregations and, after thorough consideration, it was accepted. This was in the fall of 1879. During the coming winter my father sold all his land, as well as the *Hof* (farm yard) with its inventory and the cattle. Since he was the first to sell, he received a relatively high price. However, many who then followed his example were forced to accept lower prices.

Several years prior to these events my Uncle Claas Epp, my father's brother-in-law, had caused all manner of schism in the congregation because of his millennial teachings concerning the Second Coming of Christ. Many accused him of spiritual pride. Since I do not wish to go into great detail here, I refer the reader to the pamphlet *Unser Ausgang nach Mittelasien* (Our Migration to Asia Minor), written by Franz Bartsch, a former teacher in Lysanderhoeh, Samara. It may be ordered from Echo Publishers, North Kildonan, Manitoba, Canada. Teacher Bartsch was a dear friend of ours and, since he had no property, Father placed a new wagon and two horses with harness for his use. He traveled with our group, but before we could leave they had to bury their little daughter.

CHAPTER 2

▼

FROM HAHNSAU TO KOPLENBEK

On July 3, 1880 we left our beloved home. As our caravan of ten families in 18 wagons reached the highland above Hahnsau, we all stopped, stepped out of our wagons and looked back once more into the valley below, where our former homes were hidden among the trees. Many tears were shed. Many relatives and friends had accompanied us for some distance. After we had stayed overnight in the village of Hussenback, most of them left us and returned to their homes. Uncle Epp stayed with us the longest, but finally he also returned home. Not until two years later did he and his family join us.

We had four wagons with seven horses. The first was the largest, our family wagon, drawn by three horses. It had a door in the rear. This was the lead wagon and I was the driver. The driver of the second wagon was Jacob, son of Jacob Toews, who came with us because he would have entered the service in the fall. Our other drivers were brothers Gerhard and Bernhard. They each drove one horse who simply followed the wagon ahead.

By way of Nowousenk we reached the Ural River, which we crossed over a rough wooden bridge near the town of Ilek. Then we proceeded to the large and beautiful city of Orenburg, the last city in Russia. So far we had, for the most part, passed through well-populated regions, especially the beautiful area around Uralsk. In this beautiful Cossack city the inhabitants were very friendly and sold us hay and oats, milk and bread and other necessities. These Cossacks were Orthodox in faith, called *Starowertze* in Russian, and always wore uniforms.

In such places, when we lodged for the night, the *Attemann* or mayor would often come to us and inquire what sort of people we were and where we were going and other information. Several of us, including Father, who spoke Russian, would tell them that we were German people of the Volga region, who, because of our faith were moving to Turkestan, where we were promised more freedom. Then they would say: "You are a holy people because you have such high regard for your faith."

Since Father was the accepted leader of our group, our family wagon was invariably in the lead. When we stopped for the night I drove off the road and we formed a large circle with our wagons, forming a *Wagonburg*, with a large space within the circle. In our wagon there was a hand bell. Exactly by the clock, I had to ring the bell on Father's orders, whether to wake our people in the morning, indicate time for watering the horses, or after breakfast when we were to start in the way again. The bell also rang for the morning and evening devotions, for which we gathered within the *Wagonburg*. We did not travel on Sunday; then we had worship services in the morning and afternoon. There were two ministers in our midst, the Brethren Wilhelm Penner and Jonas Quiring, both spiritual men.

In Orenburg we rested for several days. Here the horses were shod, the wagons repaired, and the supplies bought for the journey ahead. From here the road would lead almost directly southward where we would find fewer villages and cities. Orenburg is a junction city. Almost without interval, camel caravans came through with goods from Turkestan and the Far East. Out of Siberia came furs as well as herds of horses that were especially large and well built, very tough and used to the extreme cold. Here also gathered great varieties of people year in and year out. From the west the railroad brought all manner of European goods. At that time the railroad terminated at Orenburg, there being as yet no Siberian railroad. In this famous world marketplace, one could hear a maze of languages, some of which we could not even name.

The Orenburgers and the Cossacks, because of their great gallantry and valor, always played an important role in the affairs of the Russian Empire. They were very religious and no one ever heard them curse or swear. They never shook hands with those of another faith. For guests they provided their own *samovar,* or tea urn, also glasses, plates and silverware. They never used these themselves. On the other hand, no foreigner was allowed to touch their personal tableware. They were, however, always friendly and hospitable. From age seventeen all men were in the military service, stationed in their home area.

The Ural River is the boundary between Europe and Asia, as well as between West and East Russia. In the East are many nomadic and thieverish tribes of Kirghaz people who must be guarded against. It was the duty of the Cossacks to provide this protection. They were therefore nearly always in the saddle and in uniform. Their women did the field work.

Without great incident our train proceeded southward. Finally we arrived at *Iletzkaja-Saschtchita,* where the large open salt mines are located. On the way we had already met long ox caravans, bringing the pink salt to Orenburg. There were also many camel caravans on this stretch of road, which was also an official Post road, therefore a good one.

Soon we arrived at the great *Torgei Steppes.* Here there were very few villages but rather the tents of the Kirghiz tribes who grazed their livestock here. They had large herds of sheep, horses and camels. We could not buy hay here so our horses had to graze. For quite a stretch we followed the small stream Ilek, which provided good water. When we stopped to rest near a great *Aula* or hall, our camp was soon surrounded by these tent-dwellers. We could not understand their language, but since our teacher, Bartsch, spoke some Tartar, and his wife even more, they could act as interpreters and we could acquire some much-needed supplies, for our stores were running very low. Sheep were very cheap, and when the fat of their tails was rendered, this lard was used to preserve meat quite well even in summer heat.

One day we arrived at the Russian fort of Aktjubinsk, where we could buy oats for the horses and bread for ourselves from the Cossacks and the Infantry. In the same manner we also acquired provisions at the Fort Karabutsk. However, it was much more difficult to find water and fuel for the fires.

Finally we arrived at the last fort, the small town Irgisen, just before the large desert. Here we could get any and all the supplies we needed. Since this was the last town before getting to the 400 kilometer-wide desert, in which no grass grew, we had to take along enough oats for the horses for the entire distance. We could not load all this in our wagons, so it became necessary to hire a camel caravan to transport the oats. The caravan had to stay right with us all the way. In this manner we hoped to have sufficient supplies until we reached Kasalinsk.

While all these preparations were being made, another week had passed. From Orenburg we had now come almost 600 kilometers southward. As a result, the weather had become much warmer. This caused considerable hardship for the horses, especially since water was often in short supply. In the course of the route, several children died. In one family three children died at almost the same time. Without much ceremony, they were buried by the wayside.

And so we went upon our way until we arrived at the worst stretch of 200 kilometers. Because of the deep loose sand, we had to put two or three extra teams of horses on each wagon in order to keep going. Then we had to unhitch and ride the horses back for the other wagons. This made for very slow progress. I have forgotten how often we had to repeat this process. Finally we came to the end of this terrible stretch of road and arrived at the Aral Sea

For some time the horses seemed to notice the nearness of water. They breathed the fresh air and we, as they, could breathe anew. Arriving at the sea, we noticed a low reed, which the horses devoured as though it were the best of feed. In the meantime each of us dug a well about one meter deep and we all had an abundance of water for man and beast.

Here we rested for a day and then continued on. Soon we arrived at the first Turkestani city and fort—Kasabinsk on the River Syrdarja, an Uzbeck-Turkish Sart town. The river enters the Aral Sea here, and the city is surrounded by wonderful wine and fruit orchards. There were also large tasty melons. All produce was very cheap. Because my Aunt Gerhard Jantzen gave birth to a child here, and a few others in our group were ill, we remained here for a week longer.

As we were about ready to leave, a fine young Sarter came to us and asked Father whether he could accompany us to Taschkent, where he lived. Without much ado, Father agreed to take him along, and, by his suggestion, he came and took a seat beside me on the wagon. He spoke rather good Russian and by this means I had my first Uzbeck-Turkish language instructor. Of course, on the last stretch of the desert I had learned considerable vocabulary from our Kirghiz camel drivers, but now I learned more every day in the presence of this really edu-cated and intelligent Sarter. He was a good interpreter and was of real value to us.

We continued on to Karamachi, on a bumpy road to Fort Perowsk, a larger Sart town. All the way we had no problem with our horses since there was an ample supply of water and fuel. The road led along the Sydarja River, through much scrub forestry in which were many pheasants, foxes and beautiful deer.

After we had rested in Fort Perowsk for a day and had done some necessary shopping, our road led us through Fort Dachulusto, an old historical city of Turkestan. The city offered all manner of sights of ancient times. Here we rested again to prepare for the crossing of the wild flowing mountain stream, the River Ariss, which gave us much trouble. With the help of some *Dachigiten*, the horse-back-riding servicemen of the government, we were all able to make the crossing safely.

From here one could already see the giant Tien Shan Mountains. The Chinese name means the "Heavenly Mountains." The Russians call them the Alexander Chain and the Uzbeck Turks call them the Altai. Because of the snow, the peaks glistened in a bluish haze.

In a few days we came to Tschimkent, a large, high fort. Here we were told that at this place in the years 1864 to 1870 serious battles had taken place that led to the annexation of Turkestan to Russia. On our whole journey I was always impressed by the large numbers of Russian military forces in the forts. Now, in this fort, there was an especially large force, although the war had ended ten years earlier.

After we had made our usual purchases, we continued on our way. We trav-eled through Beklarbeck to Akdschan on the Kelles River, where we lodged for the night. At our regular evening worship we sang the song: *Nun ruhen alle Waelder* or "Evening Song."

1. Now all the world is sleeping,
Through fields the shadows creeping,
    and cities sink to rest.
Let us, as night is falling,
    upon our Maker calling,
Give thanks to God, who loves us best.

2. The radiant sun has vanished,
    Its golden rays are banished
from darkening skies of night.
But Christ, the sunny gladness,
    dispelling all our sadness
Shines down in warmest light.

3. Now all the heavenly splendor
Breaks forth in star-light tender,
    from darkening skies of night.
But we, that marvel seeing
    forget our selfish being,
For joy of beauty not our own.

4. To rest my body hastening,
I take off shoes and clothing,
    symbols of mortality;
These I take off; in contrast
    my Jesus now will dress me
In robes of glory and righteousness!

5. My head, my feet and hands, too,
    Rejoice that now is ended
    the weary work is done.
My heart, rejoice, you will be
freed from this earth's misery,
    And from the power of sin.

6. Go now, my weary body,
    Go now to seek your rest,
    asleep in your own bed.
Soon hour and time are coming
    when others will prepare you
A lonely bed deep in the sod.

7. As dark night overtakes me
    My weary eyes are closing;
where are soul and body then?
In your great mercy keep them,
    forgiving all my sin,
    O watchful eye of Israel!

8. As a hen her chickens covers,
    So Jesus o'er us hovers,
    to shield us from alarm.
When Satan seeks to harm me,
Guardian angels' songs assure me,
"This my child unharmed shall be!"

9. And you, all you my dear ones,
This night shall naught disturb you,
    no accident nor pest!
God keep you sleeping safely,
His angel hosts surround you,
    Safe in His keeping rest!

10. Though long our ancient blind-
    ness
Has missed God's loving kindness,
    and plunged us into strife.
One day, when life is over,
    shall death's fair night uncover
The field of everlasting life!

Words by Paul Gerhardt; Melody, page 496, *Gesang Buch mit Noten*, verses 1–3, and 10 from the Grace Hill Hymnal, page 564. (Verse 10 is not in my 1873 *Gesang Buch ohne Noten*). Verses 4–9, WMHF.

While we were singing, a fine Russian *Troika*, a Russian wagon drawn by three horses, drove up and two uniformed gentlemen stepped down. With bare heads, they stopped at our meeting and took part in the worship. After the service was over, one of them introduced himself: General Baron von Kaufmann and his adjutant Major Meiser. They had just come from Petersburg.

The Baron recognized my father immediately and greeted him in a very friendly manner and extended us a very hearty welcome to "my" Turkestan. He gave us instructions to leave the Post road and follow the river to Kaplanbek, where we were to have our winter quarters in a government stud farm. Then he went his way.

The next morning *Ohm* (uncle, or title of respect) W. Penner returned from Taschkent where he had gone ahead to be informed by the officials as to where we were to live. He was accompanied by several guides who were to lead us to Kaplanbek. One of them, a very corpulent man, was the overseer of the now defunct stud farm. After much effort and all manner of small mishaps with several wagons, we finally came to Kaplanbek, over almost impossible roads.

Our journey had taken fifteen weeks. On the way we had buried twelve children. We arrived at Kaplanbek on the 18th of October, 1880. Several weeks later, a second train of twenty-two families arrived, to whom we could offer ready housing. This group had also had all manner of incidents along the way, especially since it had become cold in the meantime.

After a few days of rest, we began to arrange our living quarters. There were only two houses available. The other buildings were large open shops built for horses. The rear wall was of thick stone. We then procured building materials and the natives built new masonry, while the woodwork was done by our own men. Doors and windows were hauled from Taschkent, 20 kilometers distant. Soon every family had a small home. Not only did we build for our families, but also for the group that came a few weeks later.

We were hardly settled when typhoid fever struck our people. The younger people were especially hard hit. In a short time my Uncle Heinrich Jantzen had lost his two older sons, the very handsome Abram, 25, and Heinrich, age 21. What that meant to the stricken parents one cannot utter in words. By spring we had buried eleven adults and soon after the twelfth.

It was evidently in late November 1880 when a third migration of seventy Mennonite families from Molotschna, in Ukraine, arrived in Taschkent. The government arranged homes for them in the lumber and cattle market. This was the so-called Peters-Gemeinde (Peter's congregation), who had not gone along with the chiliastic views of Mr. Epp, concerning Christ's return to earth to reign during the Millennium. They were known as the *Brautgemeinde* (a bride community or congregation), perhaps their own designation.

The Peters-*Gemeinde* and the Kaplanbek-*Gemeinde* had at first joined. But it didn't take long before they separated again because of the doctrinal stand of Uncle Epp. The further result was that the Peters-*Gemeinde* and a few members of the Kaplanbek group resettled in Aulie-ata during the next summer, where they founded four villages in the Talas Valley of the Urmural River.

In Kaplanbeck we had two teachers, Franz Bartsch and W. Penner. There were also three ministers, Uncle Jacob Toews, Jonas Quiring and Johannes Penner. The latter was a very moderate, but also an intellectual man, who had from the beginning refused to agree with the teachings of Epp. Prediger J. Penner would gather the young people around him twice a week for Bible and Catechism instruction. After each session he would retain one of the other of us in order to discuss our salvation. So it came to be my turn. He first asked me: "Hermannn, do you love me?" With all my heart I answered, "Yes." For all of us loved him sincerely since he had a heart full of love himself. He also kept himself free from all arguments and quarrels of doctrine, and the majority considered him a straightforward man, and this is what attracted young people to him. Then he continued to speak to me: "If you really love me, would you do me a favor?" Again I answered, "Yes," and he continued: "Then promise me that daily you will go to a place all alone, close your eyes and ask God: 'Lord, show me my own heart.' This all need not take over five minutes. But you must do it with all your heart." This I promised to do, and of the results I will report again a little later.

CHAPTER 3

▼

TO BUCHERA-SERABULAK

Almost weekly we received long prophetic letters from Ohm Epp. They contained pronouncements that always began with the words: "So says the Lord to the church at Kaplanbek." Then followed Ohm Epp's own opinions concerning many things, which I, after 70 years, can no longer describe. All the more I refer the reader to the pamphlet by Franz Bartsch. The result of these letters was, as referred to above, that the Peters-Gemeinde move to Aulie-ata; and then the decision of our group, on the advice of Ohm Epp, to move to Buchera.

In the region of Buchera is the valley of Schirisep. Of this area Jung-Stilling must have written in one of his books, that this valley must have been the place of refuge of the Church of Philadelphia, which, of course, we were. Sometimes Uncle Epp compared us with the "woman clothed with the sun" in Revelation 12. These "letters of prophecy" as we young people called them, resulted in continuous differences of opinion and quarrels in the church.

And so it came about that in mid-summer of 1881 we started for Buchera. This happened in spite of a negative report, which the delegates, Brother W. Penner and my father, brought back from Buchera. "The open door of Revelation 3:8 cannot be closed to us even by the Emir or Khan of Buchera" so said our men of Kaplanbek. My poor father, who in all this was more a practical man of the mind than a spiritual advisor, had to accept many accusations from the brethren.

Our journey then led to the River Syradarja, which we crossed at Tschina by ferry. By so doing we found ourselves in the co-called *"Hunger Steppes,"* Uzbeck-Turkisch Haarstsultanig Tsulli. I do not recall how many days we traveled in this region of little water and feed. But finally we reached the beautiful little city of Dschisak, where we rested our poor horses and enjoyed the wonderful fruit and other produce of the region. We then proceeded through mountainous terrain into the Saraf Valley. By great effort the Dachigiten succeeded in getting us across the Saraf River. Then the road led through the boulevards of great trees offering shade to the traveler and to the historic city of Samarkand. On both sides of the road were irrigation ditches that tended to cool the air, so that there was hardly any dust on the road. Often we passed great, beautiful, shady *caravansaries*, or stopping places that invited one to stop and rest. Even as much as 15 kilometers from the city we met a Russian official who had heard of our exodus, and had come to guide us to a suitable place of lodging in this great city.

We were lodged in various *Sartenhoefen* or courtyards. These were very clean and surrounded by shade trees, which provided us with a beautiful resting place. In the center of each court there was a pond of clear mountain water which was brought in by small canals, called Arek, from the Saraf and flowed through all the ponds.

We remained here about two weeks. During this time we visited the grandiose Medressen built of glazed bricks. These are Muslim Schools of Theology. We also visited the many mosques with their minarets, or tall spires, as well as the Mausoleum of one-time world conqueror Tamerlane, whom the Uzbeck Turks called Emir Temir Pasha. The great Mausoleum is made of colored Mosaic and the gilded cupola can be seen from a great distance as the rays of the sun send its glory far and wide. We also climbed the lofty tower, also built of colored glazed brick, which according to tradition was built by Alexander the Great. As proof of this, one sees his Arabian name worked into the colored bricks.

Ever since our arrival in Kaplanbek, almost a year now, I had an Uzbeck-Turkish teacher. He went with us to the boundary of Buchera as we moved out. This instruction made it possible for me to converse very well with the Muslim people. As all Russian-Turkestan cities, Samarkand is divided into two distinct parts. There is the Muslim old city and the European modern city, and these parts are divided by a canal. While the streets of the old part are narrow, those of the *Neustadt* (new city) are wide and have small gutters of flowing water. They also have large shade trees and are frequently sprinkled, for the climate of Turkestan is sub-tropical and has very little winter. Only in the mountains does it get very cold.

Here in Samarkand we buried one of our rather special persons, Peter Pauls. At our Sunday worship service we often had visitors. Among them were many officers of the military, German Balts. Before they entered they would remove their sabers and set them in a corner outside the meeting room. The governor of Samarkand, General Dreesch, a Balt, was also the Chief of the Frontier Guard between Buchera and Russian-Turkestan. Through Baron Kaufmann he had received the assignment that he should acquaint himself with my father and warn him about crossing the Buchera frontier without permission. On several occasions my father had to contact the Governor, so a sort of friendship developed between them. This was a great advantage to us later. He also informed Father that Baron Kaufmann had charged him to give special attention to our well being. Because of all these favors, we were especially sorry to learn that the Baron had died of a stroke. He never regained consciousness before his death. We had lost much by this tragedy as F. Bartsch also reports in his pamphlet.

Finally we started moving again toward the boundary. Sixty kilometers before the boundary is the last Russian city, Katta-Kurgan. We camped outside the city. By order of Governor Dreesch, Father announced our arrival to the Chief of the Frontier, who, with very friendly words, again warned about crossing the border. However, all this advice went unheeded by our people. After all, did we not stand before the "open door which no one may close to us?"

We moved on and crossed the boundary about 5 kilometers behind the old-Arabic village of Serabulak and proceeded immediately about 10 kilometers into the land. Since it was late in the evening, we camped here. The next morning we were driven back out of the area by colorfully clothed soldiers of Buchera. They left us in a well-watered valley, which, we discovered, was a no-man's land of one-kilometer width, where no one was to bother us.

Quickly we built sod huts, for winter was at hand. Hardly had we settled by our warm stoves when it began to snow and it became colder. Then, entirely without warning, one day the Buchera soldiers appeared to drive us out. Protests were of no avail. Since Father was the leader, the roof of our hut was the first to be torn off and all our boxes and chests were loaded on two-wheeled carts, of which they had about 100 with them. They bound me and placed me on top of one of the loaded carts and drove off toward Sarabulak. We had hardly begun to travel when I became numb with cold. I begged the soldier who was with me to untie me. It was obvious that I could not escape in the deep snow. He ordered a halt, untied me, and allowed me to run beside the wagon until I was out of breath and of course also warm. Then he stretched out his hand and pulled me up onto his horse beside himself. He threw his long wide fur coat over my head, which covered me completely. I stuck my head out behind his neck so that I could get air, and on the warm horse, under the warm fur, I was not cold anymore.

Shortly before dark we reached Sarabulak. There by the Aksakal everything was unloaded. My protector delivered me to the Aksakal with the words: "This is the son of the Aksakal of the frontier-breakers. Take good care of him, give him a warm bed, as is becoming for a Musselman, one of the Muslim faith, and watch him carefully. I shall ride back into the mountains and tomorrow we will bring the whole group. Inform your Russian Chief of the Frontier, the Natschalnik in Kata-Kurgan, immediately concerning this matter."

Thereupon he disappeared into the dark. The Aksakal led me into his warm guestroom, served me with the best, after which I lay down according to the customs of this people, on the heavily carpeted and quilt-covered floor for the night's sleep. He placed a warm cover over me and I went to sleep very soon. Late the next morning I awoke and arose, fresh and strong. The Aksakal, a very unusual man, ate breakfast with me, after which he took me to the market place, since this was the day of the market. Here he bought me all sorts of sweets and delicacies.

Soon after this, one cart after another came into the village with our people and belongings. On order of the Governor we were lodged in the caravansary. The large mosque of the village became our church and a building nearby became our school.

For a while now things were quite peaceful among our older men. Then suddenly the conflict for or against Epp flared again, which led to further divisions. Soon hereafter letters came again from Ohm Epp, this time from Ikan, near the city of Turkestan, where their train had stalled in the snow.

I recall that at this time our dear teacher and minister, J. Penner, who had kept himself out of the divisions and quarrels, was asked what he really thought about the condition of the Gemeinde, and he was encouraged to make his feelings known. He arose and gave a very firm lecture against all the controversies and disputings. He also condemned the "letters of Prophecy" of Ohm Epp, whose curse and bitter results we could all see. To quote further, "Therefore I call on all of you and entreat you: become sober before the Lord; He will reveal the correct truth in time. I would be the 'dumb dog' of Isaiah 56:10 if I were not to warn you with great firmness."

These are my own words as I recall them. But the results were that he was completely misunderstood and had to stand aside. I do not recall whether he left the church voluntarily or whether he was put out of the church. Even though he was now in many ways a bystander, the weekly catechism training and the blessed Bible lessons continued under his direction. Ohm Penner became even dearer and more precious to us young people, which gave him much satisfaction.

Finally the winter was over; spring came and with it also the train of Ohm Epp. Epp now made great effort to bring the different groups and divisions together again. With many he was successful; others doubted the wisdom of the whole matter and drew back. Among those who left the group was also Franz Bartsch. They moved to Taschkent, then to Aulie-ata, where they settled in the four Mennonite villages.

Because of the service of Ohm Penner several of the girls and boys became converted, I being among the group. One evening as I slept outside the wagon because of the heat, I prayed again, as I had once promised Ohm Penner: "Lord, show me my heart." How often I repeated the words I do not recall, but now came the answer. The Lord revealed my heart to me and I became convinced of my lost condition in such a manner that, in my anguish of soul, I jumped from the wagon and ran into the low hills behind Sarabulak. There, in a small valley I agonized in prayer until dawn. At that instant a miracle happened, which I cannot describe. In my heart it was as though a voice spoke: "Arise, your sins are forgiven; for they have been paid long ago on Calvary by Jesus Christ."

An indescribable peace now filled my heart. Then I ran home again. As I arrived at the door my father just stepped out. He was about to waken us, as was his custom. However, I was already outside the door and fell on him and embraced him and recounted briefly what I had experienced during the night. I was very much disappointed with what he said.

"Well, my boy, what sort of soul searching you must have gone through I cannot understand. You have not been such an 'extraordinary' boy. Of course, you played pranks as boys will. That you should be so worked up about it, I do not understand." Just then Mother appeared and overheard us. She understood much better. She embraced me and wished me luck and blessing.

On Sunday those of us who had been recently converted were baptized and taken into the membership of the church, whereupon we received the Holy Communion. Minister Jacob Toews and Johan Jantzen, my father's brother, baptized us. At that time the form of baptism was by sprinkling. We who were baptized were very happy, and I believe to this day that the Lord looks at the heart and not the form of baptism. Many years later I baptized many people by immersing, doing this because I, as well as the candidate believed on the basis of God's Word, that the symbol of baptism is best expressed in Romans 6:4: "Therefore we are buried with him by baptism into death."

My Turkish Christians I baptized by immersing them three times—in the name of the Father, and of the Son, and of the Holy Ghost. Why? Because a Muslim does not believe in the Trinity. So through this form of baptism, the understanding of the Trinity was brought to their hearts, and by the grace of God to a firm conviction. For me, as mentioned above, the main thing is not the form, but the condition of the heart, and I believe that this is true with the Lord also.

CHAPTER 4

▼

AMONG THE JAMUDEN

At this time my father received a letter from General Dreesch in Samarkant. He informed us that, through the good offices of the Baron of Grottenhelm, General in Petroalexandrowska, he had made arrangements for us to settle near the Chiwenese border, on the Amudarja River. Muhamstrachim Bagadur Khan, the Lord or Officer of Chiwa, had indicated his permission for us to settle in his Kingdom. He advised, however, that first a delegation should be sent to Chiwa, in order to clear every detail with the Khan.

Thereupon Brother Emil von Riesen, Ohm Epp and my father were chosen as delegates, who, accompanied by a guide, began the 1000-kilometer long journey to Petro-Alexandrowska and Chiwa. The trip over and back took several months. Everything went well. Baron von Grottenhelm received them in a very friendly manner and was especially glad to be able to speak German with our men. He furnished them with an able interpreter and a letter of recommendation.

After they had crossed the Amudarja by boat and after a 40-kilometer ride, they arrived in Chiwa, where the Khan received them gladly and lodged them well. In the course of the discussions the Khan came up with just one condition of settlement. Which? Our men had to promise that they would not raise hogs. This promise they gave, no doubt with inner mirth. The place determined for the settlement lay 160 kilometers downstream, on the navigable irrigation canal, Lausan.

After the delegation had informed the Gemeinde of all that they had learned, Father was instructed to send a letter to General von Dreesch informing him of what they had found and telling him that we were ready to move immediately, there being only one question: How? For the road that our delegation had traveled by horseback was impassable for wagons. After a few weeks we received a reply: "Strike out! At the border of Buchara, near Schirinchatin, you will be given an escort of Buchari soldiers, who will take you safely through all of the Buchara State to the border of Amudarja. There you will find enough boats for your whole group, furnished by Chiwa, to continue on the journey. Bon voyage!"

Forthwith we started on the 1200-kilometer journey with our 60 families and many wagons. I do not recall the number. We were forced to take a detour because the wagons could not use the riding path, which was the shorter route. As we reached the boundary of Buchara, the multi-colored escort greeted us with a friendly: "*Assalum aleikum*," that is, "Peace be with you." With them as guides we traveled many days through the fruitful land of Buchara, through towns and larger market places. Everywhere at the stopping places, preparations had been made in advance for our needs. There was feed for the horses, fruit for all our needs, eggs, milk, rice, flour, mutton, and so on. Everything was very cheap.

So we finally reached the tributary of the Saraf River, which at this place was reduced to several small streams, because it delivers its water to numerous irrigation canals, until it finally runs into the Karan Kum, the Black Desert. Here our wagon trip ended. The wagons were dismantled and together with all our possessions were loaded on camels. We needed 450 of these animals, which were delivered to us in a few days by our escort soldiers. For the women and children they made a sort of sedan chair, one of which was roped to each side of the camel. Before leaving here we had to bury *Tante* (Aunt) Wiebe (Kurt Wiebe's grandmother, mother of Mrs. Elder J. Toews).

Now all the men and boys got on the horses and we struck out directly into the desert, which was about 160 kilometers wide, until it reached the Amudarja. During the day the heat was too oppressive for traveling. So we rested during the day, for which naturally the camels had to be unloaded. It was almost impossible to find water anywhere. When the sun set in the west the camels were loaded and we went on over hill and dale, and over countless sand dunes. Many of the women and children became seasick and had to vomit, and the children suffered with dysentery. Thus we spent many a night. The nights were lit by a large bright comet, with a tail halfway across the heavens. It was so bright one could read by its light. Those of us who rode the horses would sing so as not to go to sleep. The song among others was "Our road leads through the wilderness (desert)."

Finally our horses raised their heads; they were conscious of cooler air and walked a bit faster. Soon we saw trees as we approached the canal. How man and beasts were refreshed by the water!

Shortly before evening we passed through a lonely market place called an Ilekick, where only Tadzhiks lived. They spoke the Uzbek-Turkish language, however. Behind this place was the River Amudarja, where nine large freighters were lying ready for us. They had been at anchor here for several days. The camel drivers left the next morning for their homes, after we paid them.

Now came the tiring job of having each of us find our own things in the turmoil that this all presented. This alone took several days, after which we were ready to load everything on the barges. Each family took its place alongside their own goods. Included were the dismantled wagons. The younger as well as some of the older men again mounted their horses, took provisions and cooking utensils and rode downstream toward Petroalexandrowska. I was also supposed to ride with them; however, since my eyes were badly inflamed, I had to stay on the boat. Slowly and calmly we floated downstream. Each of the boats had seven sailors besides the Captain, called *Darga*. At noon we landed to cook the food, but we ate on the boats. At night we stopped on some open shore, for the area was covered with deep forests in which there was an abundance of jackals, fox and hyenas. Those who could, slept on deck. The rest of us slept on the shore. We always kept a large fire in order to frighten the animals away. But they howled and barked all night around us, so that no one slept much. However, we could make up much of the sleep during the day on the barge, called *Kajuk*.

After nine or ten days without incident, we finally came to Petroalexandrowska. From far off we saw a *Troika*, and beside it stood several persons dressed in white. It was the General, Baron Grottenhelm with his wife and half-grown children, who all greeted us warmly in German. Father and the other two delegates were received with warm handshakes. Our riders had also arrived ahead of us.

The Baron advised that, since this was the last settlement of Europeans and therefore the last business places, we should buy what building materials we would need. On the Lausan in the virgin forest we would not be able to buy these things. We followed this advice and everyone bought doors, windows, hinges and nails, et cetera. After having made all these purchases, we loaded our ships and sailed another 160 kilometers downstream until we got to the Lausan Canal. Over this distance also, the riders followed through the undergrowth of the forests along the shore after us.

As soon as the ships were unloaded and the sailors paid, we began to look for a proper location for the settlement. On both sides of the Lausan were high dikes, behind which we now cleared the primeval forest of undergrowth to make room for buildings. After laying out a straight village street, each family built a home on either side. These were sod huts, although there was plenty of wood for lumber for more permanent buildings. Lumber and cane for the roofs were in abundance and there was plenty of wood for fuel. It had gotten quite cold in the meantime. So it wasn't long until we all sat inside by a warm stove. The barns for the horses were built of cane, and soon they too had a roof over their heads. The feed for the horses, Luzern clover, was brought to us by the Uzbeks, who lived about 5 kilometers upstream. They also brought foodstuff such as flour, rice, oil, chickens, eggs and other food items. Everything was very cheap. From the other side of the stream, fishermen brought us wonderful fish. A sturgeon one meter long cost only 25 *kopeks*.

For us the winter passed in a rather calm manner, only that the howl of animals often disturbed us at night. Even a tiger was often heard nearby. He finally got to be so brave as to take a walk down the street of the village in the morning. However, he never attacked either persons or horses. His Royal Majesty was not hungry at the moment, since there were many animals in the forest for him to feast on.

About 5 kilometers downstream lived the Jamuden, also called Turkmenen, who grazed their herds of sheep, camels, and horses on the large forest-free pastures. They are a nomadic, thievish folk who live in tents. They are never unarmed, carrying Russian repeater rifles as well as a dagger in the belt. Though they speak their own dialect, they also speak Uzbeck well. Since they could not be trusted, we had, by the order of the government, a small troop of soldiers with three officers who lived in tents nearby. One of the officers gave me daily lessons in order to perfect my command of the Uzbeck-Turkish language.

The winter was very cold so that the two-kilometer wide Amudarja River froze over solid and we could ride our sleds on the ice. The flow of the stream is toward the north, where it flows into the Aral Sea. In 1883, when the spring thaw came, the ice broke and the floes came to our village, where the river was stopped by the piles of ice. Because of this, the river rose so high that it overflowed its banks. Then we realized the importance of the dikes. As the water flowed on top of the ice, the ice was broken with thundering noise, and many huge chunks were hurled over the dikes on the land. After two or three hours the water level sank again. As we got out of our beds the next morning we stood almost knee-deep in water. This showed us that we could not remain where we had settled, so we moved one kilometer inland onto a hill, and built a new settlement.

This time we built our dwellings, as well as the barns, of brick. However, we did not remain as one settlement. About 20 families who opposed Ohm Epp, among whom were Ohm J. Toews, Johann and Heinrich Jantzen, and our dear Pastor J. Penner, and others, moved about four kilometers away and built a settlement on another hill. They surrounded their village with a wall. In the meantime, the eldest son of Jakob Toews, also named Jakob, married my oldest sister Marie. They lived next to us.

The native Jamuden often rode through our village without ever taking anything that belonged to us. So the small troop and the three officers were withdrawn. On our hill we had already planted vegetables—potatoes, beans and more. But now the Jamuden began to steal. They had noticed that we did not have guns. After all, do not the wild animals, the deer, antelope, wild boars, hyena, and jackals run right underfoot without anyone shooting at them. At first they stole our horses. Then they tried to steal the young wife of Heinrich Abrams, during which episode he was murdered. It got so bad that they would drive the residents of a house out, and take whatever caught their fancy. We hardly had a quiet night anymore. Several times some of us younger men, and also some of the older men, tried to defend ourselves with homemade swords. During such times, the older men were on their knees with Ohm Epp in prayer. When I came home in the morning, somewhat wounded, I would have to listen to Father's reprimand. In the lower village, where the other twenty families lived, things remained quiet. They had hired two Uralkosaks, who lived on the other side of the river. This kept the Jamuden from entering the village. Ohm Epp severely condemned this practice.

One night, in bright moonlight, three Jamuden thieves appeared in our yard. I recognized one of them. We three brothers, Gerhard, Bernhard and I had, without Father's knowledge, made some spears and were standing at the window in our roomy bedroom. As they rode into our yard they gave three warning shots. Two of them dismounted and forced their way into our barn, where our seven horses were kept. They led the horses out of the barn, while a third one, with gun ready, rode up and down past our window. When we saw that they were taking all of the horses, we yelled loudly and stormed into the entry of the house, and wanted to stop them from taking the horses. As we came to the outside door, Father stepped into our way with stern warning, as follows:

"Aren't you ashamed of yourselves to resist evil in this way? Because of the principle of non-resistance, our people have left one country after another, until we have come here with such difficulty. It becomes necessary for us to be what we have always claimed to be, and you want to deny the faith of your fathers by striking one blow. Back to bed! As long as God lives, who also sees the theft of our horses, He will not let you starve, even without the horses." With tears, though with inner rebellion, we went back to bed. But Father had passed his non-resistance exam. That the battle within him had been intense, we and mother came to realize much later.

In the meantime, those other twenty families were preparing to leave Chiwa and migrate to America. One night I dreamed, while standing at our well in the middle of the yard, that I was looking in the direction of the other village. I saw Ohm Jakob Toews on the road to our village. As he got near to the well, he lay hold of my shoulders and said, "My dear Hermann, you are busily learning the local language. In spirit I see you as a missionary to the Muslims, to preach to them the Gospel of Jesus Christ. As a young person, you are still careless, and you will go through many serious experiences before the Lord will get you to the place to do His will."

The next morning I told my dream to my mother, in whom I could confide. I cannot recall what her comments were. How amazed I was when, a few days later, I saw Ohm Toews approach me, exactly as I had dreamed, coming to the well, grabbing me by the shoulders, and repeating the same words. Mother stood by the open window and heard his remarks. Not until twenty years later was the prophecy fulfilled.

One day an officer of the Cossacks, with his hunting party, came into our yard where I happened to be. He asked me whether the *Strachina* or village elder lived here. As I answered in the affirmative, he observed me carefully and asked, "*Junge* (boy), are you ill? You seem so pale and thin." I answered him, "How can one look different when one hardly ever sleeps through the night and then works in the fields during the heat of the day? Almost every night the thieving Jamuds attack us and steal our horses. They took ours along too." Just then Father came out of the house. After a short greeting, the officer said to Father, "I hear now that you are allowing the Jamuds to rob you. Didn't you report this to the Khan in Chiwa?" Father answered, "According to the Word of God we cannot do that. We are people who do not resist force with force."

"But God has provided governments to protect the righteous. How can we protect you if you do not report to us? But now I know why God has sent me to you today. I will provide you with people who will protect you from such further violence." With that he rode away and continued hunting a few more days in our vicinity, after which he disappeared. Perhaps a week later, there came a troop of Chiwanese soldiers, headed by a well-dressed gentlemen. He was Kassim Diwan. Sternly he asked my father whether he was elder or leader of this village. For, in the meantime, the other group had left the region to migrate to America.

After Father answered him in the affirmative, the Minister had his fine tent set up in our yard. It was furnished with beautiful carpets. A separate tent was put up for his kitchen, in which tea and other food items were prepared. He invited Father, and me as interpreter, into his tent, where he had already been seated on the rug. We were also invited to be seated. Bread, sweets and tea were served on a cloth.

Over the cup of tea he addressed my Father: "What foolish people are you, that you allow the Jamuden to plunder you. You do not even report this to the government! So we had to learn of these conditions through the Russians over in Petroalexandrowska with their criticism. Why don't you report such things to us?" Father gave him the same answer he had previously given the officer of the Cossaks. But the Minister could not comprehend such a point of view.

In the meantime, Mother had baked some *rollkuchen* (roll-cookies, deep fat fried) and prepared some tea, so she invited us into the house in order to offer our hospitality. The Minister accepted the invitation. He was a tall man and the customary fur cap made him appear even taller. In the house he stepped to Mother's serving table on which stood a beautiful canister. After viewing himself in the glass cover, he asked who had made this box. Father informed him that his brother-in-law had made it as a birthday present.

"How could the man fasten the glass to the box in such a clever way? One can see no seam or crack, as though it were fashioned out of one piece. Even the color of the wood can be seen through the glass." After a pause, he added, "Are there more men among you who can do such work?" Father said there were, and he continued: "His Majesty the Khan was in Petersburg a few years ago and there he saw a large parquet that was covered with glass in this manner. Now he would like very much to have such a parquet. Therefore, I would like to discuss this with your master craftsmen."

Thereupon Father asked five or six of our cabinet makers to come and he presented them to the Minister. He pointed to the canister and asked, "Which one of you made that?" My uncle Gerhard Esau stepped forward and said: "I did."

He was asked to explain how he had fastened the glass to the wood. My uncle explained that this is not really glass, but a liquid, a varnish or luster, called *politur*. First the wood is polished to a very smooth surface, then the liquid is rubbed on with wax balls. In this way the wood becomes mirror-like.

As a result, two of our masters were designated to ride to Chiwa with them and show the box to the Khan. Further developments would naturally follow. I was to accompany them as interpreter.

The following morning I rode, accompanied by his Secretary, to Chiwa, about 150 kilometers distant. On the third day we arrived and the Secretary presented us, together with our precious box, to the Khan. He admired it very much and obviously liked it. For the night we were lodged at the home of the Minister of

Building Trade, whose name was Mamut Diwan. Our horses were taken care of and we received royal treatment.

The next morning Mamut rode with us, by order of the Khan, to the *Nurlawes* or Palace of the Khan, where the latter personally showed us a large newly built hall, but where the floor was missing. He wished to have a parquet floor laid, with inlaid stars of light and dark wood, and then polished or glazed.

Our craftsmen promised to complete the task if the Khan would furnish the necessary dark and light wood. This would have to be dry enough and the *politur* would have to be brought over from Petroalexandrarowsk. He agreed to all this and then asked how long it would take to complete the work. Our men, with ten helpers, set the time at six months. The floor must first be covered with ordinary wood and polished smooth. The major task would be the construction of the small pieces for the pattern of stars, using two kinds of wood. After agreeing with all these conditions, the Kahn added, "Your whole village of forty families will be brought to Akmettschet into a large park of my brothers. Here you can build houses and live a peaceful life; for there are no robbers here."

CHAPTER 5

▼

AKMETTSCHET AND AULIE-ATA

At the conclusion of these discussions with the Khan, the Secretary and the rest of us returned to our village. During our absence, the Minister had concluded his hunt with falcons, during which he shot many pheasants and ducks. After satisfying himself and his entourage, he gave the balance to our people. During the night they set out guards and no more vandalism occurred.

A few days later, several hundred high-wheeled carts were brought by their owners, with orders to move us and all our possessions to Akmettschet near Chiwa. The drivers were peasants who were brought in from surrounding villages. In about two weeks, we and all our goods, including building lumber and cane or reeds, were moved. Nothing was left behind.

Then we began to build our new homes. In the Nobleman's large park, surrounded by a stone wall, within which many apricot and peach trees grew, we built our houses in a great square. Within the square, a large open area, we built the church, a school and a teacherage.

At this time, fourteen of our men started to lay the floor in the parquet. This took about five months. In the meantime, our women also received work assignments from the Nobelman, in his large household. As is customary in Asia, he had many relatives living with him.

In the year 1885 I had become so fluent in the Uzbek-Turkish language that, after our arrival in Akmettschet I was appointed as interpreter by Khan Seit-Muhametsha-Sim Bagadur. The city of Chiwa was only six or seven kilometers away from our village, so that I could be at the court during the day and ride home in the evening. The Khan had presented me with a stallion, a trotter or pacer. On Sundays I was at home. In addition to the continuing language study, I was also instructed in the Koran, the Muslim bible, and other literature.

Unfortunately, there were always new schisms in the church, which hurt my spiritual life. In this, we that were younger could not understand our parents, which naturally pained them greatly. Finally Ohm Epp was denied opportunity to speak in the congregation, so he was cut off with only ten families, including my parents. We four brothers and one sister, all married by now, remained in the church. Thus we were severely chastised by Ohm Epp, to which our parents had to give approval. This cut deep wounds in our hearts—how deep only the Lord knows.

This was experienced by all families who remained within the church. We had much wealth as we left our beautiful home in Hahnsau. Father had sold his three farms and sacrificed it all to this "*Irrsinn*" or heresy. To the glory of God and our Savior, let it be said: we never became bitter toward our parents; for this we loved them too much. But Uncle Epp caused me great struggle. For more details I refer the reader again to the Barsch pamphlet.

All these tensions, added to the glamorous and loose life at the court, injured my spiritual life so much that I realized that I must leave. So my young wife and little son Abram and I, together with three other families, moved to Aulie-ata. This was in 1890. By this time several hundred families had settled here in four villages. As early as 1881 they had broken away from Ohm Epp.

We had hardly arrived when we noticed that here, too, quarrels and differences were present. Here the matter of immersion was the bone of contention. This resulted in a division through which the Mennonite and the Mennonite Brethren Churches were formed.

All this caused me severe inner harm and I withdrew from spiritual things. My soul suffered greatly. We spent the winter in the village of Nickolaipol in the house of Ohm Jacob Janzen, my father's cousin. His son, Peter, who was about my age, was also married and lived with us in the same house. Ohm Janzen lived about two kilometers away in his waterpowered mill.

Daily Peter and I worked in the mill. Our youngest son, Abram was still in school, but already the future preacher could be detected in him.

In the following spring, the government developed a new village plan. So Peter and I, with ten other young families, left the four villages to build up a new settlement named Orlof. I soon noticed that I did not have sufficient funds to build up a household. After putting a roof over the house and barn, I ran out of money and I didn't know how to proceed. Since living costs were very low, we could keep above water. At this critical time, the Chief of our district, Chef Kalauer, visited us to see how the young Mennonite farmers were progressing in their building. He also came to me and saw that progress had been halted and said, "How now, Brother, evidently your money ran out and you cannot complete your buildings." "So it is, your Highness," I answered. "Where did you learn such good Russian?" "In our private school on the Volga."

He had three interpreters with him, since in Aulie-ata district three different languages were used. I soon conversed with these three in their own languages, which I had learned at the Khan's court. This surprised the Chef, and after some thought he said, "You are short of money for your building. I will provide for you by appointing you as forester in our district. You will receive enough salary so you can finish your buildings and establish your farmstead. Of course, in between time, you must ride through the hills and inspect the forests."

I answered, "But I have never had training in forestry. How can I be a forester or forest ranger?"

"I will provide you with books through which you can get the necessary information. Added to that will be the actual practice. What is most important to me is that you will need no interpreters."

So I became the forester and in three years I passed the examination and became Chief Forester. This was in 1895.

The church, now that I was an official of the State, promptly put me off the membership roll, for I now had ten subordinates in the various precincts to watch over and whose services I had to examine. Not only did we superintend the forests, but we also had to assign the grazing rights among the nomadic Kurgisen and other tribes in the surrounding hill of the Tjanschen Mountains.

CHAPTER 6

▼

CONSPIRACY AND ITS CONSEQUENCES

One evening three village mayors came to me, each of whom governed 100 to 150 nomads. Although they were Kirghiz, I had learned to know them as honorable men. They told me of a "great secret." From Fergowa, the former Muslim capital of Kokan, Israelchanture, brother of the former Khan Chuderjarchen, had come into our area. He was spreading the news that God had revealed to him that the time had come for him to liberate the Muslims of the principality from the Russians. He is now agitating the people in the hills against the Russians. He is announcing himself as a Holy One and therefore wears only the holy pilgrim garb, the long *kaftan* or mantle, woven out of camel hair, and the red fez with a white turban over it. No layman, especially no Kirghiz, may wear this type of dress.

They reported further that Prince Israelchanture Ischan (the Holy One) had large sheets of paper with him that contained many signatures, stamps and fingerprints of prominent men of the larger cities: Namangen, Margelan, Audischen, Osch, Orotube, Chodschend as well as many of the larger market places. Included also was the whole province of Aulie-ata on the south side of the Tjan-schan Mountains. These men felt obligated to report all this, since they were oath-bound officials of the province.

After I had listened to the whole matter, I told them that this is a serious political problem and that they are surely duty-bound to report this in writing to our district Chef Kolauer. They said that they would be willing to do this, but they master only the Turkish language. If they reported the matter in Turkish, the interpreter Bekschurof would be asked to translate it into Russian. Since he himself is part of the planned revolt, he would naturally reveal the whole matter. Therefore they asked that I should write the report in Russian, which they would sign and seal. I fulfilled their request and sent them with the report to the District Chef at Aulie-ata.

After they had gone, I dressed myself in Kirghiz attire, rode into the mountains to Kunischtak-Schlucht, where Israelshautuk was said to be hiding. I found him there in a large *Aul* or tent-village, together with many wealthy chiefs. I dismounted and entered the tent. There sat the Ischan dressed in his sacred pilgrim robes on beautiful rugs. They were at the point of officially opening their meeting.

I bowed and greeted them with their customary *"assalom salleikum tachsir"* meaning: "Peace be to Your Highness." Thereupon the Khan insisted I be seated behind him. I suppose that my noble fox fur cap, cut to Kirghiz pattern, in addition to my Kirghiz clothes, brought me his hospitality. I accepted his invitation and took a seat beside him, after which we exchanged a few words of greeting.

Then he said, "Your blue eyes indicate that you are a Russian, but because of your excellent Usbek-Turkish speech, in spite of your blue eyes, you must be a Tartar."

He then turned to all those present and spoke of the revelations of God, as a result of which he must free the Muslim people of Fergowa and, if possible, all of Turkestan from the Russian yoke. He then showed them the papers with the many seals and signatures, and insisted that every Musselman, that is every loyal Muslim, should sign their names. At the designated time they would join all Musselmen in driving out the unbeliever, that is, the Russians who would then lose all their possessions. He emphasized that I, as a Tartar, would not be expected to sign.

After I had learned as much as I deemed necessary, I left as quietly as I had come, and rode home. After three days the Schulzen, or village mayors, came back from the city and informed me that Kreis-Chef Kalauer was very angry at them and shouted, "For twenty-five years I have been Chef here in the Aulie-ata district and there had never been any such disturbance. I do not believe anything you have reported to me. There is another reason behind this. It must be your personal hatred of the Ischan."

The whole conversation between Kalauer and the *Schulzen* (mayors) was interpreted by Beckschurof. The Chef gave them written orders to arrest Ischan, with his eight loyal followers who always traveled with him, and deliver them to the Chef.

It took ten days of searching before they found the Ischan and his followers to bring them to the city. It became evident that the interpreter had secretly sent messengers to warn Ischan, even during the time of the hearings before Kalauer.

After the Ischan and his men were in prison, Kalauer turned further investigation over to his assistant, Captain Lascheschnikof. In the meantime, the Kirghiz servants and workers left their posts of duty in our village, as well as all the larger Russian villages, with the threat, "As we have had to serve you, so now you shall serve us, for our Savior has come."

One day Captain Lascheschnikof came to me saying that he would like to go among the Kirghiz in order to determine the extent to which the agitation by the Ischan had taken hold. He didn't bring his interpreter because he did not fully trust him.

He asked me to accompany him into the hill country to investigate the extent of the rebellion. This seemed laughable to me and I assured him that this would help matters very little. But since he wished it, I agreed to go with him.

We visited a few of the notorious Auls without getting any information. So I advised him to go to some of the farmers in the large village of Dimitrofka and other villages too, and question them concerning the attitude of the Kirghiz. He interviewed a number of the peasants including eight in our villages. All of them informed him that all Kirghiz had left the villages, voicing the threat mentioned above. With these results he went back to the city.

In the meantime, Kalauer, with his cabinet, spent 17 days from morning till night, grilling the three Schulzen until they became pliable enough to sign a paper prepared by Kalauer. It was signed and sealed, and the content was about as follows: "We three Schulzen of this and that Auls had a personal grudge against the former Prince Israelchanture and we didn't know how to get our revenge. Since Herr Forester Jantzen is a good friend of ours, we asked him for advice. He told us that since the Prince has a high position in the community, we could hurt him most by accusing him of planning a people's revolt."

After this declaration was signed and sealed, Kalauer had them taken to prison. Then it was my turn. He ordered me to the city and read me the statement of the Schulzen. Thereafter he jumped up in a rage, made the sign of the cross before the Ikon and swore an oath: "As truly as you see me make the sign of the cross before the image of the Holy Saint, so surely will I get you on the long road to Siberia."

Then I had to surrender my official badge to him, and with another curse, he dismissed me. But that was not enough. He issued to all our magistrates and church elders a strict order in the form of a declaration, which was to be announced from all pulpits to all our citizens. The declaration was as follows: "Forester Jantzen has caused a completely innocent Prince of Fergowa, Israelchanture, to be politically suspect. However, I have proof, black on white at hand, that the former Forester Jantzen, in order to do a favor to three Auls Schulzen, plotted all this falsely. There is therefore no truth in all this tale of a revolt. This declaration is to be publicly announced to all citizens. In the future no one is so much as to greet Jantzen."

In addition, the *Schulze* or mayor of our village of Orlof received the order to make a church resolution asking Kalauer to free the congregation of this liar Jantzen, and that the members of the congregation were to sign the resolution. Our congregation Orlof was composed of 125 members, half of whom were Lutherans. They refused to follow Kalauer's order because of the behavior of the Kirghiz in recent days, which had clearly shown that they were possessed by a spirit of rebellion. The congregation refused to do as Kalauer had ordered.

About a week before Easter, Captain Lascheschnikof went to the prison in order to question the Ischan. In the course of the interview, he succeeded in pulling out of the shaft of Ischan's boot the following letter addressed to the interpreter Bekschurof:

"Honored Sir and Brother Bekschurof: I have reports from the outside that our plans are to be carried out anyway. It has been determined that our people will attack the city and the barracks on Easter Sunday morning, since at that time soldiers are ordered to be in church. Our people will capture the barracks with all the weapons and then will proceed against all non-Muslims. Since you wear European clothes, it could easily happen that in the melee you could be killed also. I advise you therefore to take your family and leave town early on Easter morning."

Mr. Lascheschnikof now had in hand undeniable proof of the planned revolt, but he had to deliver the letter containing the plans for the plot to his superior Kalauer. The latter was naturally frightened and the question rose: what can be done in order to avoid trouble? Mr. Lascheschnikof came to me and asked my advice. It seemed to me that it would be best to arrest all the leaders and nothing would happen. I further advised him to have this suggestion come from himself and not from me. This procedure was followed and the revolt was avoided.

In the meantime, however, Kalauer had reported this whole affair to the higher authorities of Taschkent, capitol of Turkestan. As a result, investigating officials came to our area and the Ischan, the three Schulzen and I had to appear before them repeatedly for questioning. Finally the highest court of three Troikas from Taschkent came to give a verdict.

I noticed that none of my eighteen defense witnesses were called in. I protested this omission, but the court ignored my protest and thus the verdict was given. I was sentenced to twelve years in Siberia "for having falsely accused a Prince of Fergow, Israelchanture, of high treason."

I refused to sign this verdict of the court and demanded on legal grounds a hearing before the Court of Appeals, for a review of the verdict. This was granted me by the court and would stay the sentence for six months. While the Ischan was acquitted, the three Schulzen were given 1½ years in prison for "false accusations" which Kalauer had forced them to sign.

Thus the trial ended and Polkowik Kalauer won the victory. Greatly depressed, I returned to my quarters where I was visited regularly by our Mennonites. During these days many came by. They had heard the verdict of the court and eyed me suspiciously.

In the evening, as we sat around the large table drinking tea, a young Sartar lad came in and asked if I were Jantzen. As I answered in the affirmative, he handed me a letter and said, "I must bring you to the district notary Wassieljew." I went into another room and read the letter written by Count Anitschkof. He asked me to come to him immediately with the bearer of the letter. He said he is a member of the High Court and has quarters with Wassieljew. He wished to discuss various matters of interest to me.

I followed his request immediately. At the home of Wassieljew, who was also an old acquaintance of mine, I met the Count and another gentleman. All of them greeted me with a warm handshake, and seated me beside the Count, who then said:

"Mr. Jantzen, I was very happy that you refused so stubbornly to sign the verdict and thus received a six month period for your appeal. I am a very young jurist and came from Petersburg. I was placed here as a member of the Oblastnoi Court for Turkestan. I have carefully studied the whole affair of the Ischan on my own and have discovered that you have been shamefully tricked. I still do not know the reason for this. I have written an appeal, which will be forwarded to three offices. It contains the history of this whole matter as well as the request that the whole trial be reopened and that your 18 witnesses should also appear. The request is based on Article so and so. One copy will be forwarded to His Imperial Highness, the Tzar, a second to the Senate, and a third to the Oblastnoi Court. You are, of course, already acquainted with the latter. At the end of each copy of the appeal it is noted that a copy goes to the two other offices. This is to avoid having the matter pigeonholed and forgotten. Six months will pass quickly. If you will sign the three copies, I will see to it that they will be forwarded without delay."

I signed the petitions with great relief and thanked the Count. But he didn't wish to be thanked, adding: "I have learned from Mr. Wassieljew and others that Polkonik Kalauer has relieved you of your post as forester and has persecuted you in other ways, in spite of the fact that the whole city of Aulie-ata believes that you saved them from a Muslim rebellion. For your sake, I believe that you should accept a position as forester in the Taschkent District and thus escape Kalauer's persecution. I will see to it that you get such an appointment. First, however, we must complete this trial and secure your acquittal."

I now took my leave and, after mutual "good-byes," I returned to my quarters. To this day I believe that I slept well that night.

When I arrived home I found my wife in great concern and fear. The news of my banishment to Siberia had preceded me to Orlof. Many Mennonites and Lutherans came to me to voice their concern. However, for a while I did not appear in the other four villages. I waited quietly for two or three months. The Kirghiz workers returned to their former jobs. Kalauer had issued visas or passports to the Ischan and his eight followers, with which they disappeared to Kaschgar in Chinese-Turkestan.

Suddenly I received the news that the three Troikas, with the officials of the High Court, had returned to Aulie-ata to review the Jantzen case. Soon the 18 witnesses were heard and I was acquitted.

That evening I had to go to see Wassieljew again, where the Count greeted me with great joy and wished me well. Immediately he placed in my hand the appointment as Forester in the Taschkent Mountains. He had taken care of all matters with the Kreis Chef in Taschkent, Mr. Kisseloff. Many citizens of the city, as well as my forester friends, came to congratulate me.

I hurried home in order to celebrate a *Dankfest* (Thanksgiving feast) with my loved ones. I would like to say here, that although in my conscience I admitted having wandered from the Narrow Way and that I had lost my inner peace, yet through the years I had never forsaken prayer and that the Lord had answered many prayers, in spite of the fact that I went my own ways. As much as possible I had observed the morning and evening altar. After all, this habit had been practiced since my youth.

Now it became necessary that I should quickly prepare to move to my post at Taschkent. I left my wife and children temporarily in Orlof. By wagon I rode to my designated forest district in Newisch Perkenterollost, about 90 kilometers from Taschkent in the Hindukusch Mountains.

The people are mostly Tadzhiks. They speak their own language and live in closed villages surrounded by vineyards. The forests were made up mostly of walnuts, cedars and wild fruits. Since none of the natives were allowed to own guns there was an abundance of wildlife in the mountains: wild boars, deer, mountain sheep and ibex. The Tadzhiks were a rather wild people and rather vindictive. I was reminded of Matthew 5:5, so I dealt with these people gently. In a year or so I understood the truths of these words, for I had won the confidence of all the tribes of the six large villages in my district. Since hunting was enticing, I became a passionate hunter, and through the years we lived here I shot numbers of wild boar and other wild animals.

After four months my wife and children joined me. Since it was very hot in the village in summer, we lived in a spacious tent in the cooler regions of the hills. However, during the third year my wife became so seriously ill that I had to send her, with all the children, back to Aulie-ata. That was a journey of 490 kilometers. One of her brothers took them there in a well-furnished wagon. I accompanied them on horseback over the first 120 kilometers, but then I had to return to my post.

The following day there appeared a hard-riding courier and handed me a large envelope from the Secretary of War from Oblastnoi in Taschkent, which contained orders that I accompany the courier to the Chancellery in order to report to him on political matters. As I read this, my heart sank and I asked myself: "What can be wrong now?"

Three years before, I had barely escaped one political noose and now comes the second one. However, there remained no alternative; I must report to him. So I mounted my horse again and rode to Taschkent, where the adjutant of His Excellency in the First Chancellery of the Secretary of War received me warmly, which of course made me breathe more easily. He informed me of the reason for ordering me to appear, when he said, "Whether you may have heard of the terrible event which happened in Adischen four days ago, on the 19th of May, I do not know. On that day many thousands of the masses, incited by one Israelchanture Ischan, in a surprise attack on the city, murdered some fifteen thousand Europeans—non-Muslims."

I responded, "Who would have informed me of it up in the hills?"

He further reported that the garrison was also murdered. Somehow the reports concerning these events had leaked through by way of Namagen. Thus the garrisons from Namagen, Margulen and Kokan were dispatched to Andischen. After heavy fighting, the Ischan, with 100 men, were captured. Then he added, "We shall now go into the next room and meet the Governor."

As we entered, the Governor arose from his desk and came toward us. He asked my name, which I gave him. He then grasped my hand and said, "You already know the subject of our concerns. It is shocking what happened in Andischen. I have not been in this position even a year, and in a matter of days I expect my Superior from Petersburg, who is to make an inspection tour of all of Turkestan. Now this had to happen. Since I am responsible for law and order in this province, this unfortunate uprising in Andischen places me in a very difficult position. And I know of no way out. I have discovered that four years ago you had reported this Ischan as a rebel. He was imprisoned but was acquitted later by the Oblastnoi Court and was freed. Now it is evident that you were right. Therefore, I would expect of you that you would help us onto the right track in order to clear up this whole matter."

Here I was gripped by the old bitterness about this whole thing and how I had been treated. So I said, "Your Excellency, at that time I merely did my official duty and, if the High Court freed the Ischan in spite of my information, what can I do about it? If Your Excellency would be informed by the High Court as to the real reason for this, then perhaps you would get onto the right track."

At this moment a door to the next room opened and Mr. Ilinski, the First Secretary of His Excellency, stepped in. He turned to the Governor and said, "I heard everything that was said here and, since Mr. Jantzen is an old friend of mine, I would ask that you turn him over to me. I will discuss everything with him and the matter will be cleared."

With a "*Laduo*," meaning "Good," Mr. Ilinski and I were dismissed and we stepped into his office. After we were seated, Mr. Ilinski ordered some tea with refreshments. Then he said, "Dear Friend Jantzen, after hearing what you just said to the Governor, I perceive that you are still bitter, because of the shameful treatment you received from the Court four years ago. Had I been so treated, I am sure I would be as embittered as you. However, this will not get us anywhere.

We must rather make every effort to bring those happenings of four years ago into their proper focus and thus explain the uprising or revolt in Andischen. This matter places the Governor in an untenable position, since at that time he was not even here. He must now answer for this revolt for which he was not to blame. Therefore, I would ask you to give us a helping hand in clearing up these affairs."

To that I answered, "Four years ago I entered into my diary this whole Ischan story with succeeding events, complete with all dates and details. This I did that my children would some day have the information. That could give you considerable light in these matters. However, at the end of the report I added a few words for my children that you, as a Russian, would very likely not appreciate. Therefore, I believe it would be better if I did not allow the daybook to fall into the hands of strangers."

Mr. Ilinski then asked, "May I, as your old friend, know what these extra remarks to your children were? After all, they had nothing to do with the Ischan story. I give you my word of honor that I would tell no one about them."

"Good. You shall know then. I reminded my children of the difference in the concept of the importance of an oath. With us Mennonites our 'yes' is sacred, while many Russians will break an oath for a bottle of whiskey."

After some thought, Mr. Ilinski said, "As bitter as this pill is for me as a Russian to swallow, I must fully agree with you. However, as I already said, none of this shall appear on the report which I must write on the basis of your diary. I would hope and expect that you would bring me your diary as soon as possible."

After another assurance of his promise, we parted with a hearty handshake. I immediately rode to the hills to get my daybook. In three days I was back in the city. As I stepped into the Chancellery, I was met by the Governor's First Adjutant. He was very excited and shouted, "I would never have imagined such a thing of you." He showed me a large folder in which the whole Ischan episode with the court proceedings were written word-for-word and then signed with my name.

The script was as follows: "To the Governor General, appointed by Petersburg, His Excellency, General Duchowskoi:" Then followed the whole Ischan affair and the concluding sentence: "I, the former Forester Jantzen, venture to present this petition to Your Excellency upon your entrance to this high office over all of Turkestan. For I fear that if I wait a few days with this petition you might have become accustomed to the practice of purchase or bribery of officials here in Turkestan." This was followed by a clever forgery of my signature.

After I had read all this—or whether he read it to me I do not recall now—the Adjutant added, "You surely wrote this, didn't you? You will certainly suffer the consequences." With that he dragged me into the Governor's office and said, "I have the honor of presenting to you Forester Janzen." At the same time, he placed the document with my signature on the table before the Governor. He, of course, was already aware of its content.

He arose, stepped toward me and looked at me with piercing eyes. "Young man, how sad that you again have chosen to go on the long road to Siberia. In your obviously great stupidity, you will have to go on that road, for did you not write this petition?"

"No, Your Excellency."

"What proof have you?" I asked a counter question: "When and where was this paper written?"

"On May 19 in Aulie-ata."

"Your Excellency, I will not move from this place until you inquire of my superior Polkovnik Kisselof by telephone, how long I have been away from Aulie-ata, and where I was on May 19."

He took the telephone and called Kisselof. He heard the following reply to his questions: "Forester Jantzen has been at his place of service here in our hills for three years and during that time was never in Aulie-ata. On May 19, I and several others were with Forester Jantzen hunting in that area."

His Excellency hung up the receiver joyfully, took my hand and congratulated me. "You are free! I would very much like to know who wrote this petition."

"I do not know. I have no idea."

"Whoever did was no friend of yours. Now your help is so necessary to us, would you step in to see Mr. Ilinski." With that I was dismissed and stepped into an adjoining room where Mr. Ilinski was already waiting for me. He immediately rose and stretched his hand toward me, congratulating me for my acquittal. He had heard everything through the partly open door. He then told me that he had received instructions to go to Aulie-ata to investigate all Ischan-connected-matters and asked me how to proceed in order to best achieve his objective.

I said to him, "You will first have to reassign the powerful Polkownik Kalauer and his interpreter Beckschurof either to Wernie or Perwosk and announce publicly in Aulie-ata that these men would never return there again. Only then will some open their mouths and dare to give information of the Ischan affair. Otherwise you will learn nothing."

As he returned my diary to me and thanked me for my help, he said, "Tomorrow morning I will travel to Aulie-ata. I advise you not to write to your wife or relatives during my absence. It could be dangerous for you to do so."

We took leave of each other and I left the "Big House." In deep thought I slowly made my way to my night's lodging, when someone called to me. As I looked up I saw an old acquaintance of mine from Aulie-ata, Captain of the Cavalry, Zulof, who was now an Advocate. He was riding a horse that I had sold him years before. After dismounting, he patted the horse's mane affectionately and said, "This bay is the best horse that I have ever had. In four days I have put 300 kilometers behind me. However, that is secondary. I noticed that you were so deep in thought that you didn't even notice me riding beside you, until I called to you. And, of course, I realize what it is that depresses you so. However, you did not study law in vain, and you will surely find your way through these problems and obstacles." With that he jumped into his saddle and was gone. Now I was convinced who had formulated those dangerous petitions. I recalled that Zulof was an old enemy of Kalauer.

The next morning I rode back to my hills, which had become so desolate for me since my wife and children had gone to Orlof. Thus I spent three lonesome months remaining busy at my post. The most difficult part was that I had no news from home.

Then one day another courier came with orders from Mr. Ilinski to come to him without delay. He had returned to Taschkent from Aulie-ata two days before and had many things to tell me. Immediately I rode with the messenger into the city. The following morning I went to the Chancellery where I was greeted warmly by Mr. Ilinski and he related the following:

"Even before I left, Kalauer was informed by telegram that he was being transferred to Wernoie, and when I was half way to Aulie-ata I had Beckschurof thrown into prison. As I approached Aulie-ata I left the town to my left and proceeded directly to Orlof, in your hills, and visited your wife and told her all my plans. Then I had your 18 witnesses come to me and they gave me all the necessary information concerning Israelchanture. Then I drove to Dimitrofka and interviewed your ten witnesses as well as the Kirghiz Chiefs there.

Then I rode to Aulie-ata and questioned Beckschurof in prison. He finally confessed that the Ischan had given Kalauer 2000 rubles and several hundred sheep to secure his freedom and the passport to Kaschgar in Chinese Turkestan. Beckschurof then swore that as interpreter he was forced to carry out all of Kalauer's orders. He himself had received nothing and is therefore innocent. I left the prison and went to my quarters. The next morning it became known that Beckschurof was found dead on his straw mattress. A few days later it was discovered that *Frau* (Mrs.) Kalauer, who was still in town, had sent him a large bowl of fat "*Palei*" or rice soup, a favorite food of all Muslims. Beckschurof must have eaten the soup with a voracious appetite and then died during the night. And now let us go into the next room where His Excellency will inform you further."

After we entered in his presence, he greeted me warmly and said, "Mr. Jantzen, through your flawless bearing in the Ischan matter you have rendered us a great service. Therefore, I appoint you as Chief Forester of the whole Aulie-ata region with double salary. With reference to your service in this matter, I have reported everything to Petersburg and hope that soon we will have good news for you from there. And now I wish you a pleasant journey to Aulie-ata and your family."

After I had thanked His Excellency, I left his office and went back to Mr. Ilinski's department. He took me to his home where we celebrated the consummation of the Ischan episode with his wife and children. He informed me too that the Ischan, with about a hundred of his accomplices, had been hanged. The village of Mingtube, where Ischan had been entrenched, had been leveled with artillery fire.

The following morning I started on the way to my hills. After a few days I received my release and the position was transferred to my successor. All this took about a week. However, my beloved Tadzhiks were very unhappy about my leaving. They brought me all manner of gifts for my wife and children. There were large sacks of walnuts that grow wild here, several large goatskin containers of grape syrup and an endless amount of honey. I finally left with a heavily laden wagon on my trip home. Many of these dear people stood by the road and wept.

May I insert here that fifteen years later I again visited these Tadzhik villages and lived among them as a missionary, this time about spiritual matters.

On my way home, when I arrived at the village of Golowatschofke, the last station before Aulie-ata, I was greeted by dear old friends, the Doctor Allisejewitsch and the Forester Berdeschof. They had come this far to meet me and received me with great joy. Many others had also come out and they cheered loudly: "Our deliverer-friend Jantzen has come back. If it had not been for him, we would have been massacred four years ago at Easter time by the Muslims, as they have now done at Andischen."

This tumult was too much for me, so I gave my wagon over to my brother Heinrich who had also come to meet me. I got into the wagon of the two friends mentioned above and rode with them ahead of the crowd.

The next evening we arrived at Orlof, but here the uproar was even louder than it had been in the city. My whole yard was filled with people who wished to greet me. However, I cannot even describe the meeting with my dear ones; it was overwhelming. All this had happened by December 1899.

CHAPTER 7

▼

THROUGH INNER STRUGGLE

In Taschkent it was decided that I should stay at home until the following spring in order to rest from my duties, but in April 1900 the government requested that I should go to the forest near Koijantogai, about 5 kilometers from Orlof and build a house at government expense. It was to have a walled yard and include a stable. This was to be my home while in the forestry service and would subsequently be transferred to my successor.

The building was started right away so that I could move in during the summer of that year. We lived here about eleven years. In addition to the house, we also had 20 *hektar* (about 50 acres) of land for our use, which belonged to the Office of Chief Forester.

We had a cheese making plant for which my 25 registered dairy cows furnished the milk. I also raised a few thoroughbred horses, as well as fattening some pigs. At this time the price of grain was very low because there was no railroad transportation available. It was therefore more profitable to feed the grain than to sell it. The nearest railroad station was about 300 kilometers distant, therefore the ample wheat crop was hard to dispose of.

In the fall the cattle-rich Kirghiz came down from the mountains and traded some of their cattle for wheat. In this manner I came to own 100 steers, which I had traded for wheat. These I grazed in the hills on government land. We acquired 100 sheep in the same way. These I grazed in a grassy valley which the government assigned to me. Later I sold them.

In the course of years, the three older sons took care of most of the chores. Abram, the oldest, attended school in Taschkent from age 10 to 13, where he learned well. However, the growing farm business kept him home more and more, since my own position kept me very busy fulltime.

There was much grief and annoyance. The ten subordinate foresters and other officials were all Russians. As former soldiers, most of them were alcoholics, but I could not fire them. They often indulged in illegal practices, for which I was responsible to my superiors. In addition to this, the several hundred thousand Kirghiz population had many conflicts among themselves because of the division of grazing rights. They formed into groups or cliques, which battled one another because each sought his own advantage. Since they are stupid, uneducated, dishonest and very self-seeking people, they caused me much grief and I often had to help settle their quarrels.

Two official honors or certificates of merit in glittering frames came to me, which I hung in my office. The two scripts said: "In recognition of extraordinary service rendered by Chief Forester Hermann Jantzen by the Ministry in Petersburg. In the name of His Imperial Majesty, the Tzar of Russia." Signed: Minister of the Interior.

And: "To the Chief Forester Hermann Jantzen for exceptional performance and improvements in the mountains, granted by the Department of Forestry of Turkestan." Signed: General Dubinof. How proud I was of these certificates of honor and even more so of the medallion, which was added later.

However, all through the years of my wandering from the path of the Lord, there burned within me the hell of self-consciousness: "You are not in the right place. You are fully aware that you are going against the voice of the Holy Spirit within you."

In the course of time, this made me very miserable. One day, after a tiring pheasant hunt, I sat down on the stump of a tree and wept. My faithful hunting dog, Hector, was lying before me and he noticed it. He got up, looked at me sadly and lovingly licked my hand. I said to him, "Dear Hector, I envy you. You are still just like God created you—sinless—but I?" And again the tears streamed over my cheeks. Hector noticed it, jumped up and tried to console me.

In those days my dear Uncle Revered Jacob Jantzen showed great concern about me and tried to help me get back on the right track. But—shame on me! I was too proud to admit to others the truth I very well knew myself. At that time two ministers from South Russia visited our villages. They were Reverend Jacob Reimer from Rueckenau and Jacob Kroeker from Wernigerode in Germany. They held evangelistic meetings for two weeks in both congregations. Many were converted and many received more light on the truth of salvation in Scripture. We also, my wife and children and I, drove the 12 kilometers almost every day, from Koijantogai to the meetings in the nearby villages. The messages often gripped me, but that was all. I made no spiritual progress.

A little later a Mr. Broadbent from England, a great friend of missions, came to our region. He was, if I remember correctly, a representative of the British and Foreign Bible Society. It had come to his attention that, in this large Muslim country of Turkestan, no mission work was being done, in spite of the fact that there were large Christian churches among whom he felt there certainly must be some genuine children of God. He had come to organize a Muslim Mission, for which he would naturally need some missionaries. These he hoped to find in our villages, but without success.

He was told, "Our children and young people naturally master the Kirghiz languages, since they were born here and come in daily contact with these people. But they would not make missionaries and we need them here at home. However, in Koijantogai there is a Chief Forester named Jantzen, who in his youth studied the Muslim languages of Turkestan in Chiwa for eight years. He also studied the Koran. He is the man for you, Mr. Broadbent. Yet, though he is a Christian, he has strayed from the Truth and has lived for years in the world. Perhaps you can win him over for your cause."

Mr. Broadbent then came to me and told me of his interest and repeated what was told him about me. I listened to him quietly and finally I said, "I really feel sorry for you, Mr. Broadbent. Yet I haven't the slightest notion to preach the Gospel of Jesus Christ to these lying, deceitful, thieving Kirghiz people. That would be casting the pearls before the swine. I would rather send them all to Siberia, for they lie to me daily in all imaginable ways." In these words I spoke forth my bitterness.

Mr. Broadbent listened patiently and then replied, "I know that you, who know the Truth, have gone astray. But how can you be aware that, here in your neighborhood, people are dying in total darkness and you have not warned them? Don't you know what it says in Ezekiel 33:8? That is a word just for you, Mr. Jantzen: 'If you, a believer, have not warned the godless of his way and he dies, then God will require his blood (Mr. Jantzen) at your hand.' Wherever I go, I will pray for you until I hear that you have gone with the Gospel in the Turkish language to give these poor Muslim people of Turkestan the Gospel of the Cross of our Lord Jesus Christ."

With that we parted and he returned to England. But Mr. Broadbent kept his word. His prayers, and those of Uncle Jacob Jantzen, were answered. How? That took me through terrible days, but it was for my salvation.

It was on a Sunday evening that my five boys and I spent the evening in the beautiful moonlight playing our musical instruments. They all had musical talent. They played either a balalaika, or mandolin, with the two older ones on guitars or sometimes violins. I played the zither. As we concluded, I said, "Boys, the price of beef on the market is very good at present. How would it be if we were to bring home our steers from the hills? They would bring good money on the market."

The boys agreed and we decided that on the morrow the two oldest boys, Abram and Bernhard, together with our herdsmen, would ride into the hills and carefully drive our 100 steers home. After a day of rest, we would then drive them to the market in Dimirofka.

After three days the beautiful herd arrived at home. My boys had gloated over the beautiful animals all the way home. My wife and the rest of us were amazed at the fat, sleek cattle. Early the next morning the herdsman came and called me: "*Bai*, that is to say, Sir. A lung disease has struck some of the steers and several died during the night. Many more are groaning and are sick. We can't possibly take them to the market. We must quarantine them."

I got up and went with him to investigate the matter. It really was so. To make a long story short, in about six weeks, not only all the steers had died, but all 36 dairy cows. Added to that, came the death of five thoroughbred horses that died of an unknown disease. And, as though that were not enough, our dear Hermann, age 8, was down with typhus and seemed unable to live or die.

And so the Chief Forester Jantzen, acclaimed in various government circles, now sank to his knees as he faced God's judgment. And God spoke to me at length through His Holy Spirit and showed me all my sins and the injustice that I, in my pride, had committed against many people, especially the Muslims of my district. I do not recall how long God kept judging me, but completely, yes, completely broken, I lay before God and wrestled for grace and peace for the sake of Jesus Christ.

And God was merciful and answered my prayer. As a sign of His grace, He filled me with His peace that is so divine. No one can understand it who has not experienced it himself. One cannot describe such a feeling. And what is a mystery about all this to me until this day, is that all my hate and bitterness totally disappeared. Even at that time I could have embraced those Kirghiz that had become so loathsome to me and tell them, "Come with me to the Lord Jesus; He loves you and wants to save you and give you joy."

After all these experiences I said farewell to my public service and moved back into my own home in Orlof. I reduced my holdings and divided much of it among my children. Abram was married by this time. Bernhard followed him soon. A few years later Heinrich was married. That left Hermannn, Fritz, Franz and Anna, who was 26 years old by now, at home.

It took almost two years to transfer my government post to my successor. There were by then ten forestry districts in the mountains and canyons and it took that long to unwind these affairs. In the meantime, the church matters which concerned me and my past were also brought in order.

CHAPTER 8

▼

THE SERVICE OF WITNESSING

Finally I was completely free and a voice within said, "Now you must make up what you have neglected in your past." But how could I make up what I had missed? As a missionary? No, insofar as it meant to change from a secular to a spiritual vocation? Yes, if it meant that from now on I was to show how the love of God toward us sinners can be demonstrated in word and deed.

So I proceeded on the basis of my experience with God as a witness of Jesus Christ among the Muslims, with the message from Jesus Christ as Paul expressed it in I Corinthians 2:1–4: "When I came to you, brethren, I did not come proclaiming to you the testimony of God in lofty words or wisdom. I decided to know nothing among you except Jesus Christ and Him crucified. And I was with you in weakness and in much fear and trembling, and my speech and my message were not in plausible words of wisdom, but in demonstration of the Spirit and power." (R.S.V.—Jantzen used the Elberfelder Bibel).

For eighteen years I had exercised my official duties chiefly over the nomadic Kurghiz, the Kasaken (not Cossacks), the Kuraminsan and other tent dwellers, who numbered into the hundreds of thousands. They were difficult to govern and in my official pride I had often sinned against them. After my conversion, I was driven by the Holy Spirit to go to them and, wherever possible, to make restitution. I confessed my guilt and asked forgiveness. This amazed them and they asked, "How is it possible that suddenly you are so changed? Formerly, while in uniform, you were so unapproachable, and, when we did not obey the Russian laws, we were often rather severely punished. And now you come to us as a civilian and beg to be forgiven, when really we were the guilty ones."

I answered, "In my anger and official arrogance, I often treated you unfairly, in that I had you punished too severely."

"But how is it that you have changed so?"

"The Lord Jesus through His Holy Spirit has brought this about. He has given me a new heart, full of love for you. He also forgave me all my sins, and now I have such perfect peace that I want you to know about it too."

This increased their astonishment and they meditated over their own condition. They asked me whether the Lord Jesus could change them too. Then I could tell them the full gospel of Jesus Christ. They forgave me my guilt and we parted as good friends.

I now traveled extensively among these peoples and in a few years several were converted. As soon as this became evident by their walk, and after I had conducted Bible study with them, they asked to be baptized.

After more study concerning baptism, we were convinced that the symbol of baptism was nowhere better explained than in Romans 6:3–4, where it is written: "We are dead with Christ, and buried into his death by baptism, then arisen with him, to walk in newness of life." They therefore desired baptism by immersion, which I administered to them, after which we had Holy Communion together.

In 1911–1912 I took a course in the Alliance Bible School in Berlin. This school had been founded by Pastor Koehler in 1903 in cooperation with brethren in Molotschna for the purpose of training evangelists for Russia and Slavic countries of the east. During World War I the school was moved to Wiedenest in the Rhineland, where it is still located. Many years later the director of the school was Brother John Warns and after his death Brother E. Sauer was its leader. After

WWI Brother Legiehn served there, but at present he is director of a Bible School in Paraguay.

After finishing this course, I accepted many invitations and traveled extensively among the Brethren in Holland and Germany, and lectured in churches and to other groups. In this way I learned to know many dear people and prominent spiritual leaders.

Shortly before my trip back to Russia, I returned to the Bible School in Berlin and delivered a farewell speech. Present at the time was my old friend Jakob Kroeker of Wernigerode, whom I had known as one of my relatives in Russia.

The next morning the whole school, with Pastor Chr. Koehler at the head, and with teachers Warns and Michener, accompanied me to the Bahnhof (train station) Tiergarten. While we all sang "God be with us until we meet again" the train pulled out of the station and brought me to Marienburg. There I was received by Brother Cornelius Andres, since deceased, who took me to his hospitable home. Brother Andres also took me to Neuteichedorf, where my father and grandfather were born. In the evening I was asked to speak before a small gathering in his home.

The next day we visited my cousin Gerhard Jantzen in Herrenhagen at his stately home. After that Brother Andres took me to Elbing. From there I walked to Augustwalde where my mother was born. I also looked up other relatives who lived in the area.

I now traveled eastward to Warsaw, where I worked for six days. By the way of Kiev, where I viewed the Lewra-Catacombs, I arrived at Sofiewke. Here I lodged with Brother and Sister Woelk, and the next day I conducted a meeting at Einlage. I went to Halbstadt by way of Prischipp, where I stayed with Brother Abr. Kroeker. He made it possible for me to visit the distribution center at Raduga.

The next station was Rueckenau, where Brother Jacob Reimer lived. It was he who, together with Brother Jacob Kroeker, had visited us in Turkestan some years earlier. I accompanied Brother Reimer to Apaulee, to the Sudermann family, where with other brethren and sisters, we spent a very blessed Sunday. The fellowship was even sweeter because of the arrival of Brother Jacob Kroeker from

Wernigerode. Here the Brother told me for the third time what he had said to me earlier in Germany:

"My dear Brother Jantzen, never forget what I will now repeat once more. As you take a determined stand for Jesus Christ, freed from all prejudice and bias, you will experience great disappointment and bitter heartbreak, because your most intimate brethren will forsake you because they will not understand you." At the time I did not understand him, but later incidents taught me what he really meant.

Then he continued, "Brother Jantzen, you have come from the so-called 'Alliance' Bible School of Berlin. My advice to you is that you never speak the word 'Alliance" in our Mennonite churches, because they all fear the word." Since the location of the school was transferred to Wiedenest, they dropped the "Alliance" designation and it is now know as the Wiedenester Bibelschule (Bible School)."

Following that Sunday, I, together with Missionary Friesen (Emeritus), visited several villages and churches, where we conducted meetings. Finally I went from there to Trakt on the Volga and to Hahnsau where I was born. I lodged with relatives in Koeppenthal. I visited with many friends of my youth in various villages, and here too we had many meetings and worship services. Unfortunately, I found little of spiritual life.

Here too, the day for departure came and I boarded a Volga steamer and traveled downstream to Astrachen. Here I boarded a lake steamer to Baku. In Baku I was heartily received by the one-time interpreter, Dr. F. W. Baedeker, who had become famous for his tireless investigations of the prisons in Russia and Siberia.

Also present was Patwaken Tarajans, an Armenian, who had studied in Kings College in London. He was a very determined Christian and was active in Baku as missionary and pastor. As a result of his work, there was formed here a considerable congregation of independent children of God whom he led. I was put up in the home of his wealthy brother, who owned several oil wells. All day long I worked among the Turks and Aserbeidisch people in the harbor of Baku, while in the evenings we had meetings in the Armenian Church of Brother Tarajans. This lasted about two weeks and then I made my way to Tiflis.

Here I must digress a bit. When I took leave from the Bible School in Berlin, Brother Broadbent from England, my old friend whom I had first met in Turkestan, was also present. As a great friend of missions and as representative of the British Bible Society, he traveled in many lands and, wherever possible, preached the Gospel. As a result of his service in Turkey, several Turks had been converted. These were severely persecuted. Two of them lay in prison for a long time, where they were tortured for not denying their new faith. The soles of their feet and their backs were slit open, rubbed with salt and then beaten with sticks.

Mr. Broadbent found out about these men. After much effort he succeeded, with the help of an English consul, to have them freed. This was in 1910. Now, two years later, Mr. Broadbent received sad news concerning these two brethren. So he asked me to look them up and give them spiritual help. This was the real reason for my going to Tiflis.

After I had given Mr. Broadbent's greetings to these men, they received me warmly. They had leased large grape and fruit orchards where they also lived. A well-to-do Armenian brother also joined us. For the night I stayed with Mr. and Mrs. Steinbrecher in the agency of the British Bible Society. I visited with the two Turkish brethren daily. They were really spiritually ill and at the verge of despair because of the attitude of rejection of the Baptist congregation who required that they be baptized again in order to be eligible for membership. This they could not understand and they said to me, "We were baptized in Constantinople in the presence of several missionaries in the Name of Jesus Christ. Why do it again?"

They believed that all children of God are one and that there are no differences among them. And now they find that their baptism is not accepted. So they were at the verge of rejecting all "Christendom." What all the torture in prison could not accomplish, now seemed to be brought about by the attitude of the Baptist Church.

One day, as we often did, the two Turks and I were sitting in the garden on a vine shaded bench overlooking a beautiful walk to the entrance of the garden. The two had repeated for me the hopeless situation they were in. Just then the gate was opened as the founder and leader of the Russian Baptist Church stepped in. He had heard of my presence in the city and came to get acquainted. He introduced himself by saying, "I am founder and director of the Russian Baptist Church in Tiflis."

My answer was: "Dear friend, perhaps you have never spoken truer words in your life when you said that you are the founder and leader of the Baptist Church and therefore not the Holy Spirit. For if He were the Founder and were He the Leader, then these two Turkish brethren would not be treated in such a negative manner, as is now the case. You surely know that they are Christians and baptized; you also know that they were imprisoned and tortured because of their faith and yet they remained true to the Savior. Their backs and the soles of their feet, which I have seen, testify to these facts. After all that I have heard until now, and as you yourself now express it, you are the one that started the church, it could not be different than it has been. Your 'I' stands in the way of the Holy Spirit." This was too much for him.

The above mentioned Armenian brother had a large house, and because he was a positive Christian, he saw to it that we could have public meetings each evening for the twelve days I was there. As the evenings progressed, more and more unhappy people found peace. The most striking thing was that the leader of the Baptist congregation never missed an evening. He was there every evening, though he remained silent. The Holy Spirit worked mightily in those, for me, unforgettable evenings.

The last day was on a Sunday. In the forenoon we had a closed service with a group of about fifteen determined children of God. These became the core of a non-denominational congregation. Since the owner of the house, this Armenian brother, was also a gifted speaker, he assumed the work of organizing the group.

In the afternoon these dear brethren arranged a farewell tea for me. Many sympathetic friends, most of whom had attended our evening meetings, were also invited. Each one was given the opportunity to express freely his spiritual situation. Many participated in this and it was revealed how mightily the Holy Spirit had worked in them.

At about 6 o'clock in the evening I spoke a few words of farewell, and then suggested that we sing the song "Come to the Savior." This song has been translated into many languages and nearly all of them know the song. And so the song was sung there in the various languages represented. There was some confusion, but it worked. I was informed that, besides the very happy Turkish brethren, Armenians, Tscherkessen, Lesgienen, Grusienen, Russians and a few Germans had attended our meetings.

After another hour of prayer, in which the two Turkish brethren also took part, they all went with me to the station. On the way over, a woman whom I had noticed in the meetings, asked me in for a cup of tea. She lived near the station. The others proceeded to the station and waited for me, while I went with her to her house. She told me that she was the wife of the Baptist minister, who had forsaken her. With deep anguish and tears, she said, "For ten years now my husband ignores me and lives in another house. Only by the grace of God, whose I am, and by prayer have I unbroken contact with Him. I still live in the joy of the Lord, my Savior."

After prayer together, I hurried to the station, where the brethren were waiting. Quickly they handed me the ticket and with another "God be with us until we meet again," I boarded the train and it pulled out of the station.

Late in the afternoon of the next day I arrived in Baku and went to the home of Brother P. Tarajans. He had announced a farewell meeting in the large church building, where a large congregation was present. After an introduction by Brother Tarajans, a few of the brethren spoke, after which I concluded the meeting. After a period of prayer, this meeting also closed with "God be with us …"

Then we went to the harbor where I boarded a boat, which took me across the Caspian Sea to Usanda. In Kransnouorlsk, I took a train through Turkmenian, a day long journey by way of Merv, Bairamali, Tschardschui, Buchara and Samar, finally reaching Taschkent.

Here I was greeted by my dear wife and our two youngest, Hermannn and Fritz, 13 and 12 years old. The joy of meeting again after such a long separation was very great. My wife had come the 400 kilometers from Orlof with our own wagon by way of Tschimkent to Taschkent. It took them six days. There was as yet no railroad connection from Orlof.

We took a taxi or *Mietdroschke* from the train station to the *caravanserie* where our wagon was left. It seemed to me that even our horses were glad to see me. As a Mennonite farmer, I was always a great lover of horses. We remained in Taschkent for a few days, visiting some friends and doing considerable shopping. Then we began our journey home, where we arrived safely and without incident. Our four married children were very happy to greet us.

On the next day many relatives and Minister brethren came from the villages of Romanofka, Nikoaipol, Gnadenthal and Gnadenfeld to greet me. Many members of the two denominations, the Kirchen gemeinde (church congregation) and Bruedergemeinde (Brethren Church), also brought hearty greetings.

CHAPTER 9

▼

AMONG MUSLIMS AND RUSSIANS

After the crop was harvested at home Brother Abram Janzen and I began a missionary journey. Brother Janzen had studied at the *Bibelschule* (Bible School) in Berlin for two years, even before I did, and was a great friend of missions. We rode horseback farther into the hills of our Talos Valley in the Tjanschan Mountains in order to preach the Gospel of Jesus Christ to the so-called Black Kirghiz.

We were on this trip for many weeks and visited the isolated *auls* (tent-groups), and were received everywhere by these hospitable and friendly people. This is typically Muslim. Many of them knew me from the days when I was a government official. They listened to us attentively and were often gripped emotionally and moved by the message.

But then they begged us for wheat so they could bake bread. They had plenty of meat but were always short of wheat. Of course, we couldn't furnish them with wheat. The purpose of our travels was entirely different. They could not understand why strangers should be interested in their salvation. But they remained friendly. On this trip through the mountains and valleys we often came upon scenes of indescribable beauty. But there were also surprises of another sort, not always pleasant.

One Saturday we were riding over a high ridge and found ourselves in a snow-storm, although it was early in August. Very carefully we crossed the ridge and walked slowly in knee-deep snow, leading our horses. We finally found ourselves in a large mountain valley called Hetmentube, where we again found our bearings. In this valley lay a large Russian village. Completely cut off by the mountains, the inhabitants had settled here some 15 years before. The village contained about 300 farms or *Hoefen*, surrounded by large wheat fields and orchards. A bit farther out they had large meadows and much cattle.

As we entered the village, Brother Abram said to me, "Where can we lodge here? There surely is no caravansary." "By the first best farmer," was my answer. So we came to a large, well-kept *Hof* (farm yard), where we saw a woman on a broad veranda, busy with a *samovar* or large boiler. There was also a table with benches around it.

We greeted the woman and asked whether we could lodge with them; we said we were traveling missionaries and evangelists. She called to her husband who was busily cleaning up the *Hinterhof* or back yard, since it was Saturday. After he had heard us and realized who we were, he welcomed us with obvious friendship and added, "For many years we have not heard the Gospel and we cannot read. If you would allow it, I would see to it that the whole village meets in this yard this Saturday evening to hear the Gospel. After all, we are Christians and need it."

We agreed with him, and the wife suggested that the *samovar* be set up so that the hungry stomachs be provided for. The man took our horses to the barn and fed them. He did not return for some time, while the wife served us with various delicacies. Finally I said to my companion, "I must go and see what is keeping our host."

I found him in the back yard busily skinning a two-year-old fatted steer that he had just butchered. When I asked why he would butcher a beef on a Saturday afternoon, he said, "After so many years, we now have important guests, who wish to proclaim the Gospel to us. They must have good food and my family and I will partake with them."

When he had finished taking care of the meat according to his methods, he came and sat with us. Just then his grown sons arrived from the field with their scythes. Our host gave orders that they mount their horses and ride from house to house to invite everyone to their house for a meeting that evening in order to hear the Gospel; that two missionary-evangelists had come over the mountains to proclaim the Gospel here also. The young men mounted their horses and hurried through the village, inviting everyone to come.

It all happened as our host had planned it. Shortly before sunset the large yard was filled with people: men and women, young people and children. Everyone wanted to be in on such a singular event. We were seated in chairs before the whole group as they sat on the grass. We read from the Gospel of John, chapters 1 and 3. We gave special emphasis on verse 16 of chapter 3 and spoke on that text, after which we closed with prayer. It was strange to them that we should speak to God without making the sign of the cross; this they had never seen. They were all deeply stirred and begged us to stay several days longer, so that they could hear more. They felt so needy. In spite of the fact that it was harvest time, they wanted to let their work rest so they could attend every meeting.

Gladly we acceded to their request and stayed several days longer. We had regular forenoon and afternoon meetings and the people attended, listened attentively and asked many questions. We answered these as the Holy Spirit gave us wisdom. Abram and I repeatedly said, "Such spiritual hunger we never met with before."

The Lord was in our midst quite visibly, which was obvious to us by the comments and questions that were asked at the close of each session. Here we had a multitude of people, who because of their isolation from culture and church, lived in their enclosed valley, untouched by numerous religious movements and denominational strife. They were genuine, free children of nature—*Naturkinder*—with no religious prejudices.

But of course we finally had to leave. After a very heartfelt farewell, we took our well-filled saddlebags and started on our way. Our host had provided us with roast beef, bread and fruit. Our hearts were filled with thanks and praise, and even now I love to think of those days. The Lord will take care of the rest, for according to Isaiah 55:11: "My Word shall not return unto Me void." Soon we arrived at home again, in good health and condition.

CHAPTER 10

▼

A VISIT TO AKMETTSCHET

In September of the following year, 1913, my wife and I traveled to Chiwa to see my father and other relatives in Akmettschet. My mother had already died by this time. It was a long trip, for Chiwa is 1700 kilometers from Aulie-ata. We went to Tschardshui by wagon and there we boarded a train that brought us to Tschardshui on the Amudarja River. Here we stayed overnight with the Konsul of Chiwa, an old acquaintance. The next day we proceeded by steamship to Chiwa, where we arrived safely after a relaxed and comfortable trip.

In Akmettschet we were cordially received, especially by Father, who was 85 by this time. Ohm Class Epp had already died. Through my letters and those of others, everyone knew that since 1905 I had been a changed man. They also were aware that I had attended the Berlin *Bibelschule*. Besides that, it was known that I traveled extensively and worked as a missionary among the Muslims as well as other nationals. Therefore, I was asked to do evangelistic work here too. It was primarily Ohm W. Penner, the minister who led the congregation, who insisted on this. The small *Epp-Gemeinde*, numbering ten families, were separated from the other congregation.

It was with a heavy and anxious heart that I accepted the call, because I knew that what I had to deal with here was the direct opposite of what Brother Abram J. and I had experienced in that large Russian village. Every evening for a whole month I spoke in the church. How difficult this became, only the Lord knows. In spite of, or perhaps because of, the many years of continued disagreements brought about, on the one hand by the teachings of Ohm Epp, and on the other by the narrow chiliastic conceptions (Christ's return to earth to reign during the Millennium), there was here great knowledge of the Bible, but one did not have the Lord Jesus Himself. The personal experience of the creative power was missing; the conscious possession of eternal life in one's heart.

The essence of my presentation is best summarized as follows: "My dear brethren, the Word of the Lord Jesus, said to the theologian and teacher in Israel, applies even to a pious Mennonite: 'Except a man be born again he cannot see the kingdom of God.' (John 3:3) In order to impress upon the heart of Nicodemus the importance of this Word, the Lord Jesus further strengthened it with an oath by using the double 'Verily, verily.' It is the requirement and demand that comes from the lips of the only begotten Son of God. In John 1:12–13 we read that God's children are not born of man but of God. Herein we see what it's all about. With all our humanistic piety or religion we get nowhere and are lost. Nicodemus was also a religious man, but that did not suffice. The Lord Jesus tells us further why He came into the world in Matt. 18:11 as well as Luke 19:10: 'The Son of Man came to seek and to save that which was lost.'

"As you all know, I was born to really Christian Mennonite parents, as you all were, and have received a Christian up-bringing. I was baptized in 1882 by sprinkling, after a genuine conversion and was accepted into church membership. There were other young people who did the same thing. At that time I had complete peace and knew I was buried with Christ in death and raised up from the dead through baptism, to walk in newness of life, as we read in Romans 6:4.

"Because of the doctrinal disputes and controversies, and influenced by the loose living at the court in Chiwa where I served as interpreter, I suffered so greatly in my inner life that I moved to Aulie-ata. There I entered government service and strayed even farther from the Lord. I lived many years with a lack of inner peace, until I experienced my second, terrible breakdown. In the bright light of God—God is Light—under His conviction of my sin, I was totally broken. But God's saving grace was greater than my sin, and He gave me perfect peace. The result of this was that I was completely freed from hate and my heart was filled with His peace. He also freed me from other matters that did not please Him.

"Thus, with His love I entered into missionary work. The Lord blessed so that several Muslims have accepted the Lord Jesus as their Savior. After further instruction, I followed their wishes and baptized them on the basis of Romans 6:4. I noticed later that they took offense to the fact that I was not baptized in the manner they were, so for their sake, I was baptized again, by immersion, when I was in the Mission school in Berlin."

When my brethren in Akmettschet heard that they exclaimed, "So now you are a Baptist." My answer was, "Not at all! Since 1905 I have obeyed the Spirit of Truth within me according to John 16:13."

One evening the main topic of discussion was the meaning of the last words of John 3:16: "To have eternal life." We mentioned that eternal life is the Life of God, for God alone is eternal. And what is God? God is Love, John 4:8 and 16. Here the Lord Jesus says: "He who believes on Him has eternal life." Then according to II Corinthians 5:19: "God was in Christ," so since through faith in Christ we have eternal life, we also have our position in God. In other words, a child of God has God in his heart with all His attributes and attitudes, and since God is love, a child of His cannot help but love all men, and certainly could not kill anyone. And that is the basis of our so-called Mennonite doctrine of non-resistance. I have experienced in my own heart that this is really so.

We also thoroughly studied I Corinthians 13, where Paul tells us what love is. Here everyone can examine himself and discover how one really applies these words of Paul to his own life.

In this line of thinking, and with the guidance of the Holy Spirit, I spoke during the weeks I was there. But it was an extremely difficult task. These hearts, filled with so much prejudice toward people who think differently, did not permit themselves to come to the correct conclusion in these serious matters. In spite of being brought up ethically Christian and pious, they still did not understand anything about genuine eternal life in a child of God. With deep sorrow I often thought of the words of Brother Kroeker, which I have alluded to earlier. To be misunderstood is very difficult to take, and yet they showed much love to my wife and me.

At the close of my work there, I was overjoyed by what my brother-in-law, Franz Pauls, with whom my dear, deaf father lived, said to me, "Schwager Hermann, now I know, too, that the Lord Jesus is my Savior. I also have experienced Him, and my heart is filled with deep peace. Now I can understand you completely." With the same message, and a radiant face, a 36-year-old sister also came to me.

Our discussions during those weeks brought our revered and much beloved teacher and minister to a state of deep meditation. One morning he asked that we take a walk in a quiet section of Akmettschet. In a secluded spot we sat down on a sand hill and Brother Penner said, "After all the search and discussion during these weeks, I arrived at the place where I must say that I am not converted at all, to say nothing of being a child of God. I lack the inner assurance we read of in Romans 8:16: 'The Spirit itself bears witness with our spirit that we are the children of God.'"

After saying this he wept, and I was so shocked and astonished that I didn't know just what to say. All this was so long ago now that I cannot recount all the details of our conversation. I can only add that Brother Penner went through terrific struggles. Finally we prayed together and went home. He lived and preached for years after this time, but he was and remained a dejected and sad man, and I am told he experienced a difficult death.

As our time had now come, we traveled back to Taschkent and stayed with Brother Abram J. Janzen, who in the meantime had been appointed manager of the depot of the Bible Society. We worked together for awhile in the Sarter and Muslim *Altstadt* or old section of the city. Then my wife and I started on our homeward journey. On the six-day trip we distributed many tracts and gospels among the Muslim populace.

CHAPTER 11

▼

MISSIONARY EXPERIENCES

It was in May 1915 that I embarked on another lengthy trip from Orlof to Taschkent. On this road one passes through many Russian and Sarter villages as well as many Kirghiz Auls. Such trips were made either on farm wagons or on horseback, as I often did. I took my time on the way, and at every station, every village or in the Auls, I preached the gospel to the inhabitants and distributed much literature.

Near the entrance to the *caravanseries* there is usually a tea room where travelers and the usual market goers sit on carpets and drink their tea. Here I also sat among them, with my bag of Russian and Uzbeck language literature beside me. Soon the tea drinkers noticed this and asked about the contents of the materials. I would take some sheets and distribute them to those who could read, since a large majority could not. Then I asked one who was most vocal to read out loud, for example, John 3:16 and as the Spirit led I would introduce other scriptures.

Many of them knew me from earlier years and heard the Word gladly, and often said so. The Word was accepted in a varying degree, but it made a strong impression upon a majority of them. For me, however, the words of Isaiah 55:11 were of uppermost importance: "So shall my word be that goes forth out of my mouth; it shall not return unto me void, but shall accomplish that which I please, and it shall prosper in the thing whereto I sent it."

And so this trip also ended with Brother Janzen in the Bible depot. As usual, I stayed for some time. We visited the Russian Baptist Church, which by now had several German members. We were welcomed with much love, as though we also belonged. We were often given opportunity to preach the Word of God there.

Taschkent, capital of what was then Turkestan, is a very large, well-situated city of over 200,00 European inhabitants. On the west side, separated by the Keless River, is found the even larger Muslim *Altstadt* or old city, where Sarters, Uzbecks, Tadschiks and a few depraved Kirghiz, working as day laborers, lived. As in the *Neustadt*, or modern part of the city, the *Altstadt* had large department stores and extended trade. It had many bazaars, located on each side of the narrow streets. During the heat of summer everything is in semi-darkness, because the streets are spanned by rush mats for shade. A stranger may easily get lost in the shadows and if he does not speak the native language his situation is not to be envied. It seems that in the "good old days" Europeans sometimes disappeared without ever leaving a trace.

In the *Altstadt* are very large Mosques and theological universities with thousands of students. Here Islamic fanaticism is always very great. On nearly all street corners were tea houses that were always occupied, since in the tropical heat much tea is consumed. One was always thirsty. Endless streams of men and long caravans of camels passed by on the narrow streets. Everyone had to be careful as he went through. And it was often very difficult to do.

We also found our way through the crowded streets with our heavy bags of books. One day we met a group of begging *Dervishes* or Monks, singing and begging in the bazaars. Among the Muslims they are considered holy men and are especially fanatic. When they saw us with our books they sprang toward us, spat in our faces and screamed, "Away with these damned Christian dogs, these *Gaururs*, that is, unbelievers." It was our good fortune that the police were there immediately and they disbursed the *dervishes*, so we could continue on our way.

Disregarding various obstacles, we distributed considerable numbers of tracts and gospels on these tours. Even in the tea houses we were able to talk with many concerning their salvation. On Sunday we went to the Baptist Church, since there were no other churches in Taschkent. They sang many beautiful hymns from the "*Guelja*," the well-known songbook by Ivan Stepanovitch Prochenof.

Because of the singing, many unconverted Russians and also German business-men came to the meetings. Several of them experienced conversion and were baptized.

In this way, a German lady accepted Christ. Her husband was in the army reserves somewhere on the Persian border. She wrote to him about her experience, but instead of being happy about it, he wrote her in his rage and threatened to kill her if she would not renounce her new religion. His name was Laubach and he was to come home on furlough soon. He owned a first class meat packing plant and sausage factory, and employed many people. He had a large house. They were Lutherans, but he was a very rough man.

Soon he came home on an extended furlough. For the poor woman it was a terrible time, for he beat and tortured her. She remained firm in her faith, which made him all the more furious. Since he was on furlough, he carried his side arms. One Sunday afternoon we heard of her distress. Brother Janzen and I went over to speak to the man. His rage was awful; it was a terrible battled within us. Together with his wife, we wrestled with the Lord for his soul. And God answered in a wonderful way.

We finally got to the point where he quieted down and we actually persuaded him to attend the meeting. Depressed and quiet, he went with us and listened attentively to the sermon, obviously gripped by it. At the end of the sermon everyone kneeled, as was the custom in this congregation. All prayed audibly as they were led.

What might the thoughts of our friend Laubach have been, we do not know. But after that he didn't miss a meeting. At home he became a quiet man. Soon he experienced genuine conversion, came to complete peace, and asked to be baptized. In his home, and especially with his wife, joy reigned supreme. She said, "I now have divine happiness."

After unanimous consent of the brethren, it was decided that he should be baptized on the following Sunday. It would be in the Salar River on the edge of the city, where the river flows by a bathing beach. On Sunday morning after the sermon and a time of prayer, the whole congregation made its way on foot to the river. On the way we sang many songs and curious by-standers joined the group as we walked along. Upon arrival at the river, as many as possible entered the bathing tent, which had an open side toward the water. Several steps led down into the water. In one corner curtains were used to form a little dressing room. After a short sermon by the church leader, concerning conversion and baptism, the baptizer, dressed in a white robe, stepped into the water. The baptismal candidate followed him; but unexpectedly he returned and re-entered the tent. Soon he came back and walked down the steps into the water and was baptized. While he and the pastor were changing clothes in the tent, the congregation sang songs and continued singing on the way back to the church, where the festivities were concluded.

Brother Janzen and I were constrained to accompany the happy Laubachs to their home. It was now evening and after tea we wanted to return to the Bible depot, but Brother Laubach insisted that I establish quarters in his house now and not always with Brother Jantzen. I agreed with him and Brother Janzen also felt this would be desirable. The following morning Brother Abram came by to pick me up, as we had previously agreed, and we went to the *Altstadt*.

As we arose from the tea table, Brother Laubach put his hand into his purse and handed me 300 rubles, then worth $150 and said, "Dear Brother Jantzen, take this money and buy food in the Old City for the hungry Sarters and give them to eat. (There was a famine at the time.) After that bring them the gospel and you will see that your listeners will heed the Word much better on a full stomach than on an empty one."

We went our way and did as we were told. The next morning he did the same thing and again on the third morning. Then I said in astonishment, "Brother Laubach, that is too much that you are doing. You do have a wife and children."

"My dear brethren, my wallet was also baptized and belongs to the Lord. Didn't you notice at the baptismal service how I returned to the dressing room before stepping into the water? The reason was this: as I was dressing for the baptism, the Spirit of God said to me, 'Adam (that was his first name), take your wallet along; it too must be baptized.' The devil whispered to me, 'But you have a wife and children.' And I obeyed him. But as I was stepping into the water, God's Spirit again said, 'Adam, stop! now or never; return quickly and get your wallet; it too must be baptized because from now on it belongs to me.' That is why I hurried back and got it. I hid it in my clothes and covered it with my hands so no one could see it. So it is that my wallet was baptized with me and now belongs to the Lord. Therefore, brethren, don't worry about me; I know what I am doing. Now have a good day in the Altstadt." With that he disappeared into his packing plant and we went on our way.

One day we were sitting in the depot and, because of the oppressive heat, we had the front door wide open. We noticed a ragged *Haji*, or Pilgrim to Mecca, who had just returned from a journey to Mecca, step into our room. One can recognize these pilgrims because they wear a specially wound white turban with a yellow-brown or tan pilgrim's mantle. This man entered and sat down on the floor, obviously very weary, and asked whether we had the large book by Luther in the Uzbeck-Turkish language. We didn't know immediately which book he meant. Then he explained that it says much about Jesus, the Son of the Virgin Mary. Then we realized that he wanted a Bible.

Brother Janzen handed him a beautiful Bible in his language. Immediately he began to read in his own language, and so fluently that we were surprised. Then he told us his story. He had made two pilgrimages to Mecca and Medina. On the second trip he returned by way of Jerusalem and Bethlehem and had prayed at all the holy places, but had not found peace in his soul. He continued through Constantinople and Crimea into the Ukraine. There he met some German people who did not attend the Russian Church with its image worship. In his broken Russian he told them of the lack of peace in his heart. They informed him that he must read the large book by Luther in which much is said of Jesus, the Son of the Virgin Mary. If he would read that, he would find peace. So he was seeking everywhere for this book in his own language.

We kept the man with us several days and studied the Scriptures with him. He was susceptible to that which we told him. After a few days he journeyed on to Andischen where he lived. A few months later, in Orlof, I received the following letter from him: "I have now found Jesus as my Savior and wish to have you baptize me."

Brother Janzen also received a copy of the letter. So I traveled to Taschkent and from there Janzen and I went to Andischen 400 kilometers away. Our newly found Brother Mussa Machmudi received us with great joy. He did have difficulty understanding that Jesus should be the Son of God when God isn't married. It took us some time to explain this to him; in fact I used the Koran as evidence. Mohammed explains this in the Koran as follows:

"Jesus was born without a human father of the Virgin Mary upon the command of God through Gabriel, as Adam also had no human father and was born only by God's Word. That is why Jesus was also called the Word of God. He lived without sin and died. But God called Him from the dead and took Him alive into heaven." Further we read in the Koran that Jesus came for the salvation of many. The Muslim book *Shariah* says this and much else very clearly.

Finally the full light of God's Word came through to our Brother Mussa Machmudi, and he received complete peace and joy. After a few more days of instruction in the Scripture, and following his express wish, we baptized him in the name of the triune God, the Father and the Son and the Holy Spirit. After that we partook of the Holy Communion with him and returned to our homes.

The witness of Brother Mussa Machmudi became a great blessing to many in his community and this especially because he was so well versed in the Muslim scriptures. Through him an educated young man of Aimkischlack, 30 kilometers from Andischen, was given a Bible in his own language by Brother Janzen. He read it eagerly. Soon we had the opportunity to visit him in his village. He was the son of a wealthy merchant.

His name was Mamedschan; he was married and the father of a lovely young daughter. As a scholarly Mullah he had an extensive library. He received us warmly and together we searched the Scriptures for some days. Brother Mussa had also joined the group. As an educated former Muslim, now a Christian with a positive witness for Jesus, the Son of the Virgin Mary on the one side, but also a Son of God on the other, he made a profound impression on the young man. After we had distributed tracts and Gospels throughout the city, we returned home by way of Chodschent, where we also distributed much literature.

A few months later Mamedschan wrote us a letter asking us to come to him, since he wished us to baptize him. Again we were warmly received and he lodged us in his library. We noticed, however, that in spite of his joy in meeting us again, he was under a heavy burden. Then he told us that he now belongs to the Lord, but that this brought him very serious consequences. His father had disinherited him and had taken his wife and little daughter from him. All domestic communication was denied him; only the library was still his. His meals were brought here and served without a word being spoken.

We stayed with him a few days. Food and drink were brought to us at his request at certain hours. We slept with him in the same room, on the heavily carpeted floor, as is the custom in this country. Daily we searched the Scriptures together and asked him many questions. We were convinced that a deep understanding of God's Word had penetrated his heart. One day we asked, "Dear Mamedschan, how is it that, as we have noticed, you answer all our questions with such a genuine smile?"

He answered very soberly, "Dear brethren, I know that for days now you have tried to determine how deeply my faith in the Lord Jesus is grounded, in order to be able to baptize me. This is your duty. For we Muslims are generally false and untrustworthy. Now I must tell you something.

"Since I have received the Bible, I have studied it a great deal. This brought me many questions that I could not answer. However, I was seeking for complete answers. In my dark despair I sat here one day and cried, 'O Lord Jesus, since you did rise from the dead and are now alive, and here in the Bible I read: I am with you always until the end of the world, then reveal Yourself to me. I am seeking for you.' To this cry He opened my eyes and I saw him standing before me, with outstretched arms and with a look on His face that I cannot describe to you. I jumped up and wanted to throw myself into His arms—but with that He disappeared. And so, dear brethren, I have seen Him and am His property and I would like to testify to this by being baptized on the basis of Romans 6:4. Do now what you think you should."

We were deeply moved by this simple testimony. That night at midnight, accompanied by the invited witnesses, Brother Mussa Machmudi and a Russian Baptist sister, we went to the edge of the city and baptized him in the river. Upon our return the five of us celebrated the Lord's Supper together with much praise and thanks. We had the conviction that the Lord was in our midst. After the sister had left, we four lay down on the carpet and went to sleep.

The question may arise as to why we baptized so late in the night instead of during the light of day. The reason is simple. We were in a Muslim city. The inhabitants would never have permitted the rite of baptism. There was the mortal danger to act in the open.

The next day we started for home, making use as always of the opportunity of distributing tracts and scripture portions among fellow passengers. This gave us many chances to speak with individuals about their salvation. The Muslims in those days were very religious and talked eagerly about religion and books of that nature.

CHAPTER 12

▼

THE REVOLT OF THE JAMUDEN

In those days of the year 1916 I was at home and read under the item of Telegrams in the Turkestan newspaper the following report: "The Turkmenen have captured Chiwa after heavy fighting. Seit-Ispendjar, his court and a German village were all murdered.

The old nobleman, Seit-Muchemet Khan, had died some time before and his son Ispendjar was now the Khan. He did not understand how to rule the Jamuden and lacked the complete authority his father had achieved. All this led to an uprising among the Turkmenen. The Uzbeck-Turks, to whom the Khan belonged, were really a peace loving people; in contrast the Turkmenen or Jamuden were proud, brave, warlike and thieverish. In a few weeks they had conquered the western part of the state including the capital of Chiwa.

At the beginning of the revolt, Khan Ispendjar had called on the Russians for help, but help came too late. The Prince, his family and many other noblemen and citizens were all killed. After reading the telegram, I started on my way to Chiwa. In Taschkent I stopped to see Brother Janzen and gave him the content of the news report. He decided to accompany me, at least as far as Tschardshui, and use the opportunity to distribute tracts and Scriptures. Our 34-hour trip took us through Tschinas, Dahisak, Samarkent and Buchara to Tschardachui on the Amudarja River. Here we wanted to see a Baptist brother, but the police arrested us and took us to the Commissar who examined our credentials. Our names are German, but my first name was in Russian, therefore not Hermann but "German" since the Russian language does not have the "H" sound. He was suspicious and called other officials in and exclaimed, "Here we have something! Even this far have the Germans penetrated and sent in their spies. Into prison with the two until morning!"

I tried to explain to him: "I am a Russian citizen, born in Russia, as was my comrade. We have lived for many years in the District of Aulie-ata and now you ask who we are." He accepted my protest but we had to spend the night in the police station. The next morning we were dismissed with apologies. We made our way to the Baptist brother, a former acquaintance, who received us cordially.

But I had in mind to get to Petroalexandrowska and Chiwa as soon as possible. The only steamer on the Amudarja had left two days before. Then the brother told me of a Ural-Cossack whom he knew, who lives in Petroalexandrowska. He would call him and maybe we could further discuss the matter. This he did, with the result that the Cossack and I would buy a fishing boat and travel to Hanka together. This town lies just across from Chiwa. He could then proceed to Petroalexandrowska.

After purchasing the boat, we left the same evening from a secret spot on the river. Everything was under war alert and the river was heavily guarded. Brother Janzen and the other brother accompanied us to the boat and we took leave from each other. Without incident, after four days' travel, we reached Hanka. Here the Cossack paid me for my half of the boat and then went his way, while I walked to Chiwa.

Wearing a long Chiwanese mantle with my travel bag on my back, I forced my way through the bushes and undergrowth on the riverbank to the village of Haake, which was about four kilometers away. A Chiwanese fisherman, with his donkey, caught up with me. I asked him whether I might ride the donkey and he allowed it. So I mounted the lazy animal while the fisherman walked alongside, urging the donkey on.

As we approached the gate to the city I noticed that Russian soldiers stopped everyone and inspected those who wanted to enter. I was successful in slipping in and I rode on to the door of the city officer, Aminbei, whom I had known for many years. His yard was filled with Cossacks who pulled me from the donkey and asked me who I was. The mantle indicated I was Chiwanese, but the blue eyes betrayed me. They were suspicious. An officer came near and asked, "Who are you?"

"I am one of the Akmettschet Germans." He was skeptical and opened a notebook that he had with him and said, "Now name all the people of Akmettschet by name in the order in which they live." After I had done that, he let me go. Just then my friend Aminbei appeared and greeted me warmly and said to the officer, "This is my friend of many years from Akmettschet." This brought our affairs in order and I stayed overnight with Aminbei. The next morning one of his horsemen helped me get to Akmettschet, about 45 kilometers distant.

My relatives and friends were overjoyed to see me. All of them were wan and tired. I told them how I had heard of their reign of terror, and was constrained to come and see how they all were and whether the reports were really true. Then they told me what had happened. They were in extreme danger, because the intention of the Jamuden was that, since they were friendly to the Khan Ispendjar, they were all to be killed, together with the court and citizens of Chiwa. Just in the nick of time a friendly Jamud came and warned them. He said, "Day after tomorrow, Monday, is the day definitely set for the Jamuden army to come and destroy everything."

Upon receiving this information, the whole congregation gathered in the church and prayed and fasted all that night and all day Sunday. That evening they finally heard the Russian cannons bombarding the city of Chiwa on the side toward Akmettschet. This drove the Jamuden to the opposite side of our village. The battle raged for two days, after which the Russians drove the Jamuden back 150 kilometers to their earlier position and broke their power completely. Of the family of Bagadur only a brother of Khan Ispendjar, Seit-Abdulla, remained alive.

Since my youth, I had known Seit-Abdulla and so I went to visit him. I congratulated him that he was safe and remained with him for four days. This was as long as I could stay. It was obvious that he was very glad to see me, as his friendly reception indicated. He was still living under the pressure of his recent experience, and said to me, "My dear Jaman Aga (my name in their language or region), my father whom you served as interpreter for many years, died a natural death; his successor, Seit-Ispendjar and all my other brothers were murdered by the Jamuden. Now I am Khan; and what will my end be?"

All day long I had to stay with him and because of his crushed and saddened condition, I had a good opportunity to talk to him about his soul's salvation. I took my Uzbeck-Turkish New Testament out of my pocket and handed him a similar one, which I had purposely brought with me. He was very happy to receive it and we sat the rest of the day on his veranda and searched in the Scriptures.

It was all so new and strange to him, but I sensed that he was receptive for everything we read and discussed. The following days we spent in the same manner. As we parted, the Khan handed me a splendid photograph, on the back of which he had inscribed: "This is for my dear Brad (Brother) Jaman Aga in memory of our intimate communion during the darkest days of my life in the year 1916 in Chiwa." Signed: Seit-Abdulla Bagadur Khan. Unfortunately, in the restless years that followed, the beautiful photograph was lost, for which I am very sorry.

I might add here that in 1918 the Bolscheviks, when they came to Chiwa, overthrew his government, too. Everything Seit-Abdulla had was stolen from him, he was given Russian clothes, and sent to the Caucasus. There he walked behind a plow for the rest of his life. That was the last I ever heard about him again.

After a hurried trip I arrived at Urgensch where the steamer was all ready to leave. I boarded and we went downstream to Tschardschui. The farewells from my dear ones were very hurried because I had so little time left. The train trip took three days from Tschardschui to Aulie-ata, the end of the railroad. From there I went by wagon to Orlof.

CHAPTER 13

▼

THE KIRGHIZ REBELLION

On the way home the conductor told me all manner of bad things. The Russian government had included all the Muslim peoples of Turkestan in military service. They were not to bear arms against the Germans, but to dig communication trenches. All the Kirghiz resisted this call; had they not always prayed to Allah in their mosques for victory for Germany over Russia? The fact that they are now to be drafted suggested to them that the Germans had shot all the Russians and now it should be their turn.

In the Russian villages all the men between the ages of 17 and 45 had been called to the colors, so that practically only old men, women and children were left. Thousands of Kirghiz were massed together and attacked these villages, murdering many people in a horrible manner, plundered the houses, and burned the villages.

All this I found to be true when I got home, and fear and panic reigned among us. Because of this, many of our people sent their daughters away. We took our daughter Anna to relatives in Samara on the Trakt River, where she remained for a year.

In this manner the Kirghiz destroyed forty Russian villages in the vicinity of Istickkul-Prisspeck, which was not far from our village. Not only were the villages destroyed, but all the fields of ripened grain and fruits were burned so that practically everything was destroyed.

One bright moonlit night a group of Kirghiz came to our village. They were fully armed, which frightened us greatly. One of them dismounted and came to my bedroom window. He evidently knew that I was sleeping there. He called my name, and after I opened the window and asked what he wanted, he said, "Our Chieftains have sent us here to ask you to come with us. Our troops are stationed on the large grassland of the Russian village Klutschofka. The Chieftains want to counsel with you, for they know that you are Germans and not Russians. Hurry and saddle your horse and come with us. The August night is short and our discussion must end by daybreak. Klutschofka is a 12 kilometer ride from here."

It was obviously senseless to resist; here polite request, serious gravity, and threat were in evidence. After I had calmed my wife and children, I rode with them at a rapid gait. On the pastureland I saw thousands of Kirghiz resting while their horses grazed. The leaders were seated on a hill, waiting for me. Politely they asked me to be seated among them, which I promptly obeyed. Then the Chief among them spoke up:

"Friend Rakmen Bai (my name in these tribes), we have asked you to come in order to discuss something with you. As you must know, we are in the process of making an end to the Russians in our area. After the Germans had killed so many Russians that they wanted to draft us into their armies, we have decided to help the Germans. We are their friends and always pray for them in our Mosques. Didn't their Pascha, Kaiser Wilhelm, visit Seit-Hamiet Pascha, the Sultan of Turkey in Constantinople a few years ago? He even attended a worship service with the Sultan in a Mosque on Friday (the Muslim Sunday), dressed in a white turban, as was the Sultan. After the German Pascha asked for the hand of the Sultan's daughter for his son (which of course was not so) we are good friends of the Germans.

"We know that the people of your eight villages are Germans and have the same attitude toward the Russians that we do. They treat you as badly as they do us, which is evident when they consign horses from us. Where a Russian farmer must deliver one horse, you must furnish two. We know that the Russians hate you as much as they hate us. But now the time of revenge is here. Forty villages have been wiped from the face of the earth. The villages of Alexanovka, Dimitrofka, Klutschofka, Wodnoioe and Alexandrofka are next in line. Your villages lie among these, but no evil shall befall you. For your protection, we have set a watch around your village for many nights now. They are not to be seen by you. But they take care, that none of our people from other communities, who do not know you, will harm you. Now our advice to you is, come with us and help avenge ourselves on our common enemy."

"My friends," so I began my answer. "I thank you for your friendliness and trust you have in us. But I must tell you, as true as it is that the treatment we get from the Russians is as you say, so true it is also, that our villagers are Christians, for whom Christ has forbidden to seek revenge. Therefore, we cannot go with you. On the other hand, I would like to give you some advice, if you will listen to it."

"We have complete confidence in you, Rakmen Bai, for we have known you for many years. No doubt your advice will be valid, so speak up freely."

"Dear friends, if you believe that the Russians have been shot in such large numbers that they must now mobilize you, then you are in error. Russia is much, much larger than you imagine and they have many troops left. You will see that. And I am not mistaken when I say that in a short time, perhaps a week, large numbers of soldiers will appear to punish you. Among them will be fathers and sons of those who died at your hands and they will seek revenge. As your friend I would advise you to take as much of your property as you can and flee into the hills as far as possible. Wait there for ten days and see whether I am right or not."

Here I was asked to step aside as the Chieftains discussed the matters among themselves. This took quite some time. Finally one of them called me back into their midst. Again the Captain arose and said, "Dear Rakmen Bai, we have decided to accept your advice and do as you suggest, because we know that you have our best interest in mind." Then they called all the men together and the Captain informed them of everything that had been discussed and also what had been decided. Then he raised his hands toward heaven and cried out, "As a sign that we have accepted the advice of our friend Rakmen Bai and will carry it out, we raise our hands toward heaven and call out together, '*Allah ya schkur*,' that is, 'Thanks be to God.'"

Like a roll of thunder, the cry came from a thousand throats. Then came the command: "Everyone to your home! Everyone flee with tent, cattle and family deep into the mountains, and remain until the next call to arms."

But there never was another call, for as I had expected, there soon appeared thousands of Russian soldiers, among them many of the fathers and sons of the victims in the villages. They took their revenge on everything that fell into their hands that belonged to Kirghiz. It was much more terrible than the Kirghiz had done to them. The soldiers penetrated deep into the valleys and hills and destroyed everyone and everything they could find. Many of the wealthy Kirghiz, with their plunder, including many girls, had fled the 5-day distance into Chinese-Turkestan.

CHAPTER 14

▼

AMONG THE BOLSHEVIKS

In the following year, 1917, came the revolution with all its terrible results. Mission work was forbidden and I had to remain quietly at home. However, the calm didn't last long. As early as July there was an order by the new government that all peoples and tribes were to elect delegates who would be sent to the capital city where they would represent the interests of their *Gemeinde* or district.

Our *Gemeinde,* composed of 12 villages, elected me since I was conversant in all four languages used in Turkestan, as well as Russia. As associates or alternates they elected the Brethren P.J. and H.M. with full voting rights. Already in July the delegates from all Turkestan were required to meet in the large government building. The incumbent governor, with his *subalterns,* had been arrested and removed from office.

Since this type of government, without a head, was strange to us we elected a chairman. He had to be a Communist and at the same time an enemy of all previous forms of government. We elected a Mr. Kerenski, who later became President of Russia. In all matters a plurality of votes decided the issue. Here stood 5% Europeans over against the 95% Muslims, who naturally decided everything in their favor.

Moscow regularly sent fluent and educated men to us, who had been embittered by the long war against the Czarist regime. They continually scolded and agitated. The sessions lasted for many days. We three Mennonites didn't have much to say. New regulations came daily from Moscow that added to the confusion.

The three of us lived at the Bible depot with Brother Janzen. In our free time we made our accustomed visits into the Altstadt and visited with our Muslim friends. But all the upheaval and unrest was so upsetting that not much could be accomplished. In the delegate sessions nothing much was said about religion, although now and then a "highly regarded" Moscow lecturer would rant and rave about the longhaired Popes, who were the fundamental cause of all evil conditions.

After we arrived home from Taschkent we were continually forced to take part in deliberations in Aulie-ata. However, in October we were called to Taschkent again, where sessions became very stormy. From the 25th to the 28th there was bloody fighting that killed many people. The contest was between the Bolsheviki and the leftist revolutionaries. The Bolsheviki were well armed; the opposition was not. In the fortress there were still soldiers loyal to the Czar. These were eliminated first. Then the victorious ones went through the city killing wantonly whoever got in their way. It didn't matter whether man, woman or child. Soon the streets were filled with corpses. The leader of the leftist party was stuck alive into the locomotive firebox and burned. He was an old acquaintance of mine, named Baronef, a director of the state bank. He was a fine gentleman and left his young wife and several children behind.

During all this time we three Mennonites sat in Brother Janzen's cellar, since many cannonballs that were shot into town struck houses nearby. When things finally quieted down again, the victorious Bolscheviks went through the houses of the so-called "rich Bonzen" in order to requisition everything that was left for the new government. "Robbing" is a capitalistic expression and was never used here.

As soon as possible we started home again, with the ever-present question in our hearts: how might things be there? As we arrived in the large city of Tschimkent we noted that here everything was calm. On our way through many Russian villages people had not heard of the events in Taschkent. At home everything was quiet also.

Soon there appeared propagandists in all the villages who held large meetings, which everyone over 16, men and women, were required to attend. They made high-sounding speeches about happiness and prosperity. They also emphasized that everyone would have to become members of the party. However, in our area they received little appreciation.

The Bible depot had to close its doors in 1918, and Brother Janzen returned to our villages with his family and lived in Nikolaipol. For awhile he was active as a teacher in Orlof, which was about 7 kilometers distant. On Sundays he often served us with the Word of God, by which we all received rich blessing.

After harvest we received strict orders to deliver everything that was not necessary for our own existence or for seed, to the village of Alexandrofka, which was 35 kilometers away. That was a heavy blow for us farmers, but that is the way it remained. A while later the despots came and took away plows, fanning mills, sewing machines and many wagons from us.

A further development required that we hold an election every three months in our district. One who was elected could not decline to serve because he would be stamped as a counter-revolutionary or as a Czarist and was treated accordingly. In such an election I unfortunately received the second highest vote for district Commissar. So I became the assistant to a former prisoner of war from Galacia, named Soroka, who became Chief Commissar. He was not a bad man but was a noble communist who had chosen to remain in Russia. Unfortunately he liked to drink. I was required to work with him daily in the *Kreis Kanzelei* or chancellery and always had to stay in the city. Evenings I often went to the Altstadt where I could discuss more important matters with my Muslim friends, than the sad conditions found in our land.

Almost daily the Commissariat held its sessions which all district delegates had to attend. Here we received new decisions after the pattern of Moscow, sent to us by way of Taschkent. As I already mentioned, 5% of us faced the 95% of the Muslims, who had been oppressed by the Czarist regime, now considered as enemies. Since Bolshevism had granted them great freedom, most of them became party members and therefore, through their larger number, controlled the *Politburo* (GPU) as well as other areas of government. For them it now became self-evident that through various actions they would get revenge of their previous rules. Therefore Soroka and I often had to take a difficult stand because many of their decisions were utterly unreasonable. The intellectuals among the Muslims stood aloof in all this and didn't care much for the spirit of Bolshevism. In any case, the Muslims, through their plurality, always had their own way, in which, for the most part, those returning from the front supported them. These returning soldiers were, without exception, very bitter. Many of them were the secretaries or scribes in the chancelleries, which were controlled by the Muslims.

In autumn the expropriation edict came to us from Moscow. With it came the order that every representative of the people was required to sign it. So all the delegates were called together again, with the announcement in advance that the words "mine" and "yours" were no longer valid. In the ensuing session the law was spread before us for signature. A large majority agreed with the order. However, I opposed it, whereupon the president asked me for an explanation.

I rose and said, "We have in our village a neighbor who came to Turkestan with his wife and two children from distant Russia about 20 years ago. During all this time, he worked hard and acquired some land. If I were to sign this law I would take his property from him. So I must ask myself: for what did this man work all these years? Added to this is the fact that he is a genuine revolutionary. And there are many such cases. According to the law of Lenin, we as Bolsheviks are to provide for the proletariat, as well as to protect him. That is why I cannot sign this law."

Here a large part of the delegation cried out, "Away with him; away with delegate Janzen! He is a counter-revolutionary, a monarchist, a capitalist." Others yelled, "He is also a missionary, who has drawn some of our people away from the mosque by his teaching," and so on.

I rose and left the hall. In my quarters, I went to bed, because it was already very late. After several hours I was awakened by a knock on the door. I got up and asked who was there. The familiar voice of the chairman of the Communist Party of the Muslims and also chairman of the GPU answered. His name was Ibraimof, a highly educated Tartar and a good friend of mine. He said, "Dear friend Jantzen, why were you so stupid today by not signing the expropriation law? Do you know what happened when you left? At the close of the session I was called into the *Politburo* because of an "important" matter. When I arrived there I noticed that the discussion concerned you. The group voted and agreed that you are to be liquidated, and that by a firing squad. At 7 a.m. the soldiers will come and take you to the execution. Naturally, as a single individual, I could not do anything for you, but as an old friend, who often was a guest at your house, where I ate bread and salt, I cannot but warn you. Herewith I sanctify the sacred law of Muslim hospitality toward you and am free of your blood, since I did warn you. I see your horse here with the saddle lying beside it. You still have time to flee. May Allah guide and protect you. Until we meet again in better times than we now have." With these words he disappeared.

Quickly I saddled my horse and rode to where my colleague was staying and told him my situation without naming the one who had warned me. I handed him the seal and the keys to the chancellery. He wished me a good trip and I rode away. The night was dark and it was 65 kilometers to Orlof.

At home I informed my wife and the children, all married by this time, of my situation. I was sure the soldiers would look for me at home, after not finding me in the city. I would therefore have to flee deeper into the hills, where I could hide among the Black-Kirghiz, who were friendly toward me and would not betray me. So I mounted my horse and rode into the mountains.

It happened as I had suspected. Soldiers searched for me at my home. They took the occasion to search the whole house, and what they liked they took with them. It was a difficult time for my family.

During the day I would spend my time in the higher regions of the hills; in the evening I would steal into one of the many Auls, making sure first that there were no soldiers within. After determining that, I would enter the best tent in order not to burden a poor family. I was always warmly received and served with the best they had. After all, they all had known me for many years. As we sat around the large cauldron in which the meat was cooking, I could bring them the gospel and talk to many about their salvation. They were very attentive and asked many questions.

During such evenings the dwellers of the tent took active part in the discussions. More than four months I lived among them, going from one Aul to another. No one ever betrayed me. One evening I was the guest of a Sarter Mullah (holy one) who was married to a Kara-Kirghiz girl and served as a teacher among these people. Suddenly I heard someone outside asking for me. I gave a start, but then recognized the voice of my dear co-worker, Brother A. Janzen. He immediately dismounted and we greeted each other within the tent. What a surprise that was for me! He had sought me for days and, after much effort, finally found me.

When I asked him what had induced him to look for me, he answered that only his love for me had forced him to do it. He wished to share my fate. I tried to make it clear to him that this would hardly be possible. Each morning I must go into the higher elevation of the mountains. It was already late in autumn and it was getting cold, besides having much rainy weather and even blizzards. We wouldn't dare build a fire because of the danger of detection.

But he insisted he would share my fate. Many days we were together. His love was a great blessing to me, but on the other hand it was depressing for me to realize the danger which threatened him, as it did me. So I said to him, "My dear Abram, I know that I am being hunted continually. Now imagine your position should they one day find me and you are with me in the wilderness. You would then receive the same treatment I would receive. That I do not wish to see, for your sake. Then, too, you have nothing to do with the authorities nor do they have anything against you." My continued remonstrance finally got through to him. The day came when we said farewell to each other and parted, much as had David and Jonathan in days long ago. He rode on home.

The weather in the mountains finally became more impossible, even for me. I became ill of rheumatism to the extent that the pain became unbearable. In my pain and despair, I said, "Lord Jesus, I cannot continue living like this. I must surrender to the Bolsheviks and give myself up to the GPU. If it is your will that they shoot me, that is good, too."

One night I rode home in a round-about way and related to my dear ones the decision I had made. They could see that there was no other way out for me. For a few days I hid myself at home. A short while before this, my persecutors had been there and searched for me everywhere, even in neighboring villages. Finally I had to leave. One night I rode into town, again by a round-about route. My youngest brother, by whom I stopped to say good-bye, came with me to bring my horse back.

When I arrived in town at the GPU the gentlemen were astonished to see me. I then explained my position: "I knew that you had given me the death sentence, although I only defended the Proletariat in our new order. I fled because I did not wish to be executed on that charge, that I acted according to my conscience. I never want to bring violence against my fellow man and therefore I felt I was innocent. Because of my illness I can no longer live in the mountains, so I came of my own free will to give myself over to you. If you wish to shoot me, there is a revolver all ready; I have given up my life and am prepared to die."

That surprised them even more. They rose and went into another room, where they evidently discussed what they should do. Upon their return they ordered two soldiers to lead me to prison, where with my rheumatism, I suffered intensely. My brother took my horse and a letter to my family, which the soldiers allowed me to write, and rode sadly home. I was taken into a small cell, without a bed, where I spent the nights on the cold asphalt floor. What that did to me I cannot describe; the Lord knows it.

I spent eleven days and nights in this situation. The food was not adequate for an otherwise healthy man. But I had no appetite and ate very little. On the twelfth day two soldiers took me from the cell; it took great effort and I had great pain. I assumed that the redeeming bullet would now come. But things turned out differently. I was led through the large prison grounds, surrounded by high stone walls, to a near-by building. Here the Prison Commissar had his residence and his office.

The Commissar was seated behind a green table with all sorts of papers before him. He looked at me and began: "Name?" "Married?" and so on. After he had recorded all this, he said, "I see that you are sick. Who arrested you?" As I was answering all the questions, he noticed that I had a book in my pocket, and asked what it was. I answered that it was my pocket Bible.

"Wasn't that taken from you when you were arrested?" When I said no, I added that my watch and my wallet had been taken, but not my Bible.

"Do you still believe in the Bible?" "Yes," I said and he laughed loudly, and said, "Good, take your Bible and read me something." So I took the Bible from my pocket, and without much thought I opened it and my eyes fell on Isaiah, Chapter 3, which I read to him.

Soon he said, "Who wrote that? That is exactly the way it is now in Russia!"

"The prophet Isaiah wrote it."

"When did he write it?"

"About six hundred years before the birth of Christ."

"How could he have known what we were to experience in Russia today? Certainly much of what he says agrees exactly with what we have here now."

"The Holy Spirit of God dictated it to him."

He was completely confused and sat deep in thought. Finally he asked whether all Bibles say the same thing. I assured him that they do. After more thought he said, "I must have a Bible." I asked him for a piece of paper and pen and said, "I am writing to my friend here in town who will provide you with a Bible." I then wrote to my friend and the Bible was delivered.

A few days later he called me in again, and when he saw me he yelled, "You lied to me. I did receive the Bible and looked through it to find that same passage. But it isn't in there." I assured him that it was and found the chapter and gave it to him to read. That surprised him and he said, "I must study the Bible. So I will have you brought to me every day. You will be my secretarial assistant and we can then study together. I see you are ill; you must have a bed."

And it was as he had said. As his scribe, I was given freedom to come and go to him forenoons and afternoons without escort, and we studied the Bible together. In the meantime, I received a court hearing and, as a result, I was allowed visitors from home, quilts, pillows and other items. I also had tracts and other literature in the Russian and Uzbeck languages brought to me. I distributed these among the other prisoners.

One day a giant of a man was brought into my cell—black-bearded, long-haired and very dark. His language indicated he was from Siberia. I was told that he had robbed churches and was a murderer. I thought: "What company!" He never talked unless forced to do so. Most of the time he lay still on his moldy straw mattress and seemed to be content. He scolded a good deal about the poor food. When they brought me food from home I always shared it with him. This he enjoyed. One day they brought us a large loaf of bread, which we were to divide between us. Since we had no knife, we didn't know how to cut it. Suddenly he grabbed under the table and pulled out a dagger, which he had secretly stuck under there. I was frightened and wondered how he could have smuggled that into the cell. He said coldly and calmly, "Just take the knife; it is still new. I have never slit anyone's throat with this one; there is no blood on it. Cut the bread; you are older than I." So I sliced it.

A little later an officer of the Cossacks was brought to us in the cell. He had a wounded leg and limped. He was a friendly and sympathetic man with an open character; he visited a lot and sang beautifully. I might insert here that the prisoners were entirely open and frank toward each other and spoke of their crimes without shame or reserve, utterly truthful. They took the attitude that we were all the same or we wouldn't be here.

Our Cossack officer was that way too. He told us that, after the overthrow of the Empire and the murder of the Czarist family, he was in such inner turmoil that from the autumn of 1917 to 1918 he was at the head of a large band that fought against the Reds. Finally he was badly wounded and fell into their hands. In order not to be recognized he had thrown away his uniform and went under an assumed name. In the cell he lay very near me and soon noticed that I prayed and read the Bible. This gave him more confidence in me and he soon expressed himself with complete openness.

"I am an apostate Christian who left the faith; once a member of a Baptist Church. During the long war I became very vulgar and rough and, after the destruction of the Czarist Empire, I fell into deep despair. I lost all spiritual life. Please pray for me because I am very unhappy."

Gladly I tried to help him and soon he began to pray again. Often he sang many of the Russian songs taken out of the Gusslja by Prochanof. He also composed many songs, which he put into a notebook and gave to me as a remembrance. His melodious voice often strengthened me.

Because of my rheumatism I slept badly at night. Toward morning I did fall asleep. At six o'clock the prisoners were awakened with a loud tumult and clanging at the gate. This was very annoying to me. In order to protect me from this noise, my colleague, with his soft voice, would sing a beautiful morning song into my ear. He did much good to me. However, one day he was taken out of the cell and shot. I hope to see him on the other side with the Lord.

My Bible lessons with the prison Commissar continued for several weeks, and I noted a visible change in him. But one day he was gone. His successor, an Austrian and former prisoner of war, told me that the Commissar had asked to be released from his post. This was granted and he went back home. Him also I expect to see with the Lord.

Every day at a given time all prisoners were allowed into the prison yard for a 20-minute stroll. One day, as I was walking, a snowball, thrown over the wall, fell at my feet and broke in pieces. I noticed that a piece of bread wrapped in paper lay there. I scraped it all together and hid it in my clothes, because we were always closely guarded on our walk. In my cell I opened the little packet and found the following poem:

> Wie schwer ist's doch, ganz still zu sein,
> Wenn Gott wir nicht verstehn,
> Wie redet man sobald Ihm drein,
> Als ob Er was versehn.
> Wie stellt man Ihn zur Rede gar,
> Wenn Seine Wege wunderbar
> Und unbegreiflich werden!
>
> Man fraegt: "Warrum mir dies und das?"
> Man seufzt: "Ach, wie soll's werden?"
> Man klaagt: "Wie geht's ohn' Unterlass
> So widrig mir auf Erden!"
> Man murrt: "Mein Unglück ist zu gross,
> Ich haett' wohl ein bessres Los verdient,
> Als mir ist gefallen zu."
>
> Dies tun wir, und der Güt'ge schweigt,
> Bis Er durch Seine Taten,
> Glorreichen Ausgang uns gezeigt,
> Dass Ihm noch nichts missraten.
> Dann kommt auch endlich unsre Stund,'

Wo vol Beschåmung wir den Mund
Vor Ihm nicht auftun moegen.

Kommt dann zum ziel der dunkle Lauf,
Tust du den Mund mit Freuden auf
Zu loben und zu danken.
Dann wird's nach der Kurzen Zeit
Recht innig dich erfreuen,
Dass du fein still gewesen bist
Und nichts hast zu bereuen.

Und endlich, nach der Schweigezeit,
Kannst du in selger Ewigkeit
Laut jubeln, Gott zur Ehre!

Translation:
How hard it is, to be quiet
When we don't understand God!
So quickly we'd contradict Him,
As if He's neglected something!
We'd even call Him to account,
When His ways are unknown,
And we don't understand them!

We ask, "Why this? Why that?"
We sigh, "Oh, how will it ever end?"
We complain, "Endlessly unpleasant
And difficult is my life on this earth!"
We grumble, "My misery's too great!
I've earned a better lot in life
Than what's coming to me!"

We do this, and the Good One's mute,
Until through His mighty deeds
He shows us by a glorious way,
That He never is mistaken!
Then finally our time comes,

And filled with shame and confusion,
We don't even want to open our mouths!

Then, when the dark way is ended,
You joyfully open your mouth
In Thanksgiving and in Praise!
Now, after that short time,
You'll be rejoicing
That you kept quiet
So now have nothing to regret!

And then, after the time of silence,
Throughout a blessed Eternity,
You'll shout with joy, "To God be the Glory!"

Later I discovered that a niece of mine had written the poem for my comfort and had tossed it over the wall; and it was a great comfort to me. It was a mystery to me that the snowball had fallen exactly at my feet, since she could not have seen me from the outside. But I thanked the Lord for it.

In the meantime, the non-Muslims in Turkestan had also organized themselves into a communist party in order to protect themselves against the revenge-seeking Bolshevistic Muslims. The leaders of the new party all knew me very well. One day this group presented a petition to the Muslim GPU in which seventeen of their leading men gave their lives as surety for political dependability and asked for my immediate release. All seventeen had signed the petition. So I was released in order to continue work as assistant Kreis-Commissar. For five months I had been in hiding and five months in prison under the death sentence. I was freed in April 1919.

From now on I had to attend all party meetings. As representative of our Gemeinde, as well as the Russian peasants in about 75 villages, my stance from the Christian perspective was a difficult one. During this time, government requisitions or confiscation increased and included grain, horses, cattle, hogs, sheep, etc. Naturally the farmers didn't like this and often would give vent to their anger by such expressions as: "That Jantzen is as much a Bolshevik as the others in the city. If he weren't, they wouldn't be able to rob us so." They could see, of course, that my five sons and I were treated in exactly the same manner as they. This was very painful to me, because I did feel so sorry for them.

CHAPTER 15

▼

THE EIGHT POWERFUL ONES

We were not released from our tensions—they remained with us. In 1920 Moscow sent eight delegates into our German villages. They were German speaking, fiery communists, Germans and Austrians who were former war prisoners. They came with highest orders directly from the Central Committee as teachers to bolshevize us in and out of schools, no matter what the cost. They pressured us with almost unbearable reign of terror. For instance, they would demand our best riding horses, at any time it suited their whims, and ride them to the point of exhaustion in a short time. Or they would demand, on fifteen minutes' notice, a spring wagon drawn by our best horses so they could chase to the Russian village Dimitrofka, 30 kilometers away. They would get back from such a tour with half dead horses. Their sole purpose was to get some whiskey, which they couldn't get in our villages. Almost daily they would conduct propaganda meetings, which every person of voting age had to attend. This caused curtailment of field work and so reduced production. Protests were of no avail; the threat of military force from the city was always present.

One day they divided our schools, with the teachers' homes, among themselves. Every thing had to be left to them, as our teachers were forced to vacate their homes. One of the wives resisted them. A Bolshevist teacher took a club and injured her back so she had to go to bed.

All these atrocities were reported to our village Commissars, which were made up of our own people, and who recorded our protests in the form of regular protocols. I would then take the concerns to the meetings of the *Kreis* or district Commissar and protest against the terrorism. But I didn't receive much of a hearing, for we dealt with men who had been sent by the highest court in Moscow and invested with full authority to act. So we accomplished nothing through the 36 protocols that I had received.

Finally I called our village leaders into session to discuss what might be done. In the meantime, the eight men had received the strictest order from Moscow to convict our own teachers as counter-revolutionaries and condemn them to Siberia. Because of all the injustice and frustrations, I had become very weary and discouraged. All my farming machinery had been confiscated and even my large house was taken from us. Our two youngest sons, with their families, were driven out and Bolshevik families moved in. So the Bolshevists had taken complete charge of my property. Our pastors and church leaders constantly begged me to go to Moscow to try to get us some degree of justice.

For a long time I opposed such a move. My wife and family were also against it, since they had already suffered so much fear and anguish on my account. But our leaders continued to implore me until one night at two o'clock they had unnerved me completely. They promised to take care of my family in my absence and I agreed to go. I said, "Very well, I'll do what you ask, if my wife and children agree with you."

"Well, Father," said my wife, "go again just this once. Everything must go to ruin in any case, so we will see what you can achieve."

The following morning I began with extensive preparations necessary for such a long trip. I had to take baked and roasted foodstuff of all kinds. Provisions of all sorts had to be taken along since there was famine everywhere. Because of the huge government requisitions of food, whole villages had died out by starvation. Finally I was ready and on December 10, 1920 I began my trip.

I could board the train right from home since, in spite of all the turmoil, the railroad had been completed to our area. In Taschkent I met a Mennonite brother from Alexanderthal, Altsamara, who had bought up some dried fruits for a cooperative and was at the point of departure for home. We agreed to travel together and left Taschkent on the same day.

The trains traveled very slowly since, in the absence of coal, wood was used for fuel. Since we were traveling northward day after day, it became much colder. In Orinburg, about 2000 kilometers to the north, there was snow and bitter cold. In order to secure fuel we were delayed here for a whole day. On the tracks and in the station we saw starved and frozen bodies all around. Sometimes one noticed those not quite dead yet, but the police didn't pay any attention to them. All this was for us a horrible spectacle. Finally the train continued westward. But about half way to Samara, at the station Tarotschinsk, the train got stuck in the snow. The conductor called out, "We cannot proceed further. Every passenger will have to see where he can go or freeze to death in the train."

We stepped out of the train and noticed a skinny farmer with a skinnier horse hitched to a sled. He said he was looking for someone that he might take somewhere and earn a little. We asked him whether he would take us to Alexanderthal to the German people there. He was afraid that his horse would not be able to make the 120 kilometers. We persuaded him to try and asked him about cost. He wanted no money, only bread to eat. Since we had our bags filled with foodstuffs, we agreed immediately. Soon the driver asked for something to eat. We gave him something and he was very happy and thankful.

As we passed through villages we stayed overnight with the police, since in other houses there were people starved and frozen to death. Since I had my credentials as Kreis-Commissar of Aulie-ata with me, I only needed to show this to the police to receive a warm room, *samovar* for heating water, and feed for the horse. So our driver was comfortable too.

To describe everything that happened on this trip would take too long. I have forgotten how many days we traveled, but finally we arrived at Alexanderthal. Here I stayed with Pastor J. Kliewer. He, his wife, and her parents, who lived with them, received us with great joy. Our *muschik* or driver and his horse were well taken care of, while he rested here a few days. The Mennonite villages had been well organized into cooperatives and, as a result, for the time being, were not so heavily requisitioned and lived relatively well.

I was forced to wait here for five weeks until the trains started running again. During this time I visited many friends and relatives, among them my cousin Johannes J. Janzen, who is now a preacher and teacher in Brazil. I also was able to meet many of my wife's relatives. Several times I was asked to speak in the churches and other meetings. Finally, with freshly filled travel bags, I was able to continue on to Moscow. Here, at the headquarters of the representatives of all the Mennonites, I found warm acceptance by the Brethren Peter Froese and Cornelius F. Klassen.

Now began the battle against the "Eight Powerful Ones" who had been sent from Moscow to Aulie-ata. The Brethren Froese and Klassen loyally helped me in our wanderings from one court to another. At first we didn't get very far, because the authorities couldn't believe that their party members would be found guilty of 36 felonies, and would sin so greatly against the Bolshevik principles. Neither could they deny the many signatures of the Colony Commissars. Therefore I stood firm in the demand that the transgressors of the Bolschevik laws be called to justice and thereby free us from our terror, and that our teachers be recalled from Siberia.

One day a representative of the Comintern was sent to me at my residence; he was also a German speaking former war prisoner. He came with all kinds of threats, but I didn't waver on the matter at hand. Finally, the Central Committee (ZIK) promised that the eight men in question would be brought to account and that our teachers would be brought home again. I asked that I receive written promise, since I couldn't return home without a written document. Finally the Brethren Klassen and Froese succeeded in getting the signed written statement. Upon receiving this I immediately started on my 5000 kilometer-long trip home. Naturally there were many interruptions and experiences along the way. The trip to Moscow and back had taken five and one half months.

The day after my arrival home "The Eight" called a meeting of all voters. I also attended and took my place directly in front of the Chairman. He got up and recounted that I had followed a mandate to Moscow in order to present accusations against the eight men. I had done this in such a manner that they were to be brought to court and very likely would be shot. All this is the result of a misunderstanding. They had drawn up a declaration, which the congregation should sign. Then the accused would be free again.

As Christians and anti-militarists we surely could not bring them to their deaths. All this is caused by the bad Christian Jantzen, pointing his finger at me, and his false presentation. His speech was very emotional and our people were moved and impressed. A few said that they really hadn't intended it that way. Finally I stood up, pointed at the protocols that I had, and asked, "Dear fellow citizens, are these protocols in my hand true or false?"

"Naturally they are true."

Then I drew my delegate-mandate out and asked again, "Is this mandate still in effect? Am I still your delegate or did you elect another?"

"No, you are still, and will remain, our delegate."

Then I turned to the accused eight and said, "Did you hear that?" Turning to the audience I said: "As your representative and delegate, I am the *Gemeinde* and none of you have anything to say. So I ask you to leave this meeting and go home to your work." Then I turned to the Eight and said, "Herewith I close the meeting. You must now do what the GPU will order you to do, or perhaps has already ordered you. You can only blame yourselves and not me for further consequences."

I then left the hall and went home. The next morning several of our preachers, accompanied by the leader of the Eight, came to me with a petition. I asked the leader to leave my home immediately. Then I had great difficulty to explain to my dear brethren that if they would sign the declaration they would declare themselves liars and at the same time condemn me to death. They finally returned to their homes. The next morning everyone heard that the "Mighty Eight" had disappeared. No one ever saw them again, not even the GPU.

After several weeks, our teachers returned from the north and moved into their homes at the schools. They were able for the present to continue their work without being molested. I had to return to the *Kreis*-Commissariat in the city.

CHAPTER 16

▼

"THAT THEY ALL MAY BE ONE"

At about this time I was greeted on the street one day by an evangelist, an acquaintance, from the Russian Baptist Church of Taschkent. Brother Schetjinin was a gifted speaker. He told me that the church in Taschkent had sent him to spend a few weeks in Aulie-ata to conduct evangelistic meetings. The Orthodox Church was being restricted or persecuted at this time, but his group could still work without being molested. So the church had decided to work while it is day; for the night will come when no one can work. He had rented a hall and posted announcements with his schedule of meetings, but no one came. Now he asked me what he might do.

I suggested, "Do you not yet know your Russian soul? I will help you. Tomorrow I will ride to our villages where we have fine choirs. I will invite them to come here to sing their beautiful Russian gospel songs. They may stay for one or two weeks." This made him very happy.

The next day I saw the director of the Mennonite Brethren Church choir and related the problem to him and invited him to bring his singers to town on Friday evening. This was on Wednesday. They should bring provisions for two weeks, *samovar*, and cooking utensils, since under present conditions there was very little to buy. They should not forget to bring feed for their horses. I promised to rent a well-known *caravanserie*, which was now vacant, where there would be plenty of room.

The director thought for awhile and said, "This evangelist is a Russian Baptist. I don't know whether my singers will be interested. But I will do my best to come. Will you invite other choirs?"

I said that I would. The next director gave me a similar answer. The next day I rode home and made preparations as I had promised. And on Friday evening there appeared one wagon full of singers after another in the large courtyard of the *caravanserie*. They came with sound and song.

Brother Schetjinin and I greeted them warmly and with great joy, especially the two elders of the churches, Brother K of the *Mennonitenkirchengemeinde* (Mennonite Church Congregation) and Brother B of the Mennonite Brethren Gemeinde. After they had unloaded everything and made order in the camp, everyone ate and drank for supper. Since it was still too early to start the meeting, I suggested that the group should march through the streets singing their songs. We soon would see what would happen. The Lord through His Holy Spirit would guide everything right.

They all agreed to this and so one choir of 30 voices with their director walked along, followed by the second one a little way behind. They all sang of the gospel and this made a great impression on the streets. Many of them followed our group to the hall that Brother Schetjinin had rented.

Here a few songs were sung which gripped the people of the city visibly. I motioned to Brother Schetjinin and he invited them all to come into the hall, since he had something important to tell them. Soon the hall was completely filled, with many standing outside listening through the open windows. Even the 60 choir members had to remain outside. After the group was settled, the Brother arose and gave a stirring sermon. After closing prayer he invited them all to return the next evening as he had much more to tell them. Most of them promised to come again and after a closing hymn they quietly left the meeting.

The following evening the attendance was equally large. Brother Schetjinin spoke with great spiritual joy; it was the same on Sunday. We were all convinced that the Lord was in our midst through His Word and His Spirit, which worked powerfully in the hearts of the hearers. This was further indicated by the statements of many who came to us after the meetings were ended.

After an especially good morning worship service on Sunday we sat around a long table for the noon meal. As I looked down that long table and noticed the happy singers and the fellowship they were enjoying, I must have smiled, because Brother Schetjinin asked me, "Dear Brother Jantzen, tell us why you are smiling as you look over this large company. If it is a holy smile, then we want to take part too. If that is not the case, you will have to confess it and repent."

That definitely brought me into a dilemma. If I were to tell the truth then the two elders sitting at the table would be embarrassed. So I remained silent, but Brother Schetjinin pressed me for an answer, as did the two elders. Finally I said, "When the scribes once asked the Lord Jesus a question which he did not wish to answer, he asked a counter question and said, 'Answer my question and I will answer yours.' Their answer was, 'We don't know,' and Christ said he would not answer them either. So I would like to ask you a question, also. If you answer me, then I will tell you why I smiled."

"Can you three students of scripture tell me why the Lord Jesus said to his disciples, 'In my Father's house are many mansions. If it were not so I would have said. I go to prepare a place for you.' So I ask myself too, why the Lord Jesus said that. I must assume that there is no cold weather in heaven, neither is there oppressive heat in summer; neither snow nor rain, so that one would hardly need a roof over one's head."

The Brethren laughed. "You really thought up quite a question there, Brother Jantzen."

"But that is no answer to my question." After some talk back and forth, they finally said, "We cannot answer you because we do not know why the Lord Jesus said this to his disciples." Then I said, "Good, I will give you until tomorrow noon to think about it; perhaps then you can answer me." They agreed. When I asked them the next day if they had an answer, all three answered, "no." "Then I'll give you my answer to my question and at the same time answer your question. Then you can judge or condemn as you please. The reason was as follows:

"I looked along our long table, saw the dear singers so happy and joyful with one another, eating and visiting. They were happy in each other's company. There were no divisions or differences; they were one in mind and spirit. But alas! If our dear Brother Schetjinin, who after all is a Baptist, would say, 'The Lord in His mercy has given us a common task here in Aulie-ata, a task which we enjoy doing under His guidance, when through singing and preaching sinners are brought to repentance. We tell them that the Lord Jesus loves them all and rejects no one. As we have observed how the Spirit works among the hearers, I now suggest to you that before we eat this food before us, we kneel together and worship Him, thanking Him that we, too, have been made new creatures, so that we are now placed in this world as God's children to witness for Him with word and song. I propose further that, before we eat, we observe the Lord's Supper with one another.'

"My dear Brethren, that is what I was thinking. So I suppose my smile became a little sad, because I knew that if Brother Schetjinin had made such a proposal, you dear Brother B, would have taken your group and left the hall by one exit, and you, Brother K, would have taken the other exit with your people. And all this in spite of the fact that we know that we are all God's children and as Paul expressed it: 'Members of the body of Christ.' Is it possible to have a closer union with Him and each other?

"Because of all this a bad idea went through my mind: Could the Lord Jesus have told His disciples what he did and add, 'I know you; because of this I will prepare dwellings for you; you really can't tolerate each other even under the greatest blessings.' My brethren, my heart bleeds when I think what the conditions among God's people really are."

With this I stopped. My three brethren sat there and didn't say a word. The singers also sat quietly and hardly said another word.

As we brought our cooperative evangelistic work to a close, Brother B rose unexpectedly and said, "I confess that I came here filled with unholy prejudices, to see that order is maintained. With this bias, so I believe, I have been a hindrance to the Lord's work, otherwise the blessings may have been much greater. I am truly sorry about this." Brother K added a similar confession.

After another prayer together, they all got into their large wagons and returned to their homes. In the evening I followed my usual custom and went into the Alt-stadt to my Muslim friends, to visit with them individually.

CHAPTER 17

▼

MORE NEEDS

In all this time it was necessary for me, whether willingly or unwillingly, to fill my place in the Kreis-Commissariat in order to do everything possible to represent the interest of ours and many other villages in the district. On the whole, only very little could be accomplished. The year 1922 was especially filled with many problems, whose contemporary results I no longer remember in detail.

Soon after the previously mentioned expropriation of property, in which the herds of the Kirghiz were also taken, a great famine developed among them. As a result, the dead bodies were lying in our fields and on the *steppes*. This caused a terrible stench, but no one bothered to do anything about it. I was reminded repeatedly of Jeremiah 25: 32–33 where we read: "Thus said the Lord of hosts, Behold, evil shall go forth from nation to nation, and a great whirlwind shall be raised up from the coasts of the earth. And the slain of the Lord shall be at that day from one end of the earth even unto the other end of the earth; they shall not be lamented, neither gathered, nor buried; they shall be dung upon the earth."

Then the question arose: Does this refer to Bolshevism? Has the time of fulfillment of this chapter come? When a few years later all religions and worship services were prohibited and the leaders were martyred by terrible torture, I was again reminded of the verses in Jeremiah. When, after 1930, I expressed such an opinion among the brethren in Europe, I was often greeted with a smile of pity.

However, today in 1950, many think differently than they did in 1930. Obviously, we have come to a time when nations don't know the answer to their problems. But I shall let the reader come to his own conclusion.

Another emergency was brought about by the outbreak of a typhus epidemic. Whole families died. Our youngest son, Franz, 15 years old, also died. Two others of our children and I were sick in bed for many weeks, but we recovered. After a long illness and much suffering, my dear brother Abram J. Janzen also succumbed to the disease. At the burial service the old brother and former teacher in Lysanderhoeh am Trakt, Franz Bartsch, spoke in a stirring manner on Jeremiah 57:1: "The righteous perish and no one lays it to heart; and merciful men are taken away, none considering that the righteous is taken away from the evil to come." As his widow and children did, I too lost much by the death of Brother Janzen. The congregation did not sense this loss so much because they considered him too "Alliance-minded." He loved all children of God equally, as does our heavenly Father, who can judge best the value or lack of value of all opinions and interpretations in doctrine. "Now we know in part," as Paul says in I Corinthians 13:9.

In those years of famine our two congregations had set up a soup kitchen. Every other day two fat steers were butchered and cut into small pieces, and cooked in large kettles holding 20–25 pails full. To the meat we added potatoes, turnips or millet. Twice a day 400–500 Kirghiz were fed a bowl of soup per person. They slept on a little straw in large, vacant granaries or barns. Between meals we told them Bible stories and helped memorize scripture verses, especially John 3:16, which they recited before each meal. Occasionally I came from the city and delivered a sermon to them. When I wasn't there, the Brothers C. Regier and G.R. Braun would serve.

We continued these projects for about a year, until it was prohibited. Nor could our people furnish so much food because of the ever-increasing requisitions by the government. This was Lenin's method of creating the new proletariat. All the grain, potatoes and other produce that was delivered to the government was placed in huge piles near the railroad stations, where the rain and snow caused it all to spoil. The piles were under strict guard at all times. Round about people, especially Kirghiz, starved to death. The Mennonite and Russian farmers were still better able to take care of themselves, but hunger is painful. All of us knew what that meant.

The greater part of the expropriated herds of cattle, horses, camels and small livestock also starved. And, as was reported to me, the half of the stock of the Black Kirghiz in the mountains died.

In the fall of the fateful year, 1922, there appeared in Tschimkent a young, fiery communist, a Jew from Moscow. He had received orders with full authority from the Central Committee (ZIK) to liquidate, that is shoot, all the Kulak which the GPU would name. The Kulaks were considered to be "bloodsuckers" or vampires in society, and were made up of all those who had at one time hired others to work for them. In Tschimkent the Muslim GPU listed only Russian farmers, about 300 in number, even though the propertied Uzbecks had always hired people to work for them. Then this authorized agent lined up the 300 in a long row and shot them all himself. No one could oppose him, since he had the whole garrison at his command.

Then he came to Aulie-ata. I didn't happen to be in town just then. Here, too, the GPU gave him a list of Russian farmers, as well as eighteen of ours, who had formerly been well-to-do farmers. I, too, was on the list. Since our district was so large, the GPU sent soldiers there to arrest the farmers in question. They were brought to the city and imprisoned.

When they brought in my neighbor Cornelius Wall, who had once owned a large store, and me, we already found 400 of our fellow sufferers in the prison. It was over-crowded. Eighteen Mennonites, with some Lutherans and others, 50 in all, were placed in one large cell. There were Russians, Armenians, Grusiner and Germans. It was so crowded that we were forced to lie on and under each other. Even under the bedstands everything was filled and the air was so stifling one could hardly breathe. The walls and the beds were full of bedbugs. At night they set a large tub in the corner for sanitation, which polluted the air still more.

Almost every evening at 9:00 the *Blutmensch* or blood-thirsty one, with his secretary, walked along the corridor, where he posted soldiers. He himself came to the individual cells, seeking his victims for butcher. As he pointed them out they had to stand in the hallway. When, according to his arbitrary whim, he had chosen enough, usually 20 or 25, they were led out into a wooded area and summarily shot. Often this was done in the presence of guards who would report it all to us the next morning at our 15 minute stroll in the fresh air of the prison yard.

One evening our cell, number 9, was next in line. As the *Blutmensch* stepped in we all sprang to our feet. We saw a young man, perhaps 27 years old and with a characteristic Jewish face. Besides two heavy revolvers, he carried a caucasian dagger in his belt. His secretary, evidently a Russian, stood beside him, carrying a large book under his arm. The man greeted us with a terrible curse and roared at us:

"I have looked for you Kulaks for a long time and now I have found you. See my authority from ZIK with orders to liquidate all of you without a trial; that is, to send you to the moon with this revolver." Then the secretary was told to open the book and read the names of those in our cell. There weren't very many. Yet each of us stood under great tension to see whether our names would be read. Such silence became almost unbearable for some in our cell. Those whose names were read had to step forward, sometimes ten, sometimes fewer. As they stood there before him he cursed them, then God and Jesus and His mother, as well as all the saints. Then he commanded three or so to step into the corridor, while he said to the remaining ones, "Tomorrow, as sure as I am standing here, I'll send you to the moon." With that he left our cell and moved to the next one, until finally we heard the clanging of the great outer iron gate being opened. Soon those who had been called out were no longer in this life and they never returned again. One day at 5 p.m. an acquaintance of mine of many years, an excellent farmer, and a Cossack, was brought in. At 10:00 that evening he was shot.

The next morning the guards gave us the following report. The wife of this farmer, with her grown children, had followed him to try and find out what would happen to her husband. He was an honest man of good reputation. She drove near the gate and after feeding her horses she inquired whether her husband was there and what would happen to him. The guard said he didn't know, but that each evening some prisoners were executed. She returned to her wagon and a little later, when a group was marched out, she recognized her husband. She ran to the *Blutmensch* and implored him for mercy. He not only rejected her plea but asked her children to come along too. At the place of execution she and the children were forced to dig his grave, but not too deep (they were told) so his arm would protrude from the grave. Thus the crows would find his body. The orders were carried out and to make sure that the almost-crazed wife wouldn't steal the body, a watch was set at the grave.

Our congregation sent a messenger to the prison every day, and by bribing the guards, they would determine whether our people were still alive. As soon as he had the information he hurried home and reported. At home our loved ones met in the churches every evening to pray for us. The guards told us all this. One evening one of our ministers asked all those who could leave their homes to meet and for 35 hours they fasted and prayed for our release. The Lord answered their prayers, though of course we in prison knew nothing of this.

And so it happened, as a number of farmers were brought out again to be shot that a courier came galloping into town with a telegram for our executioner (Blutmensch). As he tore it open, in his nervous condition, he read it aloud in the presence of several guards: "Upon receipt of this telegram all your authority is annulled. You must return to Moscow as soon as possible."

The guards reported this to us the next morning. Soon after reading the telegram he and the entire GPU came to the prison and reported to us that he was traveling to Moscow, but only for a short time. Upon his return he swore he would kill us all and send us to the moon. Then he turned to the GPU and ordered that not one Kulak was to be released, upon the threat of death. With this he left the prison and disappeared, never to be seen here again.

We remained in prison for a long time with dire foreboding as to what would happen to us. Finally the GPU found out that our enemy would not return. It then became possible for our people to purchase our freedom with foodstuff. Of course, that wasn't so simple, since at home almost everything had been taken away. With the help of many people, the 18 of us were finally freed. Some had been in prison for nine months. I was there for six and one half months.

Emaciated and broken in spirit, I arrived at home. Since, in the meantime, the district had to elect another delegate, I was now free of this responsibility. My position on the Kreis-Commissariat was also taken from me. But I was not forgotten. Almost every week, men from the GPU examined my household with all manner of threats. I noticed that they had a special interest in me. Thus I realized more clearly than ever that I would have to disappear. My children continued to insist that I should flee. They had not been persecuted personally. But I? Where must or could I flee with my old and frail wife?

Seitmuhamet
Rachim Bagadur
Chan von Chiwa in
Turkestan
Central Asien.

Feldpostkarte 1916.　　H. Junker

Ein Andenken von meiner
Missions Arbeit unter den Kirgiesen
im Hauschangebirge Turkestan
　　　　　　　　　Zentralasien.
Der in der schwarzen Mütze mit
dem Bart nach dem Schuß bin ich.
Das am Zelt angebundene Pferd
ist mein treuer Fuchs der mich wohl
tausende Kilom. auf meinen Missions-
　　　reisen getragen hat.

Elisabeth & Herman Jantzen
1951

078C

Auf dem Kamel wird
te ich ~~werde ich~~ reisen
in den großen Wüsten
Turkestans. Der Eingeborene vor meinem Kamel
stehend ist mein Führer
oder Wegweiser, sein Ka-
mel steht vorwärts ...
ist nicht auch die Platte
gekommen. ———

Foto aus den Jahren
1913 — 1916.

H. Zautbew

Zum Andenken meinem
Neffen Henry Tantzen bei
seinem uns ganz unerwarteten
Besuch auf Einde Gooi
bei Hollandische Rading
Post Hilversum.
H. Tantzen en vrouw.   4.6.51.

Elisabeth Jantzen
Holland

076 C

Mein Sohn Fritz – so
verkleidet war er 6 Mona-
te auf der Flucht.

1934.

Fritz. nach Sibirien
verbannt 1936.

H. Tauchen 1950.

Bradler Jk. Werns
Leiter der Bibelschu-
le in Wiedenest, Rhein
ward anno 1927 ein
Jch~

Jk. Tantzen

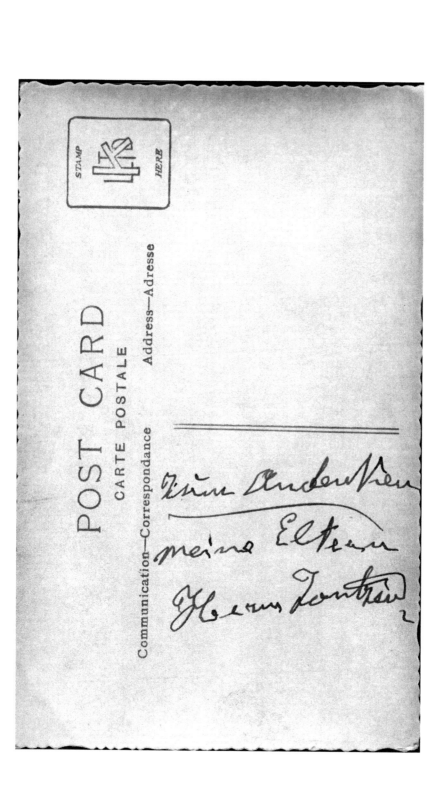

POST CARD

CARTE POSTALE

Communication—Correspondance   Address—Adresse

STAMP HERE

Zum Andenken
meine Eltern
Herm Tonträu

Типы Туркестана. Ишанъ, поднявшій возстаніе въ Андижанѣ въ 1898 году.

Israelschen Tira

<u>Ischan.</u> Geboren.

als Bruder von dem Früheren Chan oder regierender

<u>Fürst von Fergana</u> mit

der Hauptstadt Kokan

<u>Chudojarchan.</u>

Der Ischan verursachte einen Volks
Aufstand in Andischan, wobei
15000 Europäer u. vielleicht noch mehr
Eingeborene bei dem beantwortungs
Akt der Russen - das Leben verloren.

H.J.

In Triebes. Thüringen
bei Geschw. Vollrath.
im Jahre 1931.

[signature]

CHAPTER 18

▼

FLIGHT TO GERMANY

I had written to Brother Johannes Warns in Wildenest, Germany about my situation. In those days letters to foreign countries were not censored. It seemed that in Germany no one could help me. Late at night, when my wife slept, I would sometimes get up and sneak out into the calm night. For hours I sat on a little hill behind our garden and talked with my Heavenly Father. My prayers were about as follows:

"You can see that my stay here has become untenable. On the one side I get in the way of the Muslim rulers, on the other the Bolsheviks will not tolerate me because they hate You so. And now they persecute me because I often remind them of You and of their conscience. Don't you have a little corner, somewhere in your whole world, where Mother and I could spend our last days quietly and at rest?"

So several months passed. The threats did not cease. One evening my old friend Ibraimof appeared at my home. He was chairman of the Muslim Communist Party and of the GPU. Fatigued by his long ride of 65 kilometers, he sat down and said to me, "Dear Father Jantzen, a few years ago, because I had partaken of your bread and salt, I warned you about what had been decided concerning you. I advised you to flee, which you did. Even though you later gave yourself up because of your illness, you were freed again. Then last year you were imprisoned as a Kulak, when the GPU included you on their list. You were condemned to die, but again you got your freedom. But now, you are an obstacle to our Muslim Communist Party. Day before yesterday, in our plenary session, it was decided to have you assassinated. We cast lots to determine who the assassin should be. Naturally I cannot give you his name. But, as I did once before, I have come again as your old friend to warn you. I advise you to flee at all costs. You cannot escape an assassin. He will find you, no matter where you may hide."

Ibraimof stayed with us for the night. Mother served him as well as she could. The following morning, after breakfast, he bade us farewell. He was visibly touched as he gripped Mother's hand in one of his, and mine in the other, and said, "Mammascha, Papascha, do not take what I said lightly. Flee!" With that he mounted his horse and disappeared.

We stood there with one question. Where can we go? Soon thereafter I received a letter from Brother Warns with an entrance permit or visa to Germany. The letter stated: "Dear Brother Jantzen, I secured the enclosed visa for you from our government. How you can get here from where you are, we do not know. We will continue in prayer for you and your dear wife. Once you have arrived here, we will welcome you cordially."

This letter was like the fresh break of dawn after a dark night. Everything else was so obviously dark. The great question remained: how to negotiate the 9000 kilometers to Berlin and Wiedenst. We would have to get a passport to leave the country and only the GPU, who had blacklisted me, could grant us that. If I were to go there and ask for passports, I would most certainly get a bullet instead, for I was listed as counter-revolutionary. And even if I were to receive a passport I would have to get a ticket or travel permit. In Turkestan the law says that only a card carrying party member could get a ticket.

As a result of all this I sat in the dark in my hopeless situation and did not know what to do. At night I sneaked out to my quiet little hill and spoke with my heavenly Father and His Son Jesus Christ. In my struggle, I finally got to the place where I said something like this: "Lord Jesus, we read in Your Word in several places that You are the head and we the members, which I believe. You know and understand my hopeless situation. If, in spite of all this, it is Your merciful will that we get to Europe, which I believe it is, since we received the visa to Germany, then You will have to tell me how I may procure the indispensable passport. You, as the head, must reveal to me, Your member, Your plan in this. What You will tell me, I will do. I ask this in Your name."

Soon after the prayer I received the following definite instruction: "You must get from the local Colony office a certification that you have fulfilled all your obligations to the government and that you leave no debts to your district. With this, go to the GPU and have them furnish you a passport." When I told this to my wife and children they were all frightened and said, "But, Father, anything but this! You are going right to the lion's mouth that has been wanting to swallow you all along."

"I know that, yet I must act on the advice from Above."

So I went to the Colony office and received a voucher that I have no debts or obligations there and am therefore free. With this I went on my way to the city, which took me all day. As a faint-hearted man I sat in my wagon and debated: 'Isn't it madness what you are now doing? Isn't what you think you received from Above pure imagination? Will God just for your sake perform a miracle and get you the passports?' But on the other side it said to me, 'You must do what has been instructed from Above!' What a battle between light and darkness within me!

In the evening I arrived at my lodging, but I couldn't sleep. There was a constant wrestling until morning finally came. Breakfast didn't taste good at all. After breakfast I went to the GPU where, as I assumed, my persecutors were in session. As I fearfully entered, I noticed immediately that there were only strangers present at the tables. The Chairman approached me, who to my surprise was a Russian, and said in a friendly mien, "Now, Papa, you have come so early; how may I help you? What is your wish?"

"My wife and I would like to make a trip to Germany and Holland where we have many relatives and friends. For that we need passports which I must get here. At home I am free since I have filled all requirements." With this explanation, I placed my certification from the Colony office before him. He read it through, then answered, "Everything is in order; but you must be patient. Sit down for awhile. The situation is this: We are all new here and do not know you. All the GPU officials from here have been summoned to Taschkent for ten days at the plenary conference. We were sent here to represent them in the meantime.

Therefore I must first check the black list to see whether your name is on it. If it is, you know very well what would happen to you."

With this he began looking through the books that were lined up on a long table by months and alphabet. He didn't find my name in the older books, but his hand came ever nearer to the February book in which my name must surely be entered. I sat there shuddering and sighing within, "O, Father!"

Suddenly he turned to me and said, "Oh, your name surely won't be in the few remaining books either." Immediately he dictated to his secretary the necessary requisition for a passport from Moscow for both of us. He signed it and placed the official seal under his name, gave me the paper and said, "I wish you a good trip. If only I were such a capitalist as you, so I could make a trip to a foreign country to see how people live there." He shook my hand and dismissed me. I do not recall whether I thanked him or not, I was so astounded by this experience.

After arriving on the street I said, "O Father, how great Thou art in Your mercy toward such a miserable and ungodly man as I! But how shall I proceed now? How do I get the other travel requirements? How do I get the necessary party membership card?" Quietly I told my Heavenly Father these problems.

Suddenly I heard someone calling me from across the street. It was an old acquaintance of mine, a railroad official who came toward me. He shook my hand and asked, "Why are you walking along the street so early in the morning in deep thought, your head bowed low? Is it true, as your son Henry told me recently, that you wish to make a trip to Germany? If that is so, how do you expect to get a ticket, since you have no party membership card?"

"It is so; we would like to make a trip to Germany."

"As a believer you will naturally say, 'the Heavenly Father will provide for me.' But I think differently. After all, there is no Heavenly Father anymore. In this the Bolsheviks are right. Because if there were a God, He would have had compassion on our land and people long ago. However, I want to tell you something else. As you know, I am from Moscow. My mother, who is over 90 years old, still lives there in our house. I received a telegram saying that she is ill and asks that my wife and I should come to see her as soon as possible. She would like to see us once more. So we have decided to sell everything we have here and move to Moscow. We are all ready to go. Since there is much hunger in Moscow, we have secretly bought all kinds of foodstuff, and my travel papers also allow me to take two cows along. But I have no cows.

"As an official, I am provided with a whole railroad car for my trip. But so far it is only half full. And now it seems like a miracle to me that I meet you here. I know that there is no Heavenly Father. You, as a 'white' have no membership card, but I do, although I am 'red' only for the sake of food. Inside I am white too; that's why we are called '*radishes.*' Anyway, I offer you the other half of my freight car. Do as I did. Exchange all your travel money for food and also take two cows along. As a railroad man, I will furnish the feed enroute. My wife is taking her 25 hens along. We'll put them into a cage and will fasten them above the cows. Your wife and you will go along as my helpers. I have that right, and you won't need any tickets."

Because of all I heard and had been through that morning I couldn't speak right away. So he continued, "You don't say anything! Well, of course, I understand. You are thinking of your passports, that you must have, and which unfortunately you will never get. I know your whole history as well as the fact that you are on the black list."

Here I pulled out my documents from the GPU and showed them to him, saying, "My dear friend, you have just scolded my Heavenly Father since unbeknown to you, you are His servant in that you just offered me your freight car for our travel. And now, because I am showing you my passport from the GPU, you are too amazed to say anything. This is the situation: My Heavenly Father in His great mercy has decided to preserve me from my dangers. So the whole group of officials of the GPU who knew me had been ordered to Taschkent. Others who did not know me must take their places, and the substitute chairman must look through the black list and not find my name. In a few moments he has the proper papers written out, wishes me a good trip and dismisses me.

"When I got out on the street I thanked my heavenly Father with the words: 'O Father, how great is your mercy!' And the question immediately arises: What of the other travel necessities? Just then you call me from across the street and offer me everything I need, by which the matter of party membership is solved. This three-fold miracle on this one morning has astonished me so that I couldn't find any words. And your offer? Naturally I accepted it as out of God's hand and you his servant, I thank most heartily."

All this and his look at my papers had left my friend as pale as a sheet, and he called out loud, "Now I can't comprehend any of this! What you have just said and what I see is completely unnatural."

"Yes, you are right. This is supernatural. It is divine; something neither you nor I can comprehend with our minds. For God is much greater than man."

Then we quickly decided that I would have to complete all my preparations so that, by the end of the week, we could begin our journey. We parted and I started for home. But how different were my thoughts and feelings from those I had on the trip over, my pen cannot describe.

When I arrived at home they were all surprised, since they had feared never to see me again. After I had told them all that had happened, they were even more overcome with wonder. Naturally my story was told all through our villages. We bought much food stuffs as well as two cows. We hauled everything to the station, where my sons, with the instructions of the official, loaded it into the car.

But at home there were still some days of unrest. Daily the ministers came and protested my plans to leave the country. They accused me of lack of faith; that the omnipotent God could keep me safe here as well as anywhere else. They could not believe that this was the Lord's will for me. It was my own will, they said, and that I was now forsaking the churches and fleeing when they were in such difficulties. Further, they believed that the Bolshevik regime couldn't last long and that soon conditions would improve.

During that last week I had a very difficult time. At the end, even my children were against me, so that I stood all alone, misunderstood even by my own. The day before we were to leave, Brother Peter J. Janzen, brother of the deceased Abram Janzen, came to me with an offer. "Brother Jantzen, I still have a carriage and a team of relatively good horses. I will take you to the station tomorrow morning. This shall be my last service of love toward you." I accepted his offer with thanks. Early the next morning he drove over from Nikolaipol to Orlof. The time of departure was approaching. We were to part from all our children and grandchildren, from house and home, from everything we had learned to love and treasure. Mother was already in the carriage, while all our dear ones stood around the wagon and wept.

Just before leaving, I jumped down and once more ran through my two houses, my once-filled barns and granaries and machine sheds, all empty now. I ran through the fruit orchard and once more into my study. There stood my concert zither in its case. Involuntarily I must have grabbed it and taken it along, because later I couldn't recall how it had come to be with us in the wagon.

After mounting the wagon, I called out, "Be committed to God, my dear ones, until we meet again up there!" Brother Janzen drove from the yard. My wife had fainted in my arms. This was on March 28, 1923. Gradually Mother came to again and also to a mother's grief. During the drive to town she sat in one corner of the carriage and wept quietly. At the depot we were warmly received by our friend and, after saying farewell to our dear driver, Brother Janzen, we got into the train.

The next morning the train pulled out of the station. The car had been so arranged by our host that the cows stood on one end with their heads toward the middle of the car. Above the cows, the chicken crates had been fastened. The other half was divided into two parts with bamboo mats. Between us and the animals was a little space where a stove was placed, which could be used for cooking. Each of our "apartments" had a bedstead under which many sacks and boxes were placed. Above us were board shelves where the rest of the things could be placed.

At most of the stations our host telegraphed ahead so that hay and water for the cows, as well as wood for fuel, would be ready. Usually everything was promptly provided. And so our journey proceeded northward and after eighteen days we arrived safely in Moscow.

Upon our arrival I called the representatives of the all-Mennonite headquarters in Russia, Brothers C.G. Klaassen and Peter Froese, and informed them that my wife and I, with much food stuff and one cow, had come from Turkestan and asked them to pick us up. The second cow I gave to our host because of his great service in getting us to Moscow so efficiently. He was very thankful.

We were lodged in the Mennonite quarters. The cow was taken care of elsewhere. Since the price of feed was so extremely high, we soon sold her. I received several times as much for the cow as I had paid in Turkestan. I would never have thought of asking the amount for a cow that I was offered. All food rose in price daily. By this we could see how the value of money deteriorated and we sold none of what we had. Our hosts, the family Froese, Brother Klaassen, and another family Isaac, who had come from Muellerowe, enjoyed our provisions for a few weeks, when we were ready to travel on.

With great effort and much running from one place to another, in which the brethren were very helpful, I finally received a passport. This had to be registered in the German consulate, during which process the consul was very cooperative. He wished to be informed about conditions in Turkestan and about how we had gotten to Moscow. Finally he said, "Mr. Jantzen, since, because of the civil wars in western Russia and Poland, you cannot take a train to Germany, I would advise you to remain in your present comfortable quarters and wait until the next ship comes from Stettin to Leningrad. I will get information about this and will let you know when you can go that way. Then you must travel to Leningrad as quickly as possible. But I suggest that you take all provisions that you have brought here. In Germany you will need them because inflation is as extreme there as here, and the value of money falls every day."

So there was no choice for us but to stay and bide the time. We lived well in the Mennonite quarters. Within I was, of course, very restless. Continually the thought plagued me as to what would happen if the GPU should discover that we had traveled to Moscow in order to escape them. They could have me arrested by telegram and I would be done for. Then, too, when we were alone, my wife wept continually, which was very difficult for me to see.

During this time, the Mennonite Agricultural Council was organized, for which several brothers had come from the Ukraine. Among them was Brother B.B. Janz, Brother H. Riesen and another brother from Alexanderthal, Kreis Samara. On my birthday, May 28, the Council was organized; so we celebrated both together.

The next day I had a phone call from the German Consul, telling us to come as quickly as possible to his office to pick up a letter. We should be ready to get to Leningrad as quickly as possible. There the ship "Oder" was ready to leave and was scheduled to sail from Leningrad the next afternoon at 4 o'clock. I was to give the letter to Mr. Schlader, chief of the shipping company. This would enable us to get passage on the ship. There he wished us a pleasant trip.

I rushed back and told the brethren all that I knew and, after making preparations, they took us with our five sacks to the station. The express train stood ready to leave and after more good wishes we departed. At 1 o'clock in the afternoon we arrived in Leningrad. Quickly we took a cab, with our baggage, to the office of the shipping company. There Mr. Schlader asked brusquely, "What do you want?"

"Two tickets on the 'Oder' for Stettin."

"There are no more. Day after yesterday every fare had been sold," he answered rudely. I gave him the letter from the Consul, which he scanned hurriedly. Then he called into the next room, "Get two more tickets for the 'Oder' right away." He turned to me. "Please be seated, Mr. Jantzen." He quickly wrote a letter to the customs officer at the harbor, handed it to me, and said, "You must deliver this letter to the customs office. I hope that they will still let you go through customs. It is very late and they could be closed. So hurry. Here are the letter and the two tickets."

I went out and got in our cab and we rushed to the harbor. As we arrived at the customs office I saw that the gate was closed and two armed soldiers were standing guard. They didn't want to let me in but I insisted that I had to enter. The door opened and a man yelled, "What's wrong out there, that you are so noisy?"

For an answer I handed him the letter and asked whether he was the man addressed therein. He said he was and hurried into the building with the letter. Soon he returned with five strong men who carried our baggage from the cab. We followed them. Behind a long, low table stood the Chef. He pointed to the baggage and asked sternly, "What have you in those five large bags?"

"Those contain foodstuffs."

"With that you want to feed the Germans, while we almost starve here? That won't happen; they stay here and if you want to grumble about that, you damned bourgeois-capitalist, will get a bullet—which is what you really wish to avoid. We know very well who you are. What do you have in the black box?"

"That is my concert zither, that I love to play."

He laughed out loud to his comrades. "Would you listen to that! The old man drags a thing like that along, when he surely must be glad if he can get over the border with a whole skin. I really don't believe he knows what to do with the thing at all."

Another one called, "Try him out! Maybe he can play the instrument." So he demanded: "Play something for us."

After I had taken the zither out of the case, I began to play a Russian melancholy song of homesickness. I repeated it three times and when I looked up I saw that all eyes were filled with tears.

The Chef said, "Good, you damned bourgeois," and added to the men, "Stick the stamps on the baggage and get him, with his stuff, on to the ship." With a curse, he wished us a good trip and we hurried after the men to board the ship. They said good-bye and thanked me for the nice song.

As we stood on the deck, I heard someone call, "Mr. Jantzen, everything went in such a rush today that I assume you didn't exchange your money. That bothered me, so I came to exchange it for you."

I recognized Mr. Schladen, standing on the pier. He called again, "Throw your purse to me with your money." I did that quickly. He exchanged the money and threw it back to me. Again he wished us a safe journey and left the harbor.

Soon the ship was loosed from the pier and began to sail. We sat on the deck and watched Leningrad, formerly Petersburg, get smaller and smaller until it seemed to disappear in the sea. For a long time we sat there and looked toward the east, where the ruins of our lives lay, where our children with their dear ones, and many of our relatives remained.

Finally it became dark and we had to go to our cabins and go to bed. Sleep, of course, was unthinkable at first. Toward morning the ship was struck by a big storm which stayed with us for the four days of our journey.

In Stettin we first must go through customs. Here a doctor came to examine us, especially our eyes and tongue. Then he said, "My what you must have been through. Your nerves are totally kaput. Otherwise you are in good health."

Then we were allowed to proceed with our baggage to the customs office. Here a fat official greeted us, about like the man in Leningrad. "What have you in those greasy sacks?" When I said they contained foodstuff he said, "Do you think we are starving here like you did over there? Anyway, you cannot take foodstuff into the land. It must first be disinfected, because you people in the east have, the d … knows, what kind of diseases, and we will not allow our fatherland to be contaminated by them. And, after the stuff is disinfected, you will not be able to use it. What do you have in that box?"

"A concert zither," I answered. And just like the man in Leningrad, he laughed loudly and called his co-workers to him. "Think of it. Here an old man drags a zither through all the countries as though we didn't have enough of such things already. Anyway, I doubt that he can play it at all."

"Try him out. He may be able to play it," said one of them.

Upon further request, I played the well-known old German folksong, *Die Lorelei, Ich weiss nicht was soll es bedeuten, dass ich so traurig bin.* After playing it three times, I noticed that they were very attentive, so I changed to *The Watch on the Rhine.* They all cheered "Bravo" and the fat official said, "He is our man; he is our man. You are heartily welcome to the German Fatherland." With this they stuck the stamps on our baggage and several men got us a wagon that took us to the train station.

Now may I ask my dear readers: Could I have known beforehand, that twice the zither would be the method for saving our foodstuff? All of you would say "no" as I did. The Lord had something good in mind for us.

When we tried to buy tickets to Wiedenest, we were told that we couldn't get them here. The English and French occupation forces were still moving to and fro in the area. We could get tickets to Hannover, where we would find out how we could proceed. So we came to Hannover at night and couldn't get any information. As we sat there, my wife said, "Isn't this the town not far from Garden, where my sister Marie fled with her five children in 1918?" I agreed that it was so and asked the depot agent whether there is a village called Garden nearby. "Yes," he said. "There are sugar refineries there. You would have good connection on the electric streetcar and in 20 minutes you could be there."

In the morning we placed our baggage in a locker and took the electric train to Garden. In the center of the village we got out and asked a man who was working on a building project whether a widow Pauls and her children lived in that vicinity. The oldest of the children worked in the sugar factory. He answered, "Yes, she lives near by. However, she is always sick; her head is not like those of healthy people. But here comes her second son, Woldemar. He will give you more information."

As I turned around I noticed a sturdy young man approach us. "Good morning, Woldemar," I said. He thanked me and said, "But I do not know you." To which I answered, "I can understand that very well. You were just a small boy when I visited you in Waldheim in the Ukraine in 1912." He looked at me again. "Then you must be Uncle Hermann Jantzen." I agreed and, pointing to my wife I asked, "Do you know this woman?" "No, I don't, but perhaps she is Aunt Anna, my mother's sister." Then we asked him to go to his mother and prepare her a bit for meeting us. Slowly we followed him. It had been 25 years since the sisters had seen each other.

As we stepped into the house, Woldemar met us and invited us in. His mother was in the garden behind the house, feeding some chickens. After we stepped into the room we looked through a window and there we saw the sister-in-law, an old, bent, sick woman, slowly coming in. All excited, she called out, "But Woldemar, you are not at work. Must we really die of hunger? Arthur, Hilde, and Hermannn are already in bed, weakened by malnutrition and can't earn anything and you are running around and not working."

"But Mother, I went to work today. On the way I met two guests who have come a great distance, and this I wanted to tell you."

Then she called out again, "And you were to prepare me for meeting them. I am already prepared. They are brother-in-law Hermann, and Anna, my sister. For more than two months I have been praying: 'O, God, send those two people here to us; for we are all lost here in this strange land.' So I have been prepared for a long time for this visit. I am ready. I am ready."

Repeating these expressions, she stepped into the room. The two sisters fell into each other's arms and sank unconscious to the floor. Woldemar and I got them into a bed and applied cold water until they came to again. The sister-in-law kept repeating, "I am prepared. I am prepared." This showed us that her mind just was not clear. Then she added, "Now, both of you, Anna and Hermann, must stay with us and not leave us again."

Slowly we related to each other the experiences of the past few years. I sent Woldemar to the station to get our baggage. Late in the afternoon Woldemar returned with the bags. How great was the joy of this family when they saw the wealth of foodstuff. My wife, the stronger of the two women, helped unpack. There were toasted zwiebach, cheese and smoked ham, and in another sack wheat flour and rice. We also had some tea and coffee. At this, all eyes glistened.

Of course, we had to be careful that these undernourished people didn't eat too much at once. After all of them had tasted of the zwiebach and coffee, my wife cooked a weak flour soup. During the next few days they all gained strength. After a few weeks the other three children were also able to go back to work in the sugar refinery.

Now I understood the way of the Lord with the zither and why it had to be brought all this way. There is no other explanation except that here a widow, with her children in Garden, Germany, was in great need. She cried to the Lord, the preserver of widows and orphans for help, and the Lord heard her prayer. And this in such a remarkable way even for me, since I could not have known in advance anything of the conditions or happenings, since we had had no correspondence with Aunt Marie for years.

My wife and I stayed in Garden for the next few weeks, since we could not travel westward just then. In the meantime, prices kept going up. Daily I went shopping to buy what was available, because inflation kept going rapidly. Soon after we arrived I had some correspondence with Professor Benjamin Unruh in Karlsruhe. I told him of the distress this family was in and begged him, if at all possible, that something be done for them. Perhaps they could immigrate to Canada. After all, Mrs. Pauls had three strong sons who were of age. The plan succeeded so that the family left for Canada while we were still with them.

But by now all our food had been eaten and my money was used up too. Of this I didn't say anything to my wife—much more I prayed to the Heavenly Father, who had so often helped us in wonderful ways. He had so often rescued me from my problems. Quietly I said to Him, "Loving Father, you know our situation. My sister-in-law, with her children, is gone, and for us there is as yet no possibility of income in this foreign place. My money is gone too. Today I can still buy bread, but what then? We still cannot get through to Wiedenest, where we have been expected for a long time. What now, Father?"

This day passed also. Heavy hearted I went to bed. My wife lay in bed and wept for her children, which she did almost every night. Sometimes, in her grief, she sighed, "O Father, I wish I had never become a mother!" This was repeated more often as time went on. I prayed with her earnestly, which calmed her so that she could go to sleep, weary of all her grief.

The following morning, rather early, the postman brought a long letter from Brother Warns, from the Bible School in Wiedenest. In it he wrote: "Day before yesterday we were freed from the English and French occupation forces. Now the way to us is open, so that you can come to Wiedenest. At the station just before Wiedenest, Derschlag, you must get out. There you will go to the bank of Mr. Ernst Reuber, who is expecting you. He will bring you to the dwelling that has been provided for you. And, since I know that you must be in need of money, I am enclosing a small amount."

This "small amount" was several million marks, which because of inflation had only little value. Quickly I bought a little bread and after breakfast we packed our now empty bags and a few other items and went to the station. From Garden we had a direct connection to Wiedenest. The following morning we arrived at Derschlag where we went right to the office of Mr. Reuber. After a warm reception, he took us in his car to our new home, a farmhouse in a small village called Bergheusen. The owner was a relative of Mr. Reuber, but both he and his wife had died a few years earlier.

We went up the stairs and Mr. Reuber showed us four rooms. Everything was newly painted and tapestry provided. In the bedroom were two made-up beds and a large closet with men's and women's clothing. There was a commode with underwear for us. In the kitchen, which was also the living room, stood a side board filled with foodstuffs, seemingly enough for a year. In the cellar was a pile of potatoes and another pile of coal. In the yard, in a large building, there was a chicken barn with 20 hens for our use. There was also a large orchard behind the house.

After Mr. Reuber had showed us all this, we went upstairs again and he said, "My dear friends Jantzen, for two months all this has been ready and waiting for you. Milk and butter will be delivered to you, as needed, by my niece, Mrs. D., who lives in the next house. Bread will be delivered daily by our friend and Brother J., who has a bakery about 50 meters from here. You have nothing to do with paying for things at these two places. That is my business. However, I can see that you are tired and need some rest. So I will leave. In two hours I will return and take you in my car to my home in the valley where I live as a bachelor with my brother-in-law E. There we will eat our noon meal."

After he had gone, Mother and I just sat there at the table, as in a dream, not finding words to say, for everything which we experienced on this day was beyond our comprehension. We sat quietly and only sighed, "O, God, how great is your divine mercy toward us. Where can we find words of praise and thanks for everything?"

Suddenly Mother pointed her finger at the wall behind me and said, "See there!" I turned around and what did I see? There in a beautiful glass frame hung the poem which in 1919 was thrown over the wall of the prison I was in, wrapped with some bread, encased in a snowball. Here it was:

"Wie schwer ist's doch, ganz still zu sein,
   Wenn Gott wir nicht verstehn."

   Translation: "How hard it is, to be quiet
           When we don't understand God!"

I said, "Isn't this our Ebenezer: Hitherto hath the Lord helped us. As little as I understood God there in prison, so little I can fathom Him now. For His ways are wonderful and beyond comprehension for us human beings. Haven't we gone from one miracle to another on this whole trip? And now this quiet dwelling, for two months past, made ready for us by dear children of God, whom we had never seen and didn't know. In advance they have furnished us everything we have need of. Really God is incomprehensible."

But the car had come and we got in with Mr. Reuber. In a few minutes we arrived at his house, where he greeted us again, as did the family D. We were seated at a richly decked table and, as usual, when someone said a kind word to us, the tears rolled down our cheeks. Our nerves could hardly tolerate everything. So we could not eat very much either.

Our hosts told us that they, as well as most others in the community, belong to the Baptist Church in Derschlag. Here in Hundsheim, where Mr. Reuber lived, there is a chapel, where meetings were held on Sunday as well as on Tuesdays and Thursdays. Often Brother Warns and others from the Bible School came to serve with the Word of God. Wiedenest was about 8 kilometers away.

Since they have known Brother Warns so long already, they expressed the wish that as Christians we should address one another with the more intimate form of "du." This we were glad to agree to. Brother R's name is simply Ernst, his first name. Although he was 42 years old, he had never married.

After dinner Brother Ernst took us back to our home and then drove back to his office in Derschlag. The textile factory that he managed employed about 100 workers. They all called him by his first name, since they were all God's children.

The next day Brother Warns, with some of his family, came to greet us in our new home. Our reunion was naturally very cordial since we hadn't seen each other for eleven years. He invited us to come to Wiedenest soon in order to tell our student and teacher families of our travel experiences. This I couldn't promise right away, since we were both very weary and physically not very well.

It took a full year for me to rest up from all the exertions and difficulties of the past years. Then too, I had to be a strong support to my wife in her heartaches. She couldn't be comforted in the loss of our children; I was often weak myself and needed solace. All those around us put forth great effort to encourage us through all manner of deeds of kindness and love and to bring sunshine to our days whenever possible. For all this we were grateful and I thank them for it to this day.

CHAPTER 19

▼

SERVICE IN GERMANY

In the summer of 1924 we were invited to a conference lasting several days at Wiedenest. To these annual conferences many believers came from all of Germany, and some from England and Holland. I was asked to deliver several lectures at these sessions. As a result, I was asked by leaders of several of the churches to speak at their meetings. A woman at the Bible School, as well as friends of my wife at Berghausen, promised to see to it that Mother would not be left alone. Thus it was possible for me to accept several invitations and I embarked on travel that was slowly extended to six weeks.

Each year the Free Churches had two conferences. In spring it was held in Berlin and in autumn in Leipzig or Bad Homburg vor der Hoehe near Frankfurt am Main. I was always invited to these meetings. In addition to that I participated in several conferences of the Faith in Wernigenade with Brother Jacob Kroeker. He was head of the program "Light to the East." The Brethren Prochanof, Professor Marzinkowski, Professor Schlarb, Princess Lieven, Pastor Jack and several others also took part at times. On one occasion 45 Russians met and on the final day sessions were held in the Russian language.

I also visited the Blankenburger conference several times, where I became acquainted with Pastor Modersohn. He was the director of the established church movement in Germany. I spoke in several of the meetings in his circles. So it happened that in 1926 he invited me to Thueringen to serve as evangelist in his church groups. They already had a young evangelist there, but he was still rather inexperienced in the work. I accepted this invitation. The young Brother K. was a former Bible student of Brother Warns, so I had already met him. I also lodged with him in his home.

We combined three villages in this effort. He organized everything and I addressed the meetings each evening. This went on for six weeks. In the announcements for these meetings they always included the statement: "A missionary from Russian Turkestan will speak." Thus the hall was always quite well filled and we had very attentive audiences. The Lord gave much grace to speak and almost every evening souls came to faith and peace in Christ. It soon became evident that the hall in S where Brother Warns lived was too small and he felt that we should find a larger one. There was a larger one there, but it belonged to the superintendent who was not in sympathy with the work we were doing. It was doubtful that he would let us use it.

I suggested that we go and see the man and ask him for his larger hall. We went to look him up and were shown into his study. Rather coldly he asked who we were and what we might want, although he knew Brother K. The latter introduced me as a missionary from Turkestan and that I had come by invitation of Pastor Modersohn to hold evangelistic meetings. We told him that, after a week of meetings, the hall was too small to hold those who were coming, and that we had come to ask for his large meeting place for perhaps one or two evenings.

After looking at me with great interest, he asked, "Where did you study theology and what sort of gospel do you preach?" I answered, "Theology in German means knowledge of God, and in this school I am a student even now, and haven't passed the final examination yet." He looked at me again and asked, "And your gospel?" "I always do about as we read of Paul in I Corinthians 2:1–2: 'I come not with excellency of speech or of wisdom, but preach only Jesus Christ and Him crucified.'" He pondered for a bit and then said, "Good, you get the hall." After he had agreed that we would invite the five other pastors in his precinct, though he himself did not feel obligated to come, we thanked him and left.

Three days later we held our final meeting in the larger meeting place. As we stepped into the hall we noticed that every seat was taken. In the front row sat the five pastors. The theme was as always: The love of God, which even today is revealed to man through his saving grace which makes unhappy people happy. After the benediction, as everyone wanted to leave, Brother K. called them back and said, "Just a moment, please! Brother Jantzen will sing a song, accompanied on his zither, which he loves to play." With these words he placed the zither on the table. He had secretly brought it from his home. When I saw it and noticed that everyone was quietly seated again, I sighed within, "Lord, what should I sing now?" Then I said to those present, "I am completely surprised; however, if it is to be so, I will sing my life story in four short verses."

    1. Nichts hab' ich, was ich nicht frei empfing;
       Durch Gottes Gnade bin ich, was ich bin.
       Ruhmen sei ferne, doch das sei bekannt.
       Ich bin einer, den die Gnade fand.

Chorus: An mir erwiesen,
       Sei laut sie gepriesen:
       Ich bin einer, den die Gnade fand.

    2. Einst war ich ferne, in Sünden verstrickt
       Dem Gott der Gnade so weit, fern entrückt;
       Doch da kam Jesus und griff meine Hand:
       Ich bin einer, den die Gnade fand!

    3. Nicht meine Traenen, die haben's gemacht,
       Gottes Gnade had es alles vollbracht.
       Sünden vergiftet, einst abgewandt,
       Bin ich einer, den die Gnade fand.

    4. Drum lass dir's sagen mit strahlendem Blick,
       Mein Herze fliesst über von Freud' und Glueck.
       Drum noch einmal ruf ich's laut über's Land:
       Ich bin einer, den die Gnade fand!

Translation:

    1. Naught have I but what I freely received!
       By God's grace I am what I am!
       Boasting's excluded, but let it be known,
       I am one whom Grace has found!

Chorus: In me it's showing!
          Aloud I praise Him!
          I am one whom Grace has found!

2. Once far away, entangled in sin,
    Far from the God of Grace, so far!
    Then Jesus came, and grasped my hand:
    I am one whom Grace has found!

3. It's not my tears that have done this!
    God's Grace alone has done it all!
    Though once turned away, poisoned by sin,
    I am one whom Grace has found!

4. Joyfully now I tell you this news:
    My heart's running over with joy and happiness!
    So once again I proclaim o'er the land:
    I am one whom Grace has found!

I can remember to this day that it seemed as though my zither, which was stolen during the war in 1944, never had sounded so sweet and beautiful.

And what was the result? Five or six men jumped to their feet and cried, "I am lost! I am lost!" Brother K. went to them and invited them to come to his home. The five pastors stood before me and observed me with astonishment and didn't know what to say. So I said to them, "Honored Sirs, the Holy Spirit does everything well. He will do so with these men, too." Then they very politely bade me farewell, thanked me for the evening and left.

Brother K. and I took the men with us. After hours of discussion and prayer, they left for home, calm and happy. At the close of the meetings we verified that 117 persons had confessed to peace in Christ.

But now it was necessary that I return to Berghausen, where my dear wife was waiting for me. Because of her extreme grief, she became weaker and weaker. When I was home, I preached every Sunday and often two other evenings per week in the Baptist Church. But I was not permitted to remain at home very long. Since the revival in S. continued, Brother K. asked me to come there soon in order to organize the newly converted Christians into local churches. And so a larger congregation was organized in S., while in another village a small church was established. In name they remained in the established church. After some hours of Bible study quite a number asked to be baptized.

When Pastor M. heard this, our friendship ended, as it was with Brother K. He said that it wasn't his idea that we would make Baptists of the newly converted people. I could only answer that we had not persuaded them to be baptized. In our Bible study we had come to Mark 16:16 where we read: "He that believes and is baptized, shall be saved." The new converts had said that, though they were baptized as infants, they could not then have believed. Therefore that baptism didn't mean anything to them since they had not consciously believed. That is why they wished to be baptized according to God's Word, and we could not deny it to them. Therefore I had baptized them. That has nothing to do with the Baptist denomination, in which sense I am not a Baptist either, but a child of God by His great mercy, and nothing else. However, he did not understand me and the contact between us was broken.

In the fall of 1927 my wife became steadily worse and languished visibly toward her end. So, in spite of many invitations, I could not make any more trips. As I was considered a member of the Bible School and I still belonged, I had many opportunities to talk to the students. The result of this service was that, after finishing their studies, four of the students decided to go to Bulgaria to bring the gospel to the Turkish people there.

Before they left, three of them were married. It was a rule of the school that this be the procedure. The wives had previously studied the same preparatory course of study for this work. The fourth student was not ready until later, since he could not get married just then. After they arrived in Bulgaria, they had to learn the Turkish language, which took about two years.

My wife lived until June 1928 when she finally succumbed to the extreme grief of a mother's heart. In the presence of several Christians of our neighborhood, with a positive testimony of her communion with the Savior, she breathed her last. With her homegoing I had lost the last I had on earth. I cannot and do not wish to describe my grief at this point, and of course this is of secondary importance to my readers.

In spite of my protests, Brother R. arranged for a funeral service, to which the whole Bible school came to Berghausen. This procedure was self-evident to them. After a song by the students, Brother Warns was the first speaker. He was followed by all the teachers of the school. After a closing prayer and a choir rendition, the students lifted the casket on their shoulders and carried it to the cemetery in Hundsheim. It took a half-hour to walk the distance. There were many people at the house, but at the graveside many more were gathered. Many friends and church members from surrounding towns, even from Elberfeld and Barmen, took part in the service. And all this for the sake of an old, depressed and now deceased "Russian woman" who, of course, was a sister in the Lord to all of them. All this put me to shame.

At the graveside the Baptist choir sang a song, after which the minister spoke. Our dear Brother Ernst Reuber followed him. His main thought was to call attention to the blessing that the departed Mother Jantzen, by her quiet nature, had exerted on the whole community. After him several men and women testified to the influence for good she had been to them. I concluded the service. While the two choirs sang, the casket was lowered into the grave.

Before the people all separated, Mr. R. invited the students, as well as those who had come from a distance, to a chapel nearby, in order to get some nourishment before going to their homes. The chapel was filled with long tables bedecked with baked goods and coffee. Brother Reuber gave the opening prayer, since I was not able to speak. When everyone had been refreshed, the Baptist minister said a few concluding words, after which everyone went to his home. Later I was told that something like 450 people had come to the service.

Brother Warns wanted me to move to Wiedenest right away, where I already had my own room. But I declined his invitation for the time being. Then a Russian student, Brother Metnitschencko, offered to come and stay with me for a while. He had a special attachment to Mother and had always referred to us as "parents." He thought that then I wouldn't be so lonely. But this offer I also declined since I wished to be alone and have a quiet time for myself. After a few weeks I locked up my home, gave the key to Brother R, who owned it, and moved to the Bible school. There I remained in quiet seclusion for a time, receiving much consolation from Brother Warns and others.

Then one day I responded to a renewed call by Brother K that I come to S. in order to help him establish more firmly the two churches that had been organized two years earlier. The members did not feel at home in the established church. Then, too, there were a few more who desired baptism. In this way, several more congregations were organized in the villages, St ... d and St.... ch.

In autumn of that year I answered a call to Holland, where with brethren as interpreters, I traveled from place to place. I spoke in many of the Free Churches. By special invitation of the brethren in Arnheim, I remained in that city for some time. But most of the time I spent in travel and made special effort to become conversant in the Dutch language. My established quarters were with the family Abbenbrook.

CHAPTER 20

▼

MISSIONARY JOURNEYS INTO BULGARIA

In Holland I heard from our young missionaries in Bulgaria who asked me to come there as "an old specialist" to show "how one can get next to the hearts of the Turkish people." They had finished their introductory study in the Bulgarian and Turkish languages. But, aside from that, they had not accomplished much and were still treated like strangers.

In March of 1929, when I was in Wiedenest, invitations were given to the annual Conference in Berlin. I went with several other Brethren, Brother Warns being at the head of the delegation. We had a separate compartment on the train, without strangers present, and visited about many things. I turned to Brother Bohn, who had been a homeopathic doctor in earlier years and had worked in Russia also. He had visited the Brethren in Bulgaria the year before. I asked him what a trip to Bulgaria would cost. He answered, "Three hundred marks, but why do you ask? Are you planning to go there? I would advise you that, as an older man, you should take not 300 but 400 marks. You will need that much."

"Since the young men have repeatedly invited me to come and give them direction on how to reach the Turkish people, I thought, if it were the Lord's will, and He gives the necessary provision, I should accept the invitation and go there to help them." At this point Brother Bohn asked me how many marks I had in my pocket. I said, "Perhaps two hundred."

Then all the Brethren laughed and said, "Then you will need two hundred more; where do you expect to get them?" I didn't answer him. I sat quietly in one corner of the compartment and closed my eyes as though I were sleeping. The brothers continued their conversations. After a while Brother Bohn addressed me again. "Brother Jantzen, you still owe us an answer to the question, where you expect to get the two hundred marks you still need for your trip to Bulgaria; or are you asleep?"

"No, I am not asleep. I have said to my Lord and Master, who gave all missionaries the commission to go into the world and preach the gospel: 'Lord, you have heard what Brother Bohn said, that I need another two hundred marks for my trip to Bulgaria. Now I pray you, Lord Jesus, if it be your will that I make this trip, that you give me not 400 but 800 marks. You know that our young brethren there are poor, and if I come there without money for a longer period of time, I would be a burden to them.'"

Again they all laughed and one said, "Yes, Brother Jantzen, you are real bold toward the Lord Jesus." To which I answered, "That I am, because I know that He is rich." After they were through laughing, Brother Warns said to me in his calm manner, "Dear Brother Jantzen, just continue in your request; I will help you pray and He will give His answer." All became very quiet and the train rushed toward its goal, Berlin.

The Lord gave us a blessed conference. As had happened in previous occasions, I received many invitations from churches here and there to minister to them. After I accepted these opportunities I asked Brother Warns to arrange my itinerary. I followed his plan and almost every day I spoke in a different place. After six weeks I arrived at my last station, Homburg vor der Hoehe, where two brethren met me at the depot and took me to the hospitable home of Brother H. At this home the family welcomed me warmly. After we had eaten supper Brother H. smiled at me and said, "Brother Jantzen, we have received a letter from Brother Warns, in which he informed us that you want to make a trip to Bulgaria. For this you prayed the Lord, not for the 400 marks Brother B. suggested, but 800 marks 'because He is so rich.' He asks that we should examine your finances, whether you already have the 800 marks; if not, we are to make up the deficit. Mr. Warns believes that you must make this trip. So, Brother Jantzen, give us an account."

I opened my suitcase and handed the brethren all the unopened envelopes with the offerings from the churches I had visited. They opened one after another and counted the contents. The farther they went in opening and counting, the quieter and more earnest they became. When they had finished, they asked whether I knew how much was lying there on the table. I said, "No! It is a custom of mine not to count the offerings until I had reached the end of the tour. Then I thank the Lord for everything that is there. He then determines for whom or for what I should use it."

Then they said, "You have here not the 800 marks for which you prayed, but 1200 are here on the table for your trip." So we all kneeled and thanked the Lord for such evidence of His mercy. That same evening we sent a telegram to Brother Warns to tell him of the condition of my "examined treasury."

On the following morning the men took me to the train in Frankfurt. The sisters had packed several heavy suitcases with presents for the missionaries. They included all kind of foodstuffs, also coffee, etc. So I proceeded on my way to Vienna in Austria. In Vienna I was met at the station gate by Mr. and Mrs. B., where I was to stay overnight. In the evening I had opportunity to preach the Word in their meeting. The next morning they brought me to a ship which would sail down the Danube to Bulgaria. We had beautiful, bright spring weather. We sailed by way of Bratislava, capital of Slovakia; Budapest, capital of Hungary, and finally Belgrade, capital city of Yugoslavia. All these cities are on the Danube. The ship stopped at each one and many passengers embarked or disembarked at each one.

Finally we reached the border city of Lom, Bulgaria. Here my passport was checked and the baggage examined. The boat continued on past Orschowo to Rustschuck, where I disembarked. I was greeted joyfully by two young missionaries. We took a postbus and traveled southward 65 kilometers into the country to Rasgrad, where our brethren lived in the Turkish section of the city. The young wives greeted us heartily and their joy increased all the more when they saw the many gifts from their homeland. Talking and visiting continued late into the night. The next morning we went to the market and shopped for the household.

I also wanted to find Turkish clothes, purchase a red fez, a Turkish headdress—a high cap without a brim.

The merchant was surprised that I spoke to him in Uzbeck-Turkish instead of in Osman-Turkish. The latter is the language of Turkey and the Balkans. The Uzbeck-Turkish language is highly regarded here, since it is spoken and taught chiefly in the holy Buchara in Turkestan. For this reason this language is considered more holy. Only the educated Osman Turks understand Uzbeck, therefore I was always accepted by them with great respect.

Many times, as we stepped into Turkish shops, many questions were directed to me as to how I might have come to speak this holy language. I told them that I had lived in Turkestan for 45 years and that as a youth I had spent eight years in the study of the language as well as the Koran. This surprised them greatly.

Gradually I would direct the conversation toward Jesus Christ. I quoted Muhammed and what he says in the Koran concerning Jesus, who is son of the maiden Mary, born without a human father, as a result of the announcement of the Angel Gabriel to Mary. She was to give birth to a son and call his name Issa, that is Jesus. He was to come and bring salvation to many. Naturally they didn't immediately understand all this, but this heart-to-heart talk did them good and they soon trusted me.

Through these conversations with the Turks, I wanted especially to show the young missionaries that they must first of all gain the confidence and sympathy of the Turkish people. One must become Turk to them, in the style of clothing, the life style, for instance the food and drink, how to sit as they do—and the like. One must learn to live with them, feel with them, and even suffer with them. As they are, so we were at one time lost, though we were perhaps very pious and religious. Yet our homesick soul was thirsty for something. So is also the soul of the Muslim. He also has this yearning and desire; he also knows that sin separates him from God. He notices that the observance of the prescribed five daily periods of prayer which follow the ritualistic baths, and the month-long fastings do not bring rest to his soul.

When the Muslim comes in contact with the genuine love of Christ, whether through His Word or through the life of the missionary as he lives this love, he will capitulate and become a Christian if indeed he is a genuine seeker for the truth. These were some of the suggestions I made to the young friends. They later experienced the truth of these ideas in their work.

On one of the Bulgarian holidays I took a walk in the city park where a Gypsy band was playing beautiful music. I took a seat on a shaded bench a little to one side. Shortly after, another man came walking along, dressed as I was and wearing a fez. He was an important Muslim priest. After a polite "Sallom Effendi" (Peace, Sir), he sat down beside me. Soon we were in conversation, by which he, too, noticed that I was using the holy Uzbeck-Turkish-Buchara language. Then he addressed me as "Bader Effendi." "Bader" in Uzbeck is "brother." We had an hour-long conversation on spiritual matters in which he commented, "As long as the Bulgarians, who call themselves Christians, worship images and are given to drunkenness, no Muslim will accept Christ. The whole life style and the type of governing that is seen with the otherwise highly civilized Europeans, who call themselves Christians, shows that they are not such. I know the teachings and the walk of Christ in the Injil (Gospel). He did only good, nothing bad." After I had pointed out to him very personally of the truth of the Injil, we parted in a brotherly manner. Will we see each other above in the presence of the Lord? I do not know, but I hope so.

One day we traveled to Schumen, a city in the center of the country, where we visited the German missionary, Mr. H. of the established Church Mission, whose director is Professor Doctor Sch. in F. am M. This organization was never in sympathy with our Free Church mission workers from Wiedenest. Here in Schumen we found a brother filled with the love of Christ. This love does not recognize any church doctrine. Brother M. received us gladly and introduced us to the three Sisters in the mission who worked among the Turkish women. All of us from Wiedenest had much in common and stayed there several days. We even had a sort of conference where we prayed the Lord for special guidance through His Spirit. So we were preserved from doctrinal differences. The Lord Himself became very great to us, because He was in our midst, and at the same time placed us in a common field of labor.

From here I traveled alone by train to Varna on the Black Sea, where there was also a worker in the German Mission. At the station I was greeted by Pastor L, accompanied by his Turkish tutor, Mohamedin Effendi. They took me to the German Mission House, which is located near the sea on a plateau upon which the city is also built.

The house was a two-story structure on a main street. On the first floor was a large meeting hall arranged like a church with benches and a podium. Outside, above the main entrance, there was a large sign with glittering Turkish letters with the words: "Hall for Evangelism for Muslims. Everyone cordially invited." The time of meetings was also on the sign.

The Pastor and his wife lived on the second floor. She greeted me warmly. After a while we went out on a balcony from which we enjoyed a beautiful view of the sea immediately below us. While we were drinking tea, the Pastor started telling me the history of the Mission. This is now 20 years ago and I do not remember the details. He had come from Pomerania near Stettin. As a *Pfarrer* (Pastor) at home, he had had a warm heart for missions. Therefore the mission board sent him there to work among the Muslims. He had remodeled this house and, beside the hall downstairs, he had a reading room with many books and Bibles in the Turkish language. After much effort he found Muhamedin Effendi, who had been his language tutor for seven years. He now mastered the language to a degree, but in spite of all efforts, no Turks ever came to the meetings he had announced. Neither did they come to his house. All this had been very expensive and still is. So he was pretty much at the end of his rope.

I really felt sorry for the dear man and I listened to him quietly. When he had finished, after some thought, I said: "Mr. Pastor, as one who has served many years as missionary to the Muslims, who grew up among them and lived among them for 45 years, may I say a few frank words?" With his permission I continued, "First of all, I advise you to send the *Herr Pfarrer* (Mr. Pastor) back to Pomerania. Tomorrow we will go to the market and shop for a Turkish mantle and a fez. Further you must learn to sit cross-legged according to Turkish custom, and learn their habit of eating with their hands. The Lord Jesus did not say: 'You should be my theologians and pastors.' He said: 'You shall be my witnesses.' That is, we must have experienced Him in our hearts, in order to be able to witness for Him. Then he says: 'Go into all the world and teach all nations.' That does not mean that we sit in our meeting place and expect them to come to us, but we must go to them.

"Tomorrow we must dress you and then we will go into the Turkish tea house, take some tracts and scriptures along. We will sit on the rug among the people, order a pot of tea and strike up a conversation. Then things must develop on their own. At first we must win their confidence, be a Turk to the Turks, learn to feel with them. Once we win his confidence, then the Turk will open up to you. Then you will find that the Turks also have homesickness of soul, and one can talk to them."

The pastor was very willing to enter into my plans. The next morning, dressed as two Turks, we visited teahouses and visited with many people. Unfortunately, I had another attack of rheumatism, so that I was forced to remain in bed for ten days or so. During this time the Pastor's wife gave me loving care like a good nurse. May the Lord bless her for it.

During my illness Muhamedin Effendi sat for hours at my bed, and we talked about many thing that had happened in our lives. He told me much of his life in Constantinople where he was born and where he grew up. There he had attended university and Kemal Pascha was his fellow student. Kemal Pascha, of course, later became President of Turkey. So he spoke much about the reforms that he instituted in Turkey, especially in introducing Western customs which devout Moslems could not accept. Muhamedin Effendi, as a professor at a higher, theological school, protested against all the disturbances and was persecuted by his former colleague, Kemal Pascha. He was no longer safe anywhere in his own country and finally fled to Bulgaria. Here in Varna he was employed as language tutor and in this the pastor is his student. With the pastor he had read through the New Testament several times. Finally he said:

"For Jesus, the son of Mary, I have the greatest respect. He did only good and taught the same. He proved a love by his life, the like of which is not found on earth. So I feel like those men who once came to the disciples and said, 'We would see Jesus' (John 12:21). But among all that I have learned to know, who call themselves Christians, I have not seen Jesus, because they do not live as he taught. For example, Jesus taught that we are not to take the sword, and Christians make the most terrible swords and weapons, which they use against all nations who do not think as they do. And the love of which Jesus speaks is not found in them. The Europeans send us missionaries and evangelists, yet they are not like Jesus, therefore we reject it all. If Jesus Himself were to come, he could make us happy." I told all this to the dear pastor and he became very quiet and thoughtful.

After I was relatively well again I had to move on and return to Rustschuck, where I had been expected for some time. While there, I stayed with Brother H. When I arrived in Bulgaria again, Brother H. was in Constantinople, so I could meet only his wife, but I fulfilled my promise to visit them again.

Brother H. was an educated and highly talented man. He published a number of tracts and other papers in Bulgarian and Turkish, which were very popular. Through him I became acquainted with a Methodist minister who had a church in Rustschuck. He invited me to speak in his church. Since the members of his church were more or less educated people of a higher class, I could speak to them in the Russian language. Because of the similarity in the two languages, it is understandable that the Bulgarians could follow along too. I spoke there several times and each time I noticed an older couple seated in the front bench. After the first meeting they introduced themselves and invited me to their home. I accepted the invitation and soon we sat around the smoking *samovar*. While the lady served us, the man told me the following story:

"Mr. Jantzen, you spoke in your sermon about the love of God even toward people who have fallen away from Him, in the sense that God sometimes reveals Himself to such people in a wonderful way. He often answers their prayers in an unbelievable and incomprehensible way. My wife and I experienced God in the most critical time in our lives.

"As a general in the service of the Czar, I took part in the war in the Far East in 1905–07. At the end of this unfortunate war I was appointed military governor in Harbin. I filled this position until the revolution of 1917, at which time I destroyed my epaulettes and military decorations. With General Koltscheck I fought against the Reds until our army was destroyed.

"In a round-about way I finally got together with Generals Wrangel and Benikin, who were fighting the Reds in the Caucasus. This army, too, was destroyed and soldiers scattered in all directions.

"My dear, loyal wife never completely lost sight of me and always found ways to follow me at some distance. After great dangers, we found ourselves together in Odessa. There were several foreign ships there, ready to take refugees like us to a foreign country and to safety. We stood ready, guns still in hand, to board the last of these ships. However, it was overfilled already and pulled away before our eyes.

"Then in despair I said to my wife, 'Do as I do. Hold the muzzle of your gun to your forehead, close your eyes, and pull the trigger. I'll do the same, while we pray to God to save us.' So we got ready, while I prayed, 'Almighty God, you see our hopeless situation. If you are really there, save us and let the ship return and pick us up, otherwise we'll become suicides.' I prayed this prayer several times. Just then I heard small splashes and saw that the ship had actually returned to the shore and very quickly took us along. In the distance we already could see the Reds marching into Odessa. In this manner we both experienced God, and since then, under all circumstances of life, we hold onto Him and are happy in Him. The ship brought us to Varna. A little later we came here to Rustschuck, where I am a secretary to the Mayor of the city."

So far goes the narrative of my host. In the days following, I was to come to their home every day at 5:00 for tea. In this circumstance I learned to know a Russian Pope, whose wife, strangely enough, was of a Mennonite family from the Ukraine. These people, too, had come here as refugees. The Father had called together all the refugees in Rustschuck into a congregation and served as their priest.

One day Brother and Sister H. and I were invited to Sarvet, a town about 25 kilometers downstream from Rustschuck, in order to serve the church there on Sunday morning. This was a newly formed congregation which met in the home of a cabinet maker who also served as its leader. We were warmly received. Since the house was too small for those who came, we held the service outside. For us guests there was a table with some chairs behind it, while some of the audience sat on benches and others on the grass before us.

Since the leader of the church was a complete stranger to us, Brother H. asked him to tell us how he had come to this newfound faith in the Lord Jesus Christ. It is to be noted here, that the people of Bulgaria are nearly all strictly Greek Catholic. The leader prayed and then told us his story. "As all my fellow citizens know, I was for many years a confirmed alcoholic. As much as I tried to battle this evil, I had so little success in conquering it. So it happened one day that, in my drunken condition, I went to the market where I saw a bookstand with many books. I stumbled closer and looked at some of the books. My eyes fell on a used New Testament. I recalled that some people have found many unusual things therein. I was curious and bought it very cheaply, because it was well worn.

"At home I placed it on my joiners bench and went to bed to sleep off my drunkenness. When I returned to my bench the next morning, I saw the New Testament and began to read in it. I could not understand it very well, so I laid it aside and went to my work. However, I could not leave it alone. I read in it every day and gradually noticed the strange and noteworthy things in it. I read how the Lord Jesus healed the sick and raised the dead, etc. I read further that He answers our prayers. This finally gripped me so that I kneeled down beside my workbench and said, 'Lord Jesus, if everything that I read in this book is true, then I pray, free me from my drunkenness.' And He answered my prayer, as everyone will testify."

After this testimony we were asked to speak to the group, which we were glad to do. We spoke of the great love of God, which the Scripture so clearly reveals, and which is proved by such testimony of answers to prayer, which we just heard from our host. At the close we asked whether any of them had experienced Jesus Christ as personal Savior. Several of them raised their hands. We then asked them to tell us how this had happened in their lives. One man stood up and, speaking for the group, related the following:

"Because of the change in the life of the cabinetmaker, and of his testimony, we also bought New Testaments. In order to understand it better, we decided to meet twice a week to search the Scriptures. Through this we came to realize that every person has the free right to pray in Jesus' name directly, without the help of the clergy or the Mother of God. In other words, not like the priests do in the churches. So we prayed that He should make us children of God as we read in John 1:12 and 13. He heard our prayer and we are happy."

We then went to prayer and many of these simple people, men and women, spoke out clearly in praise and thanks for what God had done for them. So we had a richly blessed Sunday morning. The afternoon was very much the same. All of them met again and we had the profound feeling that the Lord was in our midst.

In the evening we were accompanied by several of the others as we went into the town and visited a Turkish tea house. We handed out tracts and then I gave an address in Turkish. As usual, a debate developed among the Muslims who were present. As we stepped onto the street to walk to our quarters at the Brother cabinet maker's house, Brother H. and I were arrested by the border police and placed in custody of two soldiers. Sarvet lies on the Romanian border.

I protested this treatment and showed my credentials, as did Brother H. These showed that we had permission from the Ministry of Sofia to preach the gospel anywhere in Bulgaria. But the police chief didn't pay any attention. We were placed on a farm wagon, which stood ready at hand. The two soldiers sat on either side of us and we drove into the night. We came to a town 30 kilometers away and were turned in as common criminals at the headquarters of the border police. There we were introduced to the secretary. He read through the protocol of the border police and said, "It is late at night and the Commander isn't here, therefore take the prisoners and lock them up." As they were about to lead us away, I said, "This will not happen until our documents have been checked, which the Bulgarian ministry has issued for us. I demand an immediate examination of the papers."

The secretary stepped into a side room, where it was immediately apparent that the Commander was playing cards. In a short time he came into the room with the secretary. He could hardly stay on his feet and yelled at me, "What do you want?"

"We were brought here from Sarvet like bandits, without one look at our perfectly legitimate papers from the Ministry in Sofia. They are in the best of order and we are to be stuck into prison. I protest that treatment and demand immediate examination and freedom."

He read the document and said, "Everything is in order and you can go free."

"We are free?"

"Yes, what more do you want?"

"We are free, but you, dear Sir, are not. What is your name?" I took out a notebook and pencil and was ready to write. He asked, "What do you want with my name? What business of yours is my name?"

"We have been illegally treated and I am going to hold you responsible to the Ministry in your government. Otherwise our papers give us no security in this land, since your subordinates do not respect them."

"Seek your rights in Holland!" he screamed. "No, but I hope to see you in the Ministry in Sofia one of these days."

After that exchange we left the chancellery and stepped out on the street. Here we found a car ready for our use, which took us to a first class hotel where, in spite of the late hour, we seemed to be expected. This matter of the auto, as well as the hotel, posed a question which was never answered. My own conjecture was that the secretary was taking care of these matters for us while I was having the discussion with the Commander.

At the hotel we were received by a lady who spoke a very fine German. After some tea and refreshments which we received, the lady sat down with us and told us that she was a native of Wuerttemberg. Her family was Catholic and she was brought up in that faith. Her husband had come to Germany as a prisoner of war. They became acquainted and later they were married. After the war they had come back here and had taken over this hotel. They were getting along right well, both in the hotel as well as in their marriage. However, she often felt a real home-sickness for Germany; but even a heavier burden bothered her day and night and very modestly she said, "I have no peace within my heart; all my praying has not helped me."

We saw in her a soul hungering for salvation and we were to show her the right way. Because of the Catholic influence, it was difficult for her at first to understand the freedom that Jesus Christ has brought. But gradually the light of life penetrated her heart. Certainly the Spirit of God was at work in her. After we had prayed with her several times, rest and peace came to her, which made her very happy. Soon the day dawned; no one had thought of sleep. We had another cup of tea and some refreshments. Then we were told that a wagon was waiting outside to take us back to Rustschuck. This seemed peculiar to me, since we hadn't ordered a car at all. Something did come into mind like lightening. "Was it necessary for us to be arrested like bandits in Sarvet to be brought here, because a homesick soul was thirsting after God and could not find her way? Did we have to be here in order to show her the way, which she followed for her own peace? O God, how incomprehensible are your ways again and again in my life."

The car into which we stepped had six seats. Sister H. and I sat in the rear seat. Ahead of us was a priest of high rank, with Brother H., and in front, beside the driver, sat a man with a slouch hat, which he wore in such a way as though he didn't want to be seen.

After we were out of town, the priest started a conversation with Brother H. by asking whether he was a Bulgarian. He said that he was a German. "Therefore you are a foreigner"—which H. admitted. Then the priest asked, "Tell me whether you heard of an incident which happened last evening in Sarvet. A Hollander was arrested and taken to the Commander of the border police, without having his papers, which were in good order, even looked at. The Hollander is said to have protested very sharply against such treatment and threatened to call the Commander to account in Sofia."

"Yes, I know about the incident, since I was there myself."

"Do you know the man?"

"Yes, I am a missionary and the man is our Inspector of Missions. He is seated behind us." The conversation was carried on in Bulgarian but I understood everything they had said. Now the priest began to implore Brother H.: "Would you be so kind and ask the man if he would please destroy the report. For, if this unpleasant business should get to the Ministry, it could go badly for the otherwise highly respected Commander. Added to this is the fact that he did not personally arrest the man."

"Alright, I will talk to the Inspector." He turned to me and said in German, that I had very likely understood what was said, and asked my reaction to it all. I answered him as follows: "In my work as Inspector of Missions it becomes my duty to make certain that our missionaries here in this country can work freely everywhere and without being hindered. That did not happen yesterday, when we were treated like bandits in spite of the fact that our papers were in good order. We were dragged to the office of the border guard and threatened with imprisonment, without having anyone look at our papers. Only after my protest did the drunk Commander agree to look at our papers and then added the sarcastic remark, 'You can get your rights established in Holland,' and then he freed us. I answered him that we would not get justice in Holland, but in Sofia. I shall go to the Home Office and report this case and ask that the Commander be made to answer to the charge. The report is all ready and in a few days I hope to meet the

Chief Minister. As a result I expect that our missionaries will be unmolested in the future."

After Brother H. had translated all I had said, the priest really began to beg, and after much discussion back and forth, I finally said, "Good. I will destroy the report, if he, as high-ranking priest will give his written guarantee that our missionaries will not be bothered in the future; this guarantee to be in writing, duly signed and sealed." After some thought, he agreed. When we arrived in Rustschuk and got out of the car, he wrote the guarantee, signed it, and stamped his official seal under his name. After he had handed me the paper, I destroyed my report and we shook hands and separated as friends. I then noticed that the man in the slouch hat was secretary of the border guard.

I spent a few days on farewell visits with my Russian friends as well as the Methodist minister. Then I said goodbye to Brother and Sister H. and boarded the steamer that took me on a six-hour sail upstream to Grechowa, where missionary K. greeted me. We took the postbus 25 kilometers into the country to Woiwodowa where Brother K. himself had built a house with a large meeting room. He was born of the family Wende in Spreewald in Germany where he owned a well-producing farm. He was not married. After his conversion he felt impelled to attend the Bible School in Wiedenest, where I learned to know him. Through my sermons on mission work in the East, he was convinced that he should go to Bulgaria as a missionary and this he did, after he had finished his school work. Since the Wendes are a Slavic people, the similarity of languages was a great advantage to him.

When Brother K. arrived here in 1926 he found a large Methodist congregation whose pastor was very friendly to him and asked him to speak in his church. After several weeks of services a revival broke out and many experienced personal salvation. They realized that it was not a certain method that is important, but the new birth through the Holy Spirit.

Unfortunately the Methodist minister didn't understand this and began to work against Brother K, to belittle him and accuse him of tearing his congregation apart. The new converts finally couldn't feel at home in their church and asked Brother K. to lead them on in Bible study. The brother agreed to this, and since they had no meeting place, he built a house with his own funds, with the understanding that as soon as possible the group would repay him and thus the building would be the property of the church.

When I arrived there, the church already had more than one hundred members who showed evidence of an active, healthy, spiritual life. Since I worked in and around Rasgrad for two months and in Rustschuk one month, I was asked to spend at least two months here also. Not only did we have two meetings on Sunday, but we also met some evenings during the week, even though it was harvest time and many people were busy in the fields. The meetings were well attended. Besides those who were believers, there were strangers: Bulgarians, Armenians, Turks, and Gypsies, of whom there are many in Bulgaria. It was surprising to see the spiritual hunger of these people, and through the weeks many were converted. Several times we had baptisms on Sunday, followed by the Lord's Supper. Here one could really see what the Lord Jesus said in John 4:35: "Lift up your eyes, and look on the fields; for they are white already to harvest."

Brother K. usually helped the peasants in the fields, swinging the scythe and setting up the sheaves. I stayed in town and made house visits where I could, since I was no longer a stranger among the people. The shopkeepers usually sat in their shops, since there were few customers during the busy season. They had much time and sipped their tea or coffee. They were always friendly to me, although I really wasn't a customer. Some came to our meetings on Sunday afternoon or evening. The atmosphere of revival touched them too, so that I could have very fruitful conversations with them.

Each week Brother K. and I went to a village 5 kilometers away, where we evangelized. The inhabitants were largely Turks and resident Gypsies. Brother K. was well known to them. Although here too people worked hard in the fields, the attendance in the evenings was very good. They were very attentive and asked many questions. We had straw-filled bags to sit on, while the audience sat on the grass. Their keen attention proved that the Holy Spirit was working in their hearts.

Our host was a blacksmith, a rather well developed Gypsy, who regarded Brother K. with special respect, which struck me as unusual.

About 12:00 one night we left the village, accompanied by some young Turks who were our friends. They came with us to the edge of the village because of some vicious dogs in that neighborhood. After they left us, with a cheery

Gehtschjarrik Salam, that is, "Good night, in peace," I asked Brother K., "Tell me, how is it that our host, the smith and his brother, treat you with such high esteem?" It was a beautiful moon-lit night, which is conducive to frank conversation. The brother said, "I do not like to talk much about it, because I might easily be misunderstood. However, to you, dear Father Jantzen (I was often so addressed), I know I can tell it. You understand the Slavic mind in me better than most of our European brothers, because you grew up with Slavic people.

"For two years now I have visited this village and taught the people the gospel. But, as you know, Muslims are hard to reach. I always stayed at the home of the blacksmith. One evening he was not at home. His wife lay sick on her bed and groaned. As I approached her bed, she wept. She didn't answer my question concerning her husband; she just kept on moaning, because of her pain. I asked whether she had tried to see a doctor to examine her and perhaps prescribe medicine. She said, 'Who should do that for me, and anyway I don't have any money to pay the doctor.'

"So I took my bicycle and rode to the next village where I knew a doctor who lived there. I told him the situation and asked him to come and examine the woman. He immediately agreed, took his bicycle and came with me. After his examination he pondered a bit and said, 'The woman must have an operation immediately. But it is 65 kilometers to Lom and how could we get her there?' I offered to hire a wagon and take her there immediately.

"While I arranged for the wagon, the doctor wrote a brief report to the head of the clinic, which he gave me, and left. By the time the wagon arrived, it was morning. I had ordered a liberal supply of straw in the wagon, so she would have some comfort during the ride. In Lom she had surgery right away and in a few weeks she was released in good health. I arranged to have her brought home.

"In the meantime, I had discovered that her husband, the smith, had stolen something and was in prison. After the woman had arrived at home, I visited her again and she asked me, 'Why did you do so much for me? You knew before hand that I could not repay you, since I have no money. The trip to Lom and back, the operation in the hospital, and the doctor here, all that has cost much money.'

"My answer was, 'The Lord Jesus ordered me to do all that.' This she couldn't fathom; it was too much for her to understand. I took my Bulgarian New Testament and read to her, how the Lord Jesus helped the sick, even those who were bad and sinful. When such people then accepted Him, they experienced a new birth in their hearts by the Holy Spirit and received an entirely new nature. This nature from Jesus desires to do only good, and this nature lives in me and told me to take you to the hospital and to provide for you. This surprised her greatly. I prayed with her in the Name of Jesus and rode home. I visited her repeatedly and prayed with her each time, until she too experienced the new birth and became a Christian.

"During this time I had opportunity to visit her husband several times in the prison. I told him everything that had happened to his wife. He too started thinking. Each time I had Bible study and prayer with him. As a result of these visits, I became acquainted with the warden and we became good friends. On one of my visits, the warden told me that something had happened to the blacksmith that he could not understand. Because of my visits the smith became a holy man, not as the Muslims, but as a Christian. He was now living like a Christian and, as a result, was a good example and model for his fellow prisoners.

"When I met him again I found a man filled with happiness and peace, for which we thanked the Lord on our knees. A little while later, he came home and worked hard at his trade. This surprised me. When I met the warden of the prison a little later, I asked him how it was the smith had been released before the time of his sentence was completed. He said, 'Because I knew of his complete change of life and saw his good walk, I became convinced that he wouldn't steal anymore. I therefore secured his release upon my guarantee, and I took the chance to let him go home."

As a result of his good walk, his brother and his brother's son were converted. As Brother K. finished his story, I was reminded of my discussion with Muhamedin Effendi in Varna, who had said to me, "We Muslims would like very much to see Jesus, not the so-called Christians and their missionaries."

As I mentioned above, always we had good meetings in Woiwodowa. One Sunday afternoon, after I had finished my sermon, a young Turk in the back row near the door stood up and asked, "May I say something?" When his request was granted he came to the front of the room and said to the congregation, "During the past few weeks I attended almost every meeting. After hearing so much about

Jesus, the Savior from sin, I was able to communicate with Him in prayer. The result was that He showed me all my sins, so that I was terribly frightened, and in despair I asked for His mercy and forgiveness. He forgave all my sins. But now He says to me that I should confess everything where I hurt people and to make good, as much as possible. This I want to do now."

Having said that, he pointed to one person and gave his name, for he knew everyone in the village, and said, "From you I stole some fruit." To another farmer he said, "From you I stole some eggs." To another, "From you I stole some chickens" and so on. Finally he said, "As far as I am able, I want to repay everyone; but I beg you to forgive my guilt." Those he had named were all Christians and were glad to forgive him and added, "You do not need to repay us; we too live only by the grace of God, which we must receive from Jesus Christ every day." After many of them expressed their joy through praise and thanks, the meeting was closed.

One day a Baptist pastor invited me to Lom, where he had a church made up entirely of Turkish Gypsies. I took a boat and came to the city, where I was warmly greeted by this intelligent young man and his wife. They both spoke rather good German since both had spent some time in Germany. They had had further education at Spurgeon College in England and were members of the Baptist World Union. Everything was ready for me to speak the same evening. After supper we started for the meeting place, which was in a village outside the city.

When we arrived there shortly before sundown, we noticed that the inhabitants were sitting around their fires on the street, cooking their evening meal. Each family invited us to eat with them, which of course we declined since we had just eaten. We stopped with one group, since they had finished their meal. They were still sitting around their fires, smoking their long-stemmed pipes. They offered us some too, which we also declined. Among them sat an old woman, smoking her pipe. She turned to us and asked, "Can a woman ninety years old still get to heaven?"

My minister friend translated her question since I could not understand her language. My answer was, "Yes, if you accept the Lord Jesus as your Savior, you will be saved and will be with Him in heaven." This surprised her very much and she asked again, "Am I permitted to attend the meetings?" My colleague answered, "Yes, you may come to the meetings."

At that moment I heard an unusual tone, as from a bell, yet it sounded different. My colleague smiled and said, "We must go; the bell is ringing." Soon we stood before a larger building. In front of it, on a post, hung a railroad rail about 2 meters long. A young man struck it with a wooden club, and that was the unusual sound. "That is our bell; we don't have watches."

In the house many Gypsies were already seated, some on benches, some on the floor, waiting for us. At the front of the room there was a sort of podium with two chairs for us. Beside it stood a parlor organ, with a Gypsy in front of it, a big cap on his head. He played the organ well, and was playing from the Baptist Hymnal.

When the room was filled, the minister announced a song. Everyone opened his songbook and sang in his own language. They all rose for prayer, removing their caps. After prayer they sat down and put their caps back on. The minister then read a paragraph from the New Testament, made a few appropriate remarks, and then gave me opportunity. I spoke in German and he interpreted for the listeners.

While the service was going on, a disturbance developed near the door. The 90-year-old Gypsy woman sat on the floor striking around her with her pipe and cried, "These boys are bothering me with their banter and teasing so that I cannot hear what is being said. I want to hear the gospel too, because I want to get to heaven." I paused for a while, as the minister went down the rows of seats and grabbed one boy after another and pushed them outside and locked the door. He came back and I continued speaking.

As I ended my sermon, I called on any of the hearers to pray publicly as the Spirit may lead them. They all rose, took off their caps, and several of them prayed. It became apparent to me how sincere they were, and how touched in their hearts. The pastor made his closing, we sang another song, and all of them returned to their homes, as we did.

The next morning a Methodist minister came to get acquainted with me. He was a Bulgarian but understood Russian well. (The similarity between the two languages is supposed to come from the fact that the Bulgarians originated near the Volga. Their ancestors were called Wolgern. Later the "W" was changed to a

"B," so that they are now called Bulgarians. How or why this happened no one can explain. Then, too, the Bulgarians are Greek Catholic like the Russians.)

How my visitor had come to be a Methodist, I do not know. There was no doubt that he was a genuine Christian, which I could detect from the questions he asked me, like one would in an examination. His questions were very thorough and deep. At the end of our conversation he seemed satisfied and invited me to speak in his church the following evening. I accepted. As my host and I walked through the streets of the city, we noticed printed announcements on many street corners, on houses, as well as in the shops. They said that on the following evening in the Methodist Chapel, a missionary from Turkestan would speak. All citizens were urged to attend, to hear this man who had come such a distance.

The following evening, as we came to the meeting place, we noticed that people were hurrying to the place, and as we entered, we found that almost every seat was taken. After opening statements by the pastor, and the singing of several songs, I was asked to speak. After I finished my sermon, I was asked to speak at two more evening meetings, which I promised to do. Each time the hall was filled. What the results were, I have not been told. My Master knows that best. For me there is always one thing to remember: I read in Isaiah 55:11, "My Word shall not return unto me void, but shall accomplish that which I please," says the Lord.

After I had finished my work in Lom, the two pastors accompanied me back to the ship that brought me back to Rustschuck. From there I returned to Rasgrad, where I stayed for several weeks to try to instruct the two young Brothers H. and G. with practical suggestions as to how they could more easily gain the confidence of the Turkish people. Then I left them and started on my journey home. All our hearts were filled with praise and thanks to the Lord, who had blessed us so abundantly during the past few months and had given us wonderful fellowship with one another. I returned to Rustschuck for ten days with Brother H.

During these days Brother H. took me to see the *derwishes* in the city. The *derwishes* are a Muslim Organization of men who live an ascetic life and are honest seekers for truth. Since I speak the language that is highly regarded by the Osman Turks, the leaders of the *derwishes* accepted me with respect and I had to speak several times in their mosques. This is not an easy task, since they are all well educated. I was glad that they all knew the Koran well.

Here I would like to insert something. When Kemal Pascha became President of Turkey he introduced all kinds of European, anti-Muslim customs into the land. He went so far as to have the Koran translated into Turkish. Originally the Koran was written in Arabic and Mohammed ordered that the Koran should never be translated into another language. This action by Kemal stirred up all the holy men, the Mufti and the Caliphs (popes of the Muslims), and caused a revolt or riot in Constantinople. But, since anything forbidden arouses curiosity, so it was there. The result is that many people read the Koran, by which Islam lost much of its fanaticism. As a result, the hearts of Turkish people are much more open to the Gospel of Jesus Christ. So God often makes use of political upheaval to open doors for His Word.

One earnest and especially educated *derwish* came to faith in Jesus Christ. Soon he said that he wished to be baptized in the name of Jesus. I had noticed, however, that he had evidenced no conviction of sin. The Koran does speak of Jesus "who was conceived in and born by the maid, Mary, in a wonderful way, who lived without sin, died, and was resurrected by God and ascended to heaven." The Koran says nothing of the cross and its significance.

So I had to remind this honest *derwish* that the Lord Jesus came only to save lost sinners; that because of them He went to the cross and died for us, in order to save us from our sins. I showed him many references in the *Injil* (gospel) in his language, that made this clear. This made him very meditative. When I accepted an invitation to come to his home again a few days later, he said, "What must I do? I have thought through all you said and I find that I have never sinned. Must I steal a horse or commit some other crime, or perhaps commit adultery, in order to become a lost sinner?"

I called his attention to John 1:6 which says that God is Light, and added that, if in continued prayer he would come to stand in God's light, then he would realize that he, too, is a lost sinner without having stolen or done other such things. But it seemed that his soul remained in the dark, even though I went to great length to get him to the Light. Finally I turned him over to the Lord and prayed that He would not leave this honorable man alone in his search for the truth.

In the meantime, late autumn had come and I had to begin my trip home. The Brethren H. and G. accompanied me from Rasgrad to Rustschuk where I said farewell to Brother and Sister H. They all came to the boat that brought me upstream to Orechowo. Here Brother K. said goodbye and I sailed in the opposite direction than I had come, by way of Lom, Belgrade, Budapest, Bratislava, back to Vienna, where I arrived in four days and was greeted by friends. I had to stay a few days, since I could not refuse to speak at several evening services. We were greatly blessed at the meetings and we made house visits during the day. Here in Vienna I had some good *arbusen* (watermelon) to eat, which are known in Germany only by name. In Holland not even by name.

Here I must include two insertions. In the spring, when I left for Bulgaria, by the grace of God I had much money in my pocket, almost like Croessus. In the fall, when I left I could leave the missionaries a few hundred marks. This was helpful under their living conditions. All that we had experienced together filled us with praise and thanksgiving. Most important was the fact that we succeeded in establishing the real mission of the church. We told ourselves that Christ did not come to establish religious movements or organizations, but as He Himself said, "to save sinners, that they may all become one."

Then I should mention that our missionaries could work actively and unmolested until the start of the war in 1939. At the outbreak of the war all missionaries were forced to leave Bulgaria. Yet they could leave the churches in the hands of Czech, Bulgarian, Turkish, and Gypsy brethren. Today no one knows how it really is with the Christians in these lands.

From Vienna my travel took me via Heidelberg to Homburg vor der Hoehe, where Brother and Sister H. took me in again. After I had spent several evenings reporting my experiences, I traveled on to Wiedenest. Here I received an especially warm welcome by Brother Warns and the many others who awaited my coming. Naturally I spent several evenings here, telling folks what we had experienced. Then I went to Holland where I again lodged with Brother and Sister H. in their home.

CHAPTER 21

▼

WITNESSING HERE AND THERE

In Arnheim as well as in other parts of Holland there were flourishing Free Churches from which I received numerous invitations to serve. They were especially glad to hear about my experiences in Russia and my work as a missionary. People were always anxious to hear about Russia. Since at that time I wasn't fluent in the Dutch language, I usually used an interpreter. I received an invitation to speak in the large state church in A a/d Ryn where the church elder Mr. L. de G. was my interpreter.

Before I say more about all this, let me inject something here as an explanation. Whenever I spoke after the year 1925, I never appeared as a theologian, but always only as a witness for Jesus Christ, or a missionary. This became all the more important as I learned on my travels in Europe that there were many "Christian" people, often very religious "pagans," who had no concept of the new birth through the Holy Spirit, as mentioned in John 1:12–13. At best, people were satisfied with a good moral life without the Spirit of God. Through humanistic effort one could ennoble oneself, for which one just didn't need the Lord Jesus, although the names Jesus and Christ were often repeated.

The *dominie* (pastor) of the state church in A. a/d R. had announced that a Russian missionary would speak. This drew many people, since they wanted to hear about Russia. I realized this but I always took the opportunity to give a personal witness of God my Savior, who had revealed Himself to me in many different ways through all manner of wonderful experiences and who also saved me out of the hands of Bolsheviks in Russia. There was always opportunity to remind my listeners of my living relationship to God that came through the new birth and by my receiving the Holy Spirit. I could therefore witness to the truth expressed in Romans 8:16 that I am a child of God and that I did not just "hope" to someday become one, as was so commonly taught.

My interpreter spoke the German language very well. As a result he could convey the emphasis or transfer the impression I wanted to make when I spoke from the heart to the heart, out of my living experiences to their lives. It was obvious that this sort of Christian experience was new to the audience and they sat in rapt attention. The *dominie* didn't make any further comment; this type of witness was new to him also.

A few weeks later I received an invitation from the *dominie* of the Reformed Church of the same city, for which I used the same interpreter. The attendance here was also very good, as was the attention to the Word. A little later I received an invitation to the Darbysten Gemeinde, or church, and again I used the same interpreter. This three-time translation of my sermons had the result that Mr. L. de G. himself was converted. This man was unmarried and invited me often to visit him in order to receive further instruction in the Scriptures. Two years later he wished to be baptized on the basis of Romans 6:4. The Holy Spirit Himself led him to this conclusion through Mark 16:16. When it became known in the community that Mr. L. de G. wished to be baptized, there was great surprise. Many members of his church didn't believe it and said, "This we must see in order to believe it."

When the day arrived on which he was to be baptized, he invited all the citizens of the city to come and see how it was done. At the appointed time we met in a large church which had a baptistry. After I had made a brief introductory remark, he addressed the group himself. "Honored citizens of A., I know that many of you accuse my old friend, Father Jantzen, of having persuaded me to be baptized. But this is not so. The Holy Spirit drew my attention to what the Lord Jesus says in Mark's Gospel: 'He who believes and is baptized shall be saved.'

These words opened my eyes to the fact that my baptism as an infant did not meet this requirement. My parents of course told me that I was baptized, but what did this mean to me as an infant? Therefore this was my decision."

After he had been baptized, and while he changed his clothes, we sang several songs together. After he returned to the group he spoke again. "Father Jantzen says that after such a serious act he is accustomed to partake of the Lord's Supper with Christians, with praise and thanksgiving. Therefore I invite all of you who are children of God to come to my apartment where we will take communion together." Then we left the hall and went to his quarters. About ten persons came with us and we celebrated together.

Because of this unheard-of step, the dear brother had to take much persecution from his church as well as others. He bore it all with true love and patience, which in time bore its fruit. His subsequent walk, as well as his love and friendship toward others, helped open the eyes of many people. The result of it all was that within two years about 35 persons took the same step. The Lord blessed the loyal witness of this brother so much that a Free Church congregation of over 100 members was organized in A. Exactly the same situation was repeated a few years later in the birth place of L. de G., where a church of some 60 members now exists.

At about this time Brother Warns and I made a tour of all of Germany and Austria until Innsbruck in Tyrol to visit all the Free Churches in the cities and villages. Evenings, and often during the day, we held meetings and were privileged to witness to the glory and working power of God through the Holy Spirit.

In 1930 I accepted an invitation to Beattenberg in Switzerland, where a World Conference of Christians of Free Churches was held. There were representatives of twenty-one countries there. Among the many hundreds of people there were blacks from Africa, brown people from India, from Arabia, China and Indonesia; then Portuguese, Spaniards, Frenchmen, Bulgarians, Romanians, Yugoslavs, Czechs, Turks, Poles, Englishmen, Brazilians, Germans, Americans, and Balts, with me as the only Russian. The theme of the nondenominational gathering was: "Where and how did you find the Lord Jesus Christ?"

The conference lasted two full weeks, since every testimony was translated into all the languages, which took a certain amount of time. Every session opened at 8:00 a.m. with a prayer meeting. This was followed by testimonies until 11:30. The afternoon sessions were from 3:00–6:00 and evenings from 7:30–10:00. At noon we all ate at a common table in a near-by hotel, while breakfast and supper was left to each person.

The testimonies were, for the most part, very impressive, and the Lord became ever greater as a result. One could see how He went after each erring soul and brought him, through self-examination, to understanding His way and leading him to Himself. He followed each person in his own way, in his own country, in varying manners, with divine patience and love. After thus receiving peace by His grace, they could not keep from witnessing to others, quietly or openly.

These two weeks were a great blessing to all of us. At the close of the general sessions the universal wish was made known that all of us should partake of the Lord's Supper together. I was selected to lead this service. With a glance at the large group, most of whom I had never seen before, I read I Corinthians 11:23–29. After a few remarks concerning the importance of the Supper, and a reminder for self-examination, I broke the bread. Then I read I Corinthians 10:15–17, offered a few remarks, after which I thanked the Lord for the wine and asked that the glasses be distributed. After the service was finished we had prayer, where each one could pray in his own language. Never had I attended so long a session in the observance of communion. After the session many were heard to say, "This was a piece of heaven here on earth, without language barrier, because we were one in spirit." And so we parted.

After this conference I traveled in Switzerland where I visited several Mennonite congregations, in addition to Free Church groups. Finally, by special request, I spent several days in the Bible School in Lausanne. Here the English Brother Eol, a friend of mine for many years, was the director. I also had opportunity to give my testimony in Methodist and Darbysten Churches in the city. From Lausanne I returned to Wiedenest where numerous invitations awaited me.

CHAPTER 22

▼

A MUSLIM MISSION CONFERENCE

From Lausanne I traveled by way of Bern and Basel to Wiedenest where I found an invitation to an inter-confessional missions conference for Muslims. Pastor von Bodelschiving gave the invitation and the place of the meeting was at Bethel by Bielefeld. Brother Warns and Bohn received similar invitations. Brother Bohn came to South Russia before World War I and worked among the Mennonite churches. Since he had studied homeopathy, he practiced that profession, continuing that until 1914 when he was banned to Siberia. After the war, he was released and could work again for a while until the Bolschevik upheaval forced him to return to Germany.

Originally it had been Brother Bohn's intention to work among the Muslims, but he found the Uzbeck language too difficult. He and another Brother named Thielmann could communicate with the Muslims, but they were not quite able to engage in public speaking in the language. Therefore, both of them worked more among the Mennonites and other German-speaking groups. Nevertheless Mr. Bohn had had considerable experience in Muslim missions and therefore had worthwhile evaluations of the work.

Several hundred people had gathered. They included professors and directors of various German and denominational mission boards and others with expertise in this field. We were able to learn to know all of them. After singing a song and prayer, the sessions were opened by a Doctor and Professor of Theology. After a discussion of the purpose of the Conference, several learned dissertations were presented. Included was the recitation of the first part of the Koran. Hearing this, those missionaries of us who were not so scholarly, smiled at each other, because the heavy German accent in reading the Arabic sounded comical to us.

For us practical missionaries the spirit of the conference was foreign. For me, who had just returned from Beattenberg, where I had had mountaintop experiences with Christians of the greatest national variety, the difference in spirit was especially noticeable. On the afternoon of the second day a man arose and reported that in one year many thousands of Muslims had been converted to Christianity in the former German colonies in Africa. When I heard that I felt peculiarly warm in heart. I raised my hand and was immediately called upon to speak with the introduction: "Mr. Missionary Jantzen, who worked for many years among the Moslems of Turkestan." Brother Warns, who had noticed my inner turmoil, told me later that he prayed for me all that time.

Being called upon to speak, I went to the podium, introduced myself as to who I was and who I am. Then I related some of my past, how I had migrated to Turkestan at age fourteen, and had studied both the language and the Koran there for eight years. Naturally I also studied the equally important Shariah (Muslim law). It was required of every student to learn first of all the *Heptijerk* or Statement of Faith and the five prayer forms which are found only in Arabic and may be prayed only in that language. I had not found the language difficult and thus had acquired the accent of the instructors. Then I gave an example by reciting the statement of faith and the First Sura.

Then I turned to the Doctor or Professor from Africa and asked whether he might tell us in greater detail concerning the mass conversions of Muslims to Christianity. I found this report a little unusual because in my 45 years in Turkestan I had learned to know them very well. Therefore I risked the opinion that those Muslims in Africa never really were Muslims.

The Doctor then replied that he would assume that the Muslims of Central Asia and Turkestan, being of the white race, therefore had a higher intelligence than the blacks of Africa, who had, until recently, lived in primitive wilderness. He reported that Arabian merchants had come to the area and offered them beautiful, colorful calico clothes if they would become Muslims. The Negroes agreed and became Muslims. When the Germans arrived the Negroes could tell that the German cloth was prettier and wore much better. The mass conversions then were pretty much tied in with the desire for the improved German dresses. Obviously the Negroes were not spiritually well developed.

I answered, "So it is obvious that the Negroes were not brought to Christ, but to German clothes. You made them Germans and nothing more." Then I told of instances in my experience of the conversion of my Muslim brothers in Turkestan, some of whom were severely persecuted and died as martyrs for their faith. They remained faithful to the end because they had accepted Christ as their personal Savior. Then I stepped from the platform.

As a result, all the missionaries present were called on individually to testify of their work. Because of these reports a prayer service for the work among the Muslim people was announced for that evening. About one hundred of the conference delegates were present, but the professors and doctors were missing. Neither could any of them be seen the next day. At the noon meal Brother Warns said to me, "Brother Jantzen, what a kill-joy you are." "Yes," I said. "But in this case I am not sorry, because the Name of Jesus, in my opinion, is not given us so we may play games with it, or use it for nationalistic or political purposes."

After the close of the convention we three from Wiedenest stayed in Bethel for several days and Pastor Bodelschiving showed us his complete institution. There were hundreds of houses, workshops and factories where epileptic men and women, boys and girls, worked. In one department they made beautiful aluminum ware, in another they wove cloth. There were also shoemaking, cabinet making, and blacksmithing among their activities.

In one room we saw a man of about 50 sitting at a table; he was a watchmaker. As he was working, he was heard to say, "I know I am not like other people, but one thing I can tell you, clock, when Paul (meaning himself) takes you in hand, then you will run right." Then he turned to us and said, "Gentlemen, Paul (he tapped his forehead) is not all there, but the clock must run well." Our guide told us that the man had worked there for many years, but almost all clocks that he worked on were well repaired.

There was much good, but also much misery, in this institution. There were several buildings where visitors were not allowed. As we walked by, we heard strange cries and horrible groanings that made one shudder. These were the totally insane. After we had left the institution, we each went our way and I returned to Holland where much work and many invitations were waiting for me.

CHAPTER 23

▼

A NEW CREATION

Now I must backtrack a few years in these memoirs. In 1928 a dominie of the Reformed Church of Holland invited me. I traveled to his town and spoke on Sunday morning in his well-filled church. I took lodging with some friends in the city.

Here I received an invitation from a lady to come and have tea with her and her husband who was a teacher of foreign languages. They said they had much to tell me. I went there, but found her home alone. She introduced herself as Mevrouw de V. and, with a radiant look, related that she had been in church the previous evening and had heard me preach. What I said caused her much thought, which brought her to the edge of despair. Then she prayed to God for mercy and forgiveness, but for hours she could find no peace, so that her husband was at a loss as to what to do. Finally they both knelt and pleaded for mercy and grace. Suddenly a great stillness and indescribable peace came over them because all their sins were cleansed by the blood of Jesus Christ. Peace now pervaded her and she had to tell me about it.

Then she asked me whether I could go and visit her father, age 62, who lived in his villa at O. In the city of L. he had a textile factory in which 400 people worked day and night. Although he was a member of the strict *Gereformerde Kerk* (Reformed Church), he had always cursed terribly. And now he feared death. I told her I could only accede to her request if the father himself would ask me to come. This she would try to arrange. With that I left her and went home.

After a few months I received an invitation by request of her father from the younger sister of Mevrouw de V. She wrote, "Father would very much like to make your acquaintance, because Mr. de V. has told him so much about you that interests Father greatly." I accepted the invitation. As I got off the train in L., Juffrouw Myn P., the younger sister of Mevrouw de V., waited for me at the gate.

The streetcar brought us within a few steps of the place where the villa was located. I noticed that my guide was very restless. Finally she asked me whether her sister had told me anything about her father. I said that she had. She then said that she didn't believe that I would get along very well with him, for he was a very singular individual. Very likely he would not receive me as I am accustomed, she thought. But I assured her that she need not worry on my account. Everything would be all right.

In the meantime, we arrived at the villa and walked in. In a beautiful hall I was warmly received by the lady of the house. Then she led me to a glass-enclosed veranda where her father sat and was reading the paper. She called to him, "Vader, here is Meneer Jantzen."

"Oh," he answered, "you are very welcome." Then he said to his daughter, "Myn, go right back into the room and close the door. When two men wish to talk to each other, they do not want any women around."

"Yes, Vader," she said and disappeared.

I was asked to be seated, while he seemed absorbed in his paper. Then, looking over the top of the paper, he said unexpectedly, "You come from Turkey where you were a missionary?"

"No, I come from Turkestan."

"Where is that located?"

"Another 1000 kilometers further east of Turkey."

"Then you saw more of the world than I have."

"That could be."

"Meneer Jantzen, that is really not the matter at hand. The reason that I asked you to come is this: My name is P. and I am 62 years old and no doubt I will soon die as other people do. I am a strict Reformed and attend church regularly, twice each Sunday. When the collection plate is passed I never put in less than 200 Gulden. But I have gone through life cursing and swearing and I cannot forgive others. And now our black-coats, the *dominie*, tell me that I cannot go to heaven but to hell. But I do not want to go there; it is too hot there."

He sprang up and continued, "I don't really believe that you will be able to get along with me. I am a peculiar, self-seeking person. However, my daughter has told us so much about you that I thought: 'Here is a neutral person, but very likely still a theologian.' They, we are told, know more about spiritual things than the likes of us. Therefore I ask you: Is it really true, as I have been told, that because of my cursing and unforgiving spirit I must go to hell? Yes or no? I want to know what you think."

"Meneer P., what I would answer to your question has very little value. Only what God says in His Word has any weight. You surely believe in God and His Word, the Bible, which you surely have in your house."

"I, a Reformed man, should not have a Bible!!" With this he opened the door and called, "Myn, bring the Bible in here." The daughter brought a beautiful Bible, placed it before him and disappeared again. Then he pushed it toward me and said, "Isn't that a beautiful Bible? I read a passage to my family every day, as it should be."

"Yes, it is a beautiful Bible," and I pushed it toward him again. "I had it brought for you. I have my pocket Bible. And now we must find the answer to your question."

"Ha, ha, ha, now just look at this! Have a Bible study? And that on a week-day?"

"Meneer P., you have asked me a very serious question, which, as I have said, only God can answer, and so please turn to Matthew 6 and read verses 12, 14 and 15 out loud." He did as I asked him, and I referred him to other verses and had him read them. Then I said, "This is the answer that God Himself gives to your question. Further we are told in II Corinthians 5:19: 'And God was in Christ reconciling the world unto Himself,' but that only on the basis of what Jesus himself said: 'If you forgive men their trespasses, your heavenly Father will also forgive you.'"

He then became troubled and strode back and forth on the veranda, while I continued. "Meneer P., a man of God whom I know (C.A. Flugge) once went to the trouble to count how often in the Bible God says to people: 'Come!' He counted a total of 1900, of which more than 1000 are in a friendly, coaxing tone. Only twice does God say in the Bible: 'Go away!' Once to the damned on judgment day and another time to those who here on earth were unforgiving."

To these words he called out loudly, "Then I am damned! I am lost, I am lost, I am lost." With these words he rushed into the room where the two women were and repeated the words over and over, while running back and forth in the room. The women sat there and wept and the lady of the house finally said, "Oh, Meneer Jantzen, if only you had never come into our house! My husband is deranged and is losing his mind; that can be seen."

"Mevrouw, you will have a non-cursing husband. The Holy Spirit is working on him. He always does things well." But she repeated over and over, "*Ick geloof er nick van*" (I don't believe any of that).

In the meantime he returned to the room where I was seated and, in his desperation, he fell on his knees beside me and cried, "O, God, have mercy on me, a blasphemer, and forgive my sins for Jesus' sake!" He repeated this prayer over and over. I had been praying silently all the while, which I always do in such cases.

Suddenly a miracle happened, which for the human mind is incomprehensible, in which the same despairing person, without apparent reason, goes from begging for forgiveness, suddenly to praise and thanks.

"O, God, You incomprehensible God, I thank You that You have saved me, too, through Jesus Christ, and I didn't realize it. But now I know it. You have opened my eyes." He prayed that way for a while, then he rose and calmly sat down beside me. Shortly after that, he gave a surprised look around, though with a radiant face, and said, "Where have I been?" Looking out of the window, he said, "How beautiful is God's nature and I have never seen it before."

Evening had come and supper was served. Quietly we sat around the well-laden table. The women, too, had become calm. Very little was said, though the host repeated, "O, God, how can I thank you for such great mercy?" Then we all retired. Early the next morning I heard that the house door was opened beneath me. As I looked out I saw Mr. P. go out. I thought to myself: Stay up here. What can you do with the women who only yesterday had been so excited? For they were quite obviously very unfriendly toward me. So I remained alone for a while, after which I ate breakfast. A short time later the host came into the room, very pale, but calm. He greeted me briefly and then said, "O, God, I thank you that I could die." Then he turned to me and continued, "Meneer Jantzen, for 15 years I have been in a lawsuit with my brother, which has cost me thousands. I wanted to force the case through to my advantage, although I was in the wrong. Because of this, I was always angry with him. But last night God instructed me to go to my brother, who lives nearby, confess my guilt to him, drop the suit, and make things right with him. This has now been done, and what is most wonderful of all is that my brother told me, after we were reconciled, that he, too, had found the Lord and has known for several years that he is a child of God. Then we embraced once again. O, how happy I am and so warm inside."

After we had taken some refreshments, I went with him to L, a twenty-minute ride on the streetcar, in order to make a tour of his factory. He went there every day and looked after things. When we arrived at the factory, his son, who was the manager, greeted us and guided us through the factory. Mr. P. stopped to say a few friendly words to each of the workers as he walked by. I noticed right away that this action of his surprised the workers. But one could see that they all enjoyed it. Previously no one could do well enough to please him and he would curse everyone. And today everything was so different. The son was naturally struck by this procedure, and he looked at me in surprise and astonishment, but he said nothing. Of course, he soon discovered what had happened.

The daughter, Myn, was president of the Reformed Christian Young Women's Association. I stayed in the house several days, since Mr. P. wanted additional information about God's Word. I noticed that Myn was also reconciled. She realized the great change that had taken place in her father. This awakened something in her, too. Finally she asked me to come and talk to her girls' group, which I did.

In the meantime, of course, many invitations were forwarded to me from Arnheim. So I had to leave there and be of service in other places. Through the following years I did keep in contact with Mr. P. About three years after the incident related above, I again received an invitation from him to come and conduct some Bible studies there. The day after I arrived, we again went to the factory in L. We sat across from each other in the tram. As we approached the bus stop, Mr. P. struck his fist against my breast and said, "Meneer Jantzen, in O. near my home lives a business friend of many years. He also has a factory here in L. For thirty years now we have met on this tram almost every morning, like you and I are doing now. A few days ago, when we got out here as usual, he struck me in the chest as I did you just now. Then he said, 'Meneer P., what has happened to you? You have been so different these past few years. Formerly, when we arrived here you were always so nervous and couldn't sit still. Even your eyes were always restless. Now you are so calm and you look so entirely different.' I didn't know what to answer him, so I struck him on his chest and said, 'I have seen Jesus!' With that I ran away and left him there speechless. What should I, as a layman, say to the man, for I really didn't understand him. Tell me, Meneer Jantzen, is there such a thing? I don't see that I am so changed."

"Meneer P., if the world sees something, then surely there must be something to be seen." He took off his hat and said out loud, "Oh, God, You who are so incomprehensible to me, how is all this possible?" and wept out loud, so that the other passengers stopped and surrounded us. So I said to him, "Let's go on quickly or we'll have a crowd around us." He was so stirred that, even as we walked together, he repeated, Oh, great God, how great is Your love and mercy toward such a loathsome blasphemer as I have been all my life, until I learned to know You. How can I ever thank You for all this?"

To see, hear and live through all this with him, and his uninhibited communion with God, stirred me to the depth of my heart. And especially so when I recalled his complete collapse that I experienced with him. Because of the total change in her husband, as well as my repeated visits and Bible studies, Mevrouw P. became entirely reconciled and was happy to have me come. So was the daughter Myn. Meneer P. lived another ten years after this. In his own personal and simple way, he prayed for his five sons and three daughters who, except for Myn, were all married.

One of the sons, named Jan, acted much like the prodigal son in the Gospel. He had received part of his inheritance from his father and had disappeared somewhere in America. His family made great effort to locate him, but all was in vain. Jan lay especially on the father's heart. When he was on his deathbed he prayed especially for Jan.

Three days before he died, I was with him and he lamented the fact that Jan had been gone for eight years now and had never been heard from. Then he prayed, "Oh, almighty God, please bring Jan back before my Homegoing." That evening I went back home. I was told later that, shortly after that, Jan walked into his father's room and greeted him. Calmly the father returned the greeting and said, "Well, Jan, you finally came back again. I knew that you would come because I had to tell you that I found the Lord Jesus Christ. Now I can go to Him in peace. Jan, forgive me for what was formerly not right between us."

"Father, I have come here from America with the same concern in my heart and for the same reason. I have come to tell my parents and my family that I, too, found the Lord Jesus over there. Forgive me all the evil and suffering that I have caused you all."

For two nights Jan sat by his father's bedside, as his brothers and sisters had done for two weeks. Then the father went to sleep, calmly and in deep peace. They telephoned the news to me and asked that I take part in the funeral service. I stayed there for several days and learned to know Jan more intimately. He related to me how the father, in full consciousness and in his simple way, had spoken to God. He was always thankful and prayed for his children and grandchildren. He included "the old Russian" whom the Lord had sent into his life, and who had lost all his children and grandchildren in that terrible land, which brings him much suffering.

About two years later Mevrouw P. was also converted, which made her very humble. She lived for several more years with her family and then went peacefully to be with her Lord. The youngest son confided in me that he wanted to enjoy the wealth of the world for a while. He was married. After a few years he unexpectedly drove his car in front of my house. With a gleam in his eyes, he stepped into my apartment.

"*Vader* Jantzen, I too have now found the Lord. I had to come and tell you, you who had gone to so much effort for my sake. I have no other business here in Arnheim and will drive right back home." We prayed together and, after we had had some tea, he joyfully drove the 100 kilometers back home again.

From time to time Juffrouw Myn and her brother A. visited me. Until now they have remained in the Reformed Church, but A. no longer feels at home there and said that he didn't know just what to do about it. I said to them, "My dears, the Lord Jesus has saved us and not the church. The Lord Jesus Himself was not very "churchy." People organized the church much later, and that in a very human way. That's why there are so many denominations and schisms. 'Seek Jesus, and His Light; all else availeth nought,' says the poet. Here in Holland it is felt that everyone must have an '*underdoek*,' something to crawl under, that is, every proper person should belong to a church."

CHAPTER 24

▼

A MISSIONS CONFERENCE
IN HOLLAND

Repeatedly through the years I traveled in the neighboring countries. In S., where Brother K was still busy, I was expected twice each year. Here, during these years, four Free Churches had been founded. I often visited Austria and Switzerland and was able to participate in several international conferences, but most often in Wiedenest.

In 1935 I received an invitation to a missions conference in W. near S. in Holland. After arriving there I found that S. was an old castle that had been renovated for conference purposes. The *dominie*, who was the director, received me warmly and assigned me to one of the several hundred rooms. When I entered the conference hall the next morning, I found there approximately 400 *dominies* and about 200 theology students. The hall could have accommodated twice as many.

A *dominie* of the Reformed Church was chairman and made the opening. Then he announced the purpose of the conference. Directors of Mission Boards of several denominations who were active in the Dutch East Indies had assembled here and were complaining about and had questions concerning the lack of unity among the churches in the homeland, which made mission work very difficult.

Each missionary had come, literally bringing his own little church under his arm, and therefore there were as many different churches there as in the homeland. This divisiveness is the best weapon of the Catholic Church in their competition with the Protestants. They point their fingers at us and say to the Indian people who are mostly Muslims, "Come with us; we do not have these divisions as you see among them."

The mission directors of the various mission societies had opportunity to speak. They spoke in about the same vein. They added to what had been said, that several mission stations had been closed because there were not funds enough to pay the salaries of the missionaries. The Catholics and the Muslims laughed at such a condition.

This was followed by leaders, directors and professors of the various mission institutes in the home countries, with the lament, "What can we do, if the churches will not send money to the mission treasuries?" One man announced that they were 125,000 *Gulden* in debt and did not know how to cover it. Another reported 150,00 *Gulden* debt, with no way to pay it. And so came one report after another.

Through all this I sat there and thought to myself: "Why have I been invited to come here? I am not a member of any of these churches and was only a foreigner tolerated in the country." Beside me sat Mr. W., member of Parliament, whom I knew as a genuine Christian from Arnheim. He was a member of the committee appointed by Minister Sl. to study the problems. More will be said about this committee later. Mr. M. had been in the Dutch Indies for 25 years as a director of missions.

In the afternoon of the third day of the Conference, I was called on by my *Schirmname* ("umbrella name"—pen name) that was used for such occasions. "Meneer Ivanov, it is your turn. We invited you as a former missionary among the Muslims in Turkestan, as a neutral observer, since you are not affiliated with any of the churches or associations represented at this Conference. Most people here know you, since you have spoken in many churches in our country in the last few years. Then, too, you understand our people. You have heard all the debates here, and now we ask you, "What do you think of all these conditions? We would like to hear from you, a specialist in missionary work. We want your advice."

Just how I felt at that moment is difficult to describe. Here I sat among all the theologians and doctors, the Princes of the church hierarchy, the representatives of Her Majesty, Queen Wilhelmina, Baron Doctor Von H. In my heart I cried to the Lord for His wisdom and courage. Then I stepped on the platform and talked as follows:

"Honored Gentlemen, since I must assume that there are many here who do not know me, I must introduce myself as to who I am and where I come from. Without knowing this, you would not easily understand what I am about to say." After I had given something of the story of my life, my conversion, and referring to the necessity of the new birth as recorded in John 3:3 and 1:12 and 13, I continued:

"As a child of God, having received the divine nature through the Holy Spirit, I was impelled through the love of God to go among the Muslim people with simple words as Paul described in I Corinthians 2:1 and 2, to tell them only of Jesus Christ and Him crucified. So, as His witness according to Acts 1:8, I went to tell the Muslims what I had experienced in Him. I went on the Lord's command and by His support. I had no mission association to finance me.

"For fifteen years I worked among the nations of the East, in Turkestan, the Caucuses, and in Bulgaria. Through this I saw the glory of the Lord and Master Jesus Christ, how He manifested the power of the Holy Spirit to many Muslims and made them new creatures. After they demonstrated by their lives that they were sincere and I had instructed them in the Holy Scriptures, I baptized them on the basis of Romans 6:4, as they requested it. In those years, until the Bolshevik regime ended all this, I never was short of money although I traveled a great deal. I never had trouble getting enough copies of the scriptures to distribute in the various languages. Neither did my family ever suffer from hunger. I say this to the honor of our Lord.

"I now turn to you students and future missionaries with this advice: first, you must be a genuine witness of Jesus Christ, and the love of God be shed abroad in your hearts as of Romans 5:5. Then you go by His command to the work that He will guide you to. He will provide all your needs. Don't wait for churches; they do not have the money, as we have heard here. And where should the church get the money? Only true children of God have a heart and understanding for missions and therefore give their support. And there aren't very many true children of God in the churches. This is made evident by the empty treasuries.

"Neither does this surprise me. As you know it is the custom that an infant is baptized soon after birth. This makes the *dominie* happy each time when he can enter another name on the church roll and the church is strengthened by one more member. Mark 16:16 has of course been set aside; the Word does not enter into the matter. After the children have grown up and memorized the Catechism they are accepted into the church as full members, and as full members it is assumed that they are also children of God. Isn't that so? This question is answered by the empty mission treasuries as well as the daily walk of many church members."

Then I turned to the *dominies* sitting before me. Many had red faces and defiant expressions. I said to them, "Honored Sirs, no one here can gainsay the truth of what I have said. But there is a way out of this situation. Mr. Chairman, you asked my advice. My advice is: we must all get on our knees and repent, pray God for His mercy and then walk according to His guidance and will. Then all will be well."

As I left the podium, I thought to myself, "Now, woe is me," because I expected that I would be asked to leave the hall. But then the Chairman called on my neighbor, who had been seated beside me. "Meneer M., Member of Parliament, you are next in line."

Meneer M. got up, took a few steps forward, turned to the audience and said in a calm strong voice, "Honored Sirs, I do not have much to say, and the little I have to say can be said from here. I agree completely with the words and the advice of the previous speaker, Meneer Ivanov, and underscore everything he has said, since that is the only way for us to take."

Then he was seated and I thanked the Lord, because with slow steps and heavy heart I had taken my seat. It became clearer to me that the words of a Member of Parliament carried much weight in this country. Then the Chairman called out, "Very Honored Meneer Baron, Doctor von A; as representative of the Queen of Holland it is now your turn." The Baron stepped to the podium and said, "Honored Gentlemen! I stand before you as one who has served for many years as Governor General of the Dutch Indies, and I speak to you in the name of Her Majesty, our Queen, as follows:

"After all that I have heard during these sessions I must agree with what Meneer Ivanov has said. There is no other way out. Further, I must repeat here what is already common knowledge. The government in the Dutch Indies is accused, and that specifically on the part of theologians, of not standing back of the missionaries and protecting them. But, we ask: what should be done by the government when the missionary, with his miniature church under his arm, comes over there? Each makes great effort to go to his particular station and first learn the language, which is obviously necessary. But then, instead of doing what the Apostle Paul and Mr. Ivanov did, they mix into the political partisanship. With scholarly wisdom they teach the people how to overcome their competitors or enemies. Since the differences among the many tribes are already very sharp, this often leads to quarrels and to murder and homicide. This is often the result of your mission. And now, if you, Honored Sirs, will give me your word of honor, that in the future these things will not happen, then I, as representative of the government, will give my word of honor, that you will be given full protection for your mission work." With the words: "*Ick habb't gesaggt,*" (I've told you) he left the platform.

After this talk there was a lengthy pause. Instead of asking me to leave, as I had expected, many students and theologians surrounded me and very respectfully asked questions. In order to answer all of them, it would require several days. The next day I resumed my travels, as there were several invitations for me to serve.

CHAPTER 25

▼

THEOLOGY OR SERVICE IN WITNESS

It was before the outbreak of the war that I received an invitation by a professor from the Hague to lecture to his students at the University. I was to lecture on the topic, "The Land, People, Customs and Fashions of Asia Minor." On the designated day I traveled there and soon found myself in a large hall filled with students. I took them on an imaginary 9000 kilometer trip by way of Berlin, Moscow, Samara, and Orenburg to Taschkent in Turkestan. Then I described the geological and meteoric make-up of the land. Here I made use of a map. Since I had lived there for 43 years, I knew the condition and make-up of the country very well. Several professors and university lecturers also took part in the presentation.

Since I recounted in Chapters one and two rather in detail the trek to Turkestan, I will not repeat that story here. What I lectured here was based upon the information in those early chapters.

Of course, many changes had come during the intervening years. The construction of several railroad lines, as well as steamships on the rivers, had opened the country to much traffic. With a pointer I showed the places on the map that were of special interest and weaved in facts about people, land and customs.

However, in the final lecture, I discussed more about my personal witness, as follows:

"In 1905 I learned to know Jesus Christ in a very personal way. Of course, I had been, outwardly at least, a well brought up Christian, as are most people here today. But there came a moment when God, through His Holy Spirit, opened my eyes so that I was convicted of my sinful and lost condition in His eyes. I fell down before Him and begged Him for mercy and that He would forgive my sins for Christ's sake. God answered my prayer. He forgave all my sins and filled me with peace and rest, and His Spirit witnessed to my Spirit that I was His child. I realized that, before that, I had not been a Christian by His standard. Now I was a different man, filled with the love of Christ, so that I was impelled to go to the Muslims in order to bring them the gospel of Jesus Christ.

"This work I was privileged to do for many years, and often I saw the glory of God, in that He made miserable people happy, and that they too knew that they were saved, because the Holy Spirit revealed it to their hearts."

As I told all this to my listeners, they were very attentive. I asked if there were any who had this witness of assurance of salvation, that they should raise their hands. Not a hand was raised. Then the Professor came to me and whispered, "Mr. Jantzen, one is not permitted to talk in this way in this place. This is not a church, nor a catechism class. I know that there must be some Christians here, since all the students are baptized and, after Catechism instruction, were received into church membership."

To that I said out loud, "Gentlemen, the Professor has just told me that such a speech and such a question are not in place here. And yet, this is the most important question for each of us on earth. It deals with the fact that one must decide whether Jesus Christ, the Son of God, died for me in vain, because I will not listen to His Spirit. If I do not give Him an ear, then woe is me. If I do listen, then I yield completely to Him and He gives me the status of being His child and enters my name in His family register. As a missionary of many years, with the realization that the Lord may call me at any time, and knowing that the eyes that see me today may never see me again, I had to ask this question, or I could not have complete peace about it. So, in conclusion, I ask you to make sure that the Holy Spirit gives you His assurance of salvation."

Very politely the Professor dismissed me. I thought: "Well, he will never invite me again," and went home. A year later I received a warm invitation from the same Professor to come to The Hague and lecture once more to his students. This surprised me greatly. In accordance with his wish, I got off the tram in front of his apartment. He noticed me coming and opened the door himself and the first thing he said was: "Meneer Jantzen, now I understand you, for God has talked to me, as He took my wife from me following a short illness. So here I was, alone with my children, and didn't know where to turn. So I had to get consolation and power through prayer, and now He is become my Father." As he gave this testimony the tears ran down his cheeks. When the time came, we went to the gymnasium where I would face many of the same students I had met the year before.

I was now allowed to speak freely and without opposition, as my heart and the voice from above would dictate. The theme of the lectures was the same: "Land and People of Central Asia." But I treated the matter more from the standpoint of missions and what this entails. At the conclusion I had the conviction that we had had a session under the Lord's guidance. On another occasion I was invited to a conference of students of Theology to lecture on "The True Theology." A short resume of what I said follows:

"Since theoretically I am not an educated theologian, but received my knowledge of God, which is what the word 'theology' means, from the actual communion with God and through prayer, I receive information to any questions through His will. By the new birth, I became a child of God, God is now my Father according to John 1:12 and 13. Therefore, I am in constant contact with Him and need not pray for myself, in the usual sense. I just discuss all my needs and problems with my Heavenly Father and He gives me guidance.

"Now this sort of theology is not very well known in this country, as my years of living here have revealed to me. This is very painful to me, therefore I cannot speak to this conference in any other way, except in the spirit that I have pursued."

Of course, the theme suggested that the truth be spoken. Since conference implies discussion, there were all sorts of questions. Of these I will refer to only one. In my first lecture I spoke about the "genuine life insurance" based on Romans 8:16: "His Spirit bears witness to our spirit that we are the sons of God."

That is a positive statement and not as is often preached from the pulpit that "we can only assume that" or "we hope someday to experience that" and that leaves us without inner assurance.

Here a female student, about age 30, rose and said, "My father, who is also a *dominie*, keeps encouraging me to pray, which I do every day, like Daniel did. Three times a day I go to my room in the attic, open the window and pray toward the east. I have done this for many years, but up until now I do not have this life insurance in my heart. Why don't I?"

I answered, "Your piety or 'religiosity' gets in your way, so that I must assume that your prayers have not gone through to God. For God is Light, we read in I John 1:5. He who really wants to come to God in prayer first sees himself in the light of God and discovers how ungodly and sinful and filthy he is: ripe for eternal damnation. Then the one who is so convicted of sin, and broken, calls on God for mercy and forgiveness. And, for the sake of Jesus Christ, He forgives him his guilt and enters him, so to speak, into membership in His large family. So He presents him eternal life as a gift, as we read in John 3:16.

"This eternal life is God's life or it could not be eternal; and this life has a living spirit, as all men have a spirit. But that spirit is God's Spirit, the Holy Spirit. He then takes control of those who are born again in this manner and gives them the witness of being children of God. This fills his heart with deep peace and great joy. Then, too, the Holy Spirit pours the love of God into his heart, which gives him a new character.

"And so, my honored listeners, and especially you, Madam, all this is not a theoretical but a very practical theology, the experience of truth for one's self. In my many years of missionary work I have seen this "God-experience" (*Gotterleben*) in all those who had a genuine conversion. This is true life insurance."

In conclusion I referred to Isaiah 57:15 where we read: "For thus says the high and lofty One that inhabits eternity, whose name is Holy; I dwell in the high and holy place, with him also that is of a contrite and humble spirit, and to revive the heart of the contrite ones."

A few weeks later I received an invitation from the father of that girl to come and speak in his church. I soon noticed that with him the important thing was to experience the circumstance under which a Christian can have this life insurance. He had much contact with German theologians and pastors, and was himself a superintendent and a personality of high rank.

The church was filled and the acceptance of the Word was good. This results from the fact that, in such circumstances, I try to talk from the heart to the heart; to speak of that taken from daily life and that applies for life, without theological expressions or foreign words. The expression "taken from life" means out of my life with God and the experiences that this brought me. I use the expression "for life" in the sense that I use scripture as I have experienced it, and by which I have become "a witness of Jesus Christ" who himself experienced what he says, and do not speak to them as do the *dominies*.

This type of sermon has through the years gripped the hearers and so it did here. The longer I spoke, the more attentive they became. Why? Because they noticed that here someone is speaking who understands them, who feels for them. I do not come with scholarly theology and stand on a pedestal above them; a theology that cannot be reached or discussed. The theologian also speaks of the Bible, but not out of the day by day experience of the listener. These are the expressions of many churchgoers in our country. After the service (in German, *Gottesdienst* or worship service), the superintendent sat and visited for some time. About the life insurance, he said not a word. The next morning we parted calmly and politely.

In my travels I met one *dominie* who was different from any other I have learned to know thus far. This *dominie* lived in a large village near a castle with much land. The owner was a baron. When I accepted the invitation to speak in his church, he received me very warmly. He was probably more than 70 years old, but looked like one in his sixties. He was not married. He had labored in this church for 50 years.

After we had taken some refreshments, he took me to his church, which was unusually beautiful. After he had showed me everything, he asked me to go behind the pulpit. He took a seat in the last row and asked me to speak. In this way he tested my voice to see that it would be strong enough.

In the evening the church was well filled. After we had sung a hymn, the *dominie* made a warm, spirit-filled introduction, the like of which I had not heard elsewhere. I also was aware that, in this audience, there reigned a different spirit. With my usual quiet sigh, "Lord, now You speak and bring Yourself honor, in that You make unhappy people happy for all eternity," I stepped to the pulpit and the Holy Spirit did his work well, which we discovered more fully the next day.

At breakfast the next morning, the *dominie* said: "Brother Jantzen, I suggest that you stay today and tomorrow and go on house visitation with me." I agreed to this and for two days, from morning until evening, we visited in the homes of the people. The most remarkable aspect for me was to see how friendly everyone greeted him. Especially the children that we met on the street ran to him and called, "*Opa Dominie*" and threw themselves into his arms. For every child he had a few kind words. I thought, "What a wonderful atmosphere!" I hadn't experienced anything like this before. When we entered a home, even the grown-ups greeted him with "*Opa Dominie*." He addressed them with the intimate "*du*." Everywhere there was evidence of honest love toward him, and he distributed his love to all.

The conversation was not always about business and property, but also dealt with spiritual matters. By this I noticed that the Word preached the night before had its effect. We also visited the old gardener at the castle, who was busy with his spade. As we stepped up to him, the *dominie* pointed to him with a radiant, loving gleam in his eye and said, "Brother Jantzen, this brother has been my God-sent helper through all the 50 years I have been here, and still is." The old gardener stood humbly by, and pointing his finger upward he said, "Good day, *Opa Dominie*; Good day, Brother Jantzen." We exchanged a few more words and then walked on. The *dominie* then told me that the gardener had taught Sunday School and Catechism through all those years and still does. The young people thought very highly of him. After about three years, the dear man went to his heavenly home. The loss was felt keenly by the whole congregation.

One day I was visited by four very fine gentlemen. The one who drove the auto was an old friend who visited me every month, though he lived quite a distance away. This time he brought his *dominie* and two elders of his church with him. All of them belonged to the strictest "*Gereformeerde Gemeente*." There are four branches of the Reformed Church, all of whom follow the doctrines of Calvin and therefore believe strictly in predestination. Since my friend had told the others about me, they had the desire to learn to know me personally.

The first question that the *dominie* asked was, "How did you come to be a missionary among the Muslims of Turkestan?" As briefly as possible, I related my life story, in which I stressed especially the wonderful guidance of God in my life. Among other things I told him that had I not had the assurance of the sonship in God, and if the love of God had not filled me, I would hardly have gone into mission work. Romans 8:16 and 5:5.

Unfortunately, to the representatives of the doctrine of predestination, the witness concerning the New Birth (John 3:3) and being a child of God was not understandable. They teach primarily the Ten Commandments and do not comprehend that Christ, according to Romans 10:4, "is the end of the law." Equally incomprehensible for the *dominie* and the elders were the miracles of God in my life and the many answers to prayer. Then, too, they couldn't see how I, though I was never ordained, could baptize so many Christians, and that not by sprinkling but by immersion.

Since the conversation led me again and again to emphasize the importance of the grace through Jesus Christ, grace which I myself had experienced, they gradually became more silent. Finally the *dominie* lamented the fact that, because of the occupation of the country through the war, people are so demoralized that many of them do not go to church anymore. He asked me whether I thought we might have a revival of our churches. I said I couldn't answer that question simply, but that the Lord through His Word could. If the *dominie* would wish it, I could answer his question in writing. He agreed to that and the gentlemen left. Our conversation had lasted about four hours. About a week later I mailed him the promised answer to his question. I asked him first to read the whole chapter of Jeremiah 25. Then I wrote as follows:

"I believe that the last part of verse 20 in this chapter pictures our time, because the Lord God is going to judge the people. The plague that verse 32 predicts, in my opinion, was fulfilled by Bolshevism, which falsely calls itself communism. We in the East literally experienced verse 25 in 1918 to 1923. The bodies of the killed and the starved were lying all around, giving off a terrible stench. The dead could not be identified. Most of them were natives from whom the government had taken the necessities of life. Daily we buried such bodies right where we found them. The verses following were also fulfilled before our eyes.

"Therefore, my honored Herr Dominie, if we believe in the truth of scripture, then we know what we can expect. We are naturally very sorry that these terrible times must fall right in our own lifetime; but there is no doubt that we have come into these times. What one has experienced and seen no longer requires faith. These are facts. Where did all the herds and herdsmen of the East go? There was a revival of true believers but it came too late. In the 30 years of Bolshevism not many herds and herdsmen are left. What they had to go through before death ended their misery, one cannot describe. Certainly you must have read in many papers the reports of some who escaped as refugees and could verify the above."

To my rather detailed letter the *dominie* only sent a short thank you note without commenting on the question further. After a full year, I was surprised to read several reports in the newspaper that this same *dominie* had been brought to the High Court of the Church Synod to answer to that body about his doctrine. For some time he had preached "free grace in Christ for all who will accept Him." This of course was against the established dogma of the church. His congregation of more than 5000 members divided into two parts as my friend, who visited me afterward, as he had before, reported to me. Dominie K. had a difficult time in his life.

CHAPTER 26

▼

HELP FOR MANY NEEDS

It must have been 1931 when I received an invitation to come to Hilversum. A government minister S, who had heard me somewhere, and a Professor G, were planning to form a relief committee for needy Christians in Russia. They asked me to take a position on the committee in order to report conditions in Russia and arouse interest in the project. I went there and the relief committee was formed.

Since there was a Minister and a highly placed Professor on the committee, it was not difficult to get the *dominies* of various churches and many wealthy people to support the committee. For this purpose many local committees were organized. I gave a lecture in a given place and then a committee was named and money collected. I traveled by car with the secretary, Meneer St. throughout the country and so quite a number of subcommittees in the cities and villages came into being. The committees were always in the hands of local chairmen who received funds and forwarded them to the central committee. The funds were channeled through the Russian *Torgsin* in Moscow for the purchase of many thousand Gulden worth of food packages to be sent to needy people in Russia. This was terminated by the Russian government in January 1936.

The thank you letters from recipients showed that packages got through safely. A little later I will report how it was that we could also get some food to dear relatives in Turkestan.

Here I must backtrack a bit more. Early in December 1929 the annual conference again held sessions in Berlin. Just before the end of the conference I read in the paper that thousands of Mennonites had come out of Russia. Some arrived in Hammerstein, some in Prenzlau and some in Hamburg. President Hindenburg took some interest in them. The report made me uneasy. So I immediately went to Hammerstein to see whether I might find some relatives from Alexanderthal among the refugees. I did meet a few acquaintances but none of my own relatives. So I went to Prenzlau. There I found a dear relative, Pastor and teacher, Johannes J. Janzen, the youngest brother of my one-time co-worker, Abram J. Janzen. He had arrived with his family and Abram's widow and her children. The latter looked so poorly that I didn't even recognize her—someone had to tell me who she was. She had come with her three children and three other families from Turkestan. But of my children, I found no one, which was a shock for me. I stayed a number of days with my dear Turkestan people, and each evening we had a worship service in the large gymnasium. Very discouraged, I proceeded to Hamburg to search in the refugee camp there, but all was in vain. After several days, and very depressed, I returned home to Arnheim.

During the spring of 1930 the conference in Leipzig was convened again. Brother Broadbent, with several members of Free Churches in England, was also in attendance. At the close of the conference, Brother Broadbent expressed the wish that I should go with him to visit several North German churches. So we arrived first in Hamburg. We took the opportunity to visit the refugee camp in Moelln, where there were many Mennonites. Everywhere they held meetings.

Many Mennonites from this camp had been helped by the M.C.C. to emigrate to Brazil and some to Canada. We also discovered that the widow of Abram J. Janzen had been held back because she had some minor children and could not join her sister in Canada. She had left the camp and was working in a children's home in Bueschen, east of Hamburg. Brother Broadbent had learned to know her very well in Turkestan, so we decided to go and visit her. We found her broken and bent by hard work. The younger children, Arthur and Hermannn, were still of school age and the mother had to work very hard to provide food and lodging for them. The older daughter also worked in a children's home, but received only her board and room. We tried to encourage the mother as best we could, and Brother Broadbent gave her some money. After we had visited congregations in Bremen, Bremerhafen and Emden, Brother Broadbent returned to England and I to Holland.

About a year after this, I received a letter from my daughter-in-law, Abram's wife, from Turkestan. At that time letters went through uncensored. She wrote: "Three months ago Abram was accused as a counter revolutionary and put into prison. He was tortured in all manner of ways. Finally he was put in a cellar with water up to his waist. On the fourth day he was taken out and shot." In the earlier years Abram had helped in mission work, and given his testimony in meetings here and there and strengthened believers with the Word. Now he left his wife and four sons and a daughter behind. I learned later that Abram's wife and her five children worked like slaves for the Bolsheviks.

A small piece of paper had been stuck in with the letter, on which Abram had penciled a short note explaining why he had been put into the cellar. These few words were so heartbreaking for me—I still have them but I don't want to repeat them. After I had read the letter—even though she tried to console me—I broke down and fainted to the floor. How long I lay there I do not know. When I finally came to, I locked the door and didn't eat anything for three days. Finally I pulled myself together and took a little food. Then I rode to Alphen, where I visited Brother de G. who had become such an intimate friend. I stayed there several days in quiet fellowship, which helped me greatly. Then I returned to my lonely apartment in Arnheim.

Shortly thereafter I received a letter from Brother de G. saying that he was taking a vacation and would like to travel to Germany with me. He thought it would be good for me. He asked that I be at the station the next morning at 9:00—which I did. We went to Wiedenest, where he wanted to learn about the Bible School. Naturally, we were warmly welcomed by Brother Warns. The next morning Brother Warns and I were alone in his study, where he wanted to share something with me.

"Brother Jantzen, I must ask for your advice on what we might do with Sister Abram Janzen. A few days ago she came here from Bueschen, completely exhausted and told us of her distress. She was denied entrance to Canada and the work in Bueschen was too hard for her. In addition to that, she was worried about the completely hopeless future for her children. Since she was a total stranger in the land, she had come here for advice. Since her husband, whom we valued highly, had been our student, we felt obligated to take her in with us. This we did gladly. There is the question, however, how this will work out in the long run. We have no home for widows or orphans. So it occurred to me that perhaps you could take her with you to Holland and tell the brethren there that she is Brother Janzen's widow and that they must provide for her. I believe that the church there would do this gladly. We have become close to them through our annual conferences."

I answered, "Dear Brother Warns, I see that you do not know the Dutch brothers very well. They would say to me, 'Brother Janzten, what do you think? Don't we have enough widows here to provide for?' No, nothing will come of this." I talked to Mrs. Janzen about this, too, but of course, she couldn't add anything to the matter.

Brother de G. and I stayed for several days, since he liked it so much in Wiedenest, and we enjoyed the fellowship of these Christians. However, I was always so depressed by the tragedy of my son that I couldn't even enjoy the food. Everyone tried to console me, but the wound was too fresh. Finally we had to continue on our trip, since Brother de G. wanted to visit the mission house in Liebenzell in the Black Forest. Before we left, Brother Bohn took me aside and said, "Brother Jantzen, I would like to tell you something. I believe that you should take Sister Janzen back to Holland, and really you should marry her. As long as you can travel, you are welcome everywhere. But once you are too old and too weak for this, who will then take care of you? So I believe it is the Lord that has led you two together, in order to make you one."

As I heard that, I was frightened inside, and felt a rebellion within, so that I said to him, "You must not be in your right mind."

He replied, "As the only relative of these children, you have an obligation to them, for Brother Abram J. Janzen was your blood relative too." My mind just seemed to go in circles, as one might say. "Just pray about what I told you," were Brother Bohn's last words.

We remained a few days in Liebzell and then rode to Moettlingen, where at one time Pastor Blumhart experienced great conflicts with the devil and with

God. His book telling of these experiences is very likely known to many readers. Great wonders and signs, with many cases of healing, happened there.

While we were there, a certain Fritz Stanger, usually called Father Stanger, was much talked about, as Blumhart had been. He had been a heavy drinker and was converted. But he had also become a great man of prayer, by whom many people received help and were healed. With the funds he received through his activities, he built a large building, called the Ark. There were always many guests and sick people living there. He even had to build a second house in order to take care of all who came there.

When Brother de G. and I arrived, we had to find lodging in the village inn. We stayed in Moettlingen for ten days and visited Father Stanger at various times and conversed with him. Among other things, he said, "Now just look at Christianity in our day. Here they come, year-in and year-out, to the old drunkard Stanger and want to be healed. As though he could do anything, and that isn't so. Even today it is as Jesus said, 'Your faith has healed you' and nothing else."

He addressed everyone with "*du*" and spoke in the Wuertemberg dialect, which often sounded very unusual. While Brother de G. and I were with him, a woman with kidney trouble came to him, groaning in pain. He looked at her and said, "But girl, where do you come from again? You were here three days ago and I prayed with you. You said then that you felt better, and here you come groaning. Go right back into your closet and ask the Lord to give you the true faith, which I cannot give you. Then come back and we will think together again."

Brother de G. enjoyed himself here, too, while I kept pretty much within myself and often quietly sighed, "Lord, reveal to me your will concerning Sister Janzen and her children." Within me I resisted the idea of marriage, what with the suffering within me, and also my age of 64 years. After great struggle I finally got to the place where I said, "Lord, if it is your will that we should marry, if only for the sake of the children, I am willing to lay my freedom as a widower on the altar, for your sake; but then you will have to provide for us."

After we had returned to Wiedenest, I discussed the whole matter with Sister Janzen and gave her three days to consider the matter. We had to return to Holland, since Mr. de G.'s vacation time had about expired. After three days Mrs.

Janzen came to my room and told me of her battles; but she, too, placed it all in the Lord's hands and said, "Yes."

We then went together to Brother Warns and announced our engagement to him. He and all the Wiedenesters were very happy over it. Brother de G. and I went back to Holland, where I arranged for entrance visas for the mother and the three children. Soon they came to Arnheim and a month later we were married. The church made a grand wedding feast for us in our chapel "Elim" where many friends took part. The two boys, Arthur and Hermannn, got into good schools and Susie is now a registered nurse. The Lord always provided for our needs, since I had no money when we got married. Therefore, I said, as mentioned above, "Then You, Lord, provide for us!" And to this time, by His grace, He has always done so.

At the beginning of this chapter I reported the formation of a relief committee for suffering people in Russia. Through the Russian trading firm Torgsin, many people received help. By this means I was able to send some packets to my sister in Akmettschet. In the same way I was able to send foodstuffs to my six married children, as well as many others in the ten Mennonite villages in Turkestan.

In February 1935 I received letters from my sister and other brethren that reported new problems. They wrote: "Dear Brother Jantzen, we have arrived upon new times here. If things continue as they have started, then our Akmettschet cannot continue to exist." In November of that year we received another letter, but from a completely different place in the vicinity of Stalingrad, north of the Hindukusch Mountains. The letter included the following:

"Dear Brother Jantzen, you will wonder how it is that these letters come from an entirely new location. The situation is as follows. On April 15 we were driven out of Akmettschet by force. We could take very little with us and were taken to Novo-Urgansk, where we were placed into a boat and taken upstream to Tschardskin. Here we were loaded into cattle cars and, after eleven days' travel we were brought to this beautiful, but so far, waterless valley. We were unloaded and were told we would have to plant cotton for the government. How to do this we don't know, since we have no equipment for it.

"On the freight car trip here we were never allowed to get out for fresh air. In the cars the heat was so terrible that on arrival we had to unload eleven bodies and quickly bury them. These eleven persons had died of thirst, and all of us were more or less sick and half-starved. The worst of it all was the continued cry of the children, here and on the trip: 'Mother, Mother, give us milk and bread.' Add to that the groans of the suffering old people among us. One cannot bear to hear all this, and prayers seem to avail little.

"O dear Brother, if the dear ones in Holland had to listen to this misery for one hour, they would surely find ways to get canned milk or other things for our children and old people. Please do what you can for us."

There I sat with these letters and didn't know what to do. Our committee treasury was almost empty; there were perhaps 200 Gulden on hand. In my help-lessness I turned to the emigrant relief committee of the Mennonite *Doopsgez-inde*, or Dutch Mennonite Church and asked Rev. Gorter, an old acquaintance, who had done much for our poor refugee people. He answered that he was sorry to say that their treasury was empty too, since they had just recently helped 400 families get from Harbin to America.

Then I said to my wife, "We must go on our knees and pray, because I cannot believe that all our dear ones over there are destined to die of hunger." So, for two days we prayed again and again, "O Lord, Thou who art so rich and mighty, have mercy and help that these poor people may be saved from starvation."

The mailman came and brought an insured letter containing money from Switzerland. When I opened the letter I found two thousand Gulden notes and a letter. A Mennonite lady, whom I had learned to know a year earlier as I traveled in Switzerland, wrote: "Dear Brother Jantzen, as you know I am employed here in the Postal Service. Yesterday I received the enclosed 2000 Gulden from an unknown source, with a letter that I am enclosing. Please read the letter and you will know what to do. With sincere greetings, Frau Gerber."

The letter she enclosed said, "Honored Frau Gerber, a few years ago I made a vacation tour of Holland. Yesterday I incidentally opened the wallet I used and found the two one-thousand Gulden bills. I thought, what should I do with this foreign money? Then I recalled that last year a touring preacher, a former mis-sionary in Turkestan, spoke in many towns and villages here in our country. He spoke in churches and to other groups as he did in your hometown, about the problems of Christians in the East. I didn't hear him, and do not know where he lives, but I assume that you no doubt know him and his address. I ask you, there-fore, to send him this money with the instructions to purchase food packets and send them to our brothers in Russia."

So the letter ended without signature. There we sat, my dear wife and I, sur-prised once again about such wonderful answers to prayer, and praised Him who had so often come to our rescue in our turbulent lives. I sat down and divided the 2000 Gulden in such a way that we could buy 85 packets. My sister had said that there were only 85 Akmettschet families who got to their new location. I assumed that the rest were dragged elsewhere. These 85 packets arrived there on the 24th of December, on Christmas Eve.

About the middle of February 1936 I received 85 thank you notes in which each one expressed himself in his own way. A résumé of all of them included: "Dear Brother Jantzen! It is impossible for you to imagine the joy in our whole camp. Each family received a wonderful Christmas gift, including canned milk, flour, bacon, lard, rice, sugar, tea, coffee and other wonders. Since we are not so closely guarded here, we had a 'Silent Night, Holy Night' celebration of praise and thanks, the like of which the world does not often see. Between the Christ-mas songs, prayers of thanksgiving were repeated again and again. 'O Lord, rec-ompense those dear givers for what they have done for us castaways. Bless them so that they can feel why You are blessing them,' etc."

They also said that those who gave for their help should be told what these gifts have meant to the recipients. They also mentioned that several more had died because of the suffering on the trip from Akmettschet and that the hunger situation continued about the same. These are the last direct reports that I ever received. I was glad to learn through a report by Brother Rempel that later they received horses, oxen and some farm machinery for their use. Whatever finally became of the group may never be known. We can only say today: hats off and let us pray for those heroes of Akmettschet!

In 1940 I received a letter from a relative of ours who was born in Turkestan. He had been a teacher in one of the villages. He reported that in 1939 all men capable of bearing arms in our villages were mobilized, he among them. All had to go to war, where all of them, except he and one other man, were killed. "Among these were your six grandsons, dear Uncle Jantzen." He wrote from a

refugee camp in Gronou, where he regained his health and finally came to his relatives in Canada.

In 1935 several families from Aulie-ata had fled with horses over the Tjan-
schan Mountains into Chinese Turkestan. There fifteen families, among them
relatives of ours, who after a week of travel arrived dead tired at two mission stations in Sinkieng, where they found shelter. One of the stations belonged to Nor-
wegian Protestant missionaries and the other was Catholic. Through the help of
these missionaries they received the necessities of life. However, a few years later
the Bolsheviks penetrated into this area too, which resulted in a terrible blood
bath. It was reported that as many as 170,000 people lost their lives, among them
all the men and boys of the fifteen families.

The women and children found shelter in the mission stations, which were
not attacked because they were the property of foreign countries. But even here,
the women were not safe, so they took flight again and finally arrived in rags and
without shoes in Urumtschi, about 400 kilometers further east. There they stood
on the street, hopeless and without knowledge of the Chinese language. When
several men in European clothes noticed them, they asked the women in *Platt-
deutsch,* or Low German, who they were and where they were from. These men
represented the M.C.C. who then listened to the long tales of the suffering of
these women.

Now they were under good care and, after they had regained their strength,
they were taken by two-wheeled carts along the southern Mongolian border via
Peking to Shanghai. From there the M.C.C. helped them get into Canada. In
this group were three of my granddaughters.

CHAPTER 27

▼

A LOYAL WITNESS FOR HIS LORD

In the years before World War II, through my extensive services in Holland, an international circle had developed. Every Monday, when I was at home, I conducted a Bible study with this group. The circle was made up of about 45 Christians from various churches, Baptist, Darbysts, as well as a Jewish Christian, my wife and I as Mennonites. One evening we discussed the problem of a paralyzed and dead Christianity. As a result, we decided that, beginning with Arnheim, we would pray for revival. These prayers were voluntary for each member, men or women, and we kneeled during this time.

The following Monday an unknown (to us) higher officer with several other gentlemen appeared in our meeting. They quietly took seats and listened attentively to our Bible discussion and remained through our time of prayer. After the meeting was over the officer came to me and said, "It appears to me that you are the leader here. Tell me, do you wish to organize another church in our already very religious Arnheim? There are already too many churches in our land. Do you want to add to this divisiveness here?

I pointed to our group members and answered, "I do not know you, Mr. Officer, but would you ask each of our participants to which Church or Confession he belongs?" In answer to that question he discovered that there were seven different denominations represented, which seemed very strange to him. Then I added, "From our prayers you must have learned that we are not concerned here with churches or that sort of thing. We are interested in a revival among the so-called Christians here in Arnheim, as well as in the whole country."

After some thought, he said, "This is all so strange to me. I would like to hear more. Would you come and see me tomorrow evening at 8:00?" I agreed to do that and he gave me his address. When I got to his home the next evening, he introduced himself and his wife as members of the strict *Gereformeerde*-Calvanistic Church. I then told them who I was and where I came from, which interested them greatly. As a result I told them much of my life's story. I also had opportunity to tell them how I had found the Lord and how He had changed my heart. I told them that I had worked for many years among the Muslims in Turkestan, Caucacus and in Bulgaria without the support of any mission society. It was just my inmost desire to bring them the gospel.

My listener, Captain W. and his very intelligent wife, followed my story very attentively. The evening seemed to pass quickly and they asked me to come again. I did that, and won their complete confidence. A few months later the Captain experienced a genuine conversion and, after a great inner struggle, became a joyous Christian. Later his wife followed the same path.

After these experiences their hearts were so full of the love of Jesus Christ that wherever they went they had to witness for Him. As a result several of their neighbors accepted Christ and became new creatures in Him. They had a get-together in their home on Wednesdays for people of the upper class. As *Vader Jantzen*, I was expected to be present. The Lord gave us many blessed evenings together.

The leaders of the Reformed Church could not understand such a situation, so they sent a well-dressed imposing church elder to visit Mr. and Mrs. W. He asked what they wanted of the "old Russian" and whether their own church was no longer good enough. Quite by accident, or so a human being might say, I came to the house and heard, through the open door, what had been said and Mr. W's answer: "Before my conversion, when I lived far from God, no dominie or church elder cared about me. But now that I no longer live for the world and attend the meetings of the "old Russian," by whose guidance I found the Lord, the church is disturbed and restless. But I see that the guilty one is just coming into the room and no doubt heard our conversation."

"Yes, in an unexpected manner," I said, and Mr. W. noted that no doubt I knew what the problem under discussion was. So I turned to the church elder and said, "I assume that when you arrive in heaven you will first look around to see if there is a *Gereformeerde Kerk*, and if you don't find one you would be ready to return to earth. For seemingly the Lord Jesus means very little to you. For us once lost sinners, but now saved by His grace, He is our one and all."

After these words the gentleman sprang from his chair and cried, "That is too much for me," and stormed out of the house.

On another Wednesday evening we again had a meeting at Captain W's home. Those who had been recently converted were given opportunity to testify what the Lord Jesus had done for them in the meantime. A former alcoholic, who was well know to all those present, stood up and said, "For twenty years I have been a heavy drinker, bringing much suffering to my wife and children. I saw my destruction coming, but I couldn't break the habit. In my despair I came to this meeting just once and heard what for me were very unusual testimonies. One person said, 'I prayed much to God but it didn't help me any, until I heard that one must pray in Jesus' name. He can save anyone from destruction who comes to Him. I did that and the Lord saved me!' This testimony gripped me and I said to myself: 'I must do that too.' So I prayed God in Jesus' name to free me from drink and He did it. I do not drink anymore and have no desire for it; I have been freed through Jesus Christ, who also atoned for all my sins on the cross at Calvary."

After he was seated another one stood, a tall, fine-looking man, and said, "I am a Catholic and must confess that I have never been in such a Protestant meeting as this. I have always attended my church according to regulation, always paid my dues, and always kept the required fast. But I could not find peace until I came here. Here I hear about such unusual things that arouse in me the desire to be freed and made happy too."

This gentleman came regularly after that evening and finally found peace through a genuine experience with God. He proved the reality of this because he took every opportunity that presented itself, driven by God's love within, to tell others of his good fortune. He lived in O., a larger city.

About a year after his conversion I received an invitation from him to come to his home on a certain evening. He wanted to have a meeting there and also requested that my wife should come. He had invited Captain W. and his wife, as well as other friends. We took the streetcar to his place and found two large rooms filled with people, none of whom we knew. The striking thing was that there was a Catholic *Pater* there and two other gentlemen; the latter were dominies from two branches of the Reformed Church. After all those invited had arrived, our dear host stood up and said:

"I was born and raised a good Catholic. As such I always tried to do my best, also toward the Church. But in spite of all my efforts I did not find peace, until I came, not through the Virgin Mary as mediator, but directly to her son Jesus Christ. He forgave me all my sins and made me a new creation. He so filled me with His love, that I cannot bear to see how so many people in my vicinity are so careless as they go through life, without ever stopping to consider the seriousness of life. Now I try as hard as possible to speak to all people of the seriousness of life.

"However, I am only a layman, and so I don't seem to understand how to witness as I should, because people go right on their way, often laughing at me. This is the reason I invited all of you, so that in your presence I can ask these three clergymen this question: What is your attitude toward all the undying souls that are placed in your care? You sit in your parsonages, do on Sunday what your synod prescribes, for which of course you are well paid. But how is it with the people for whom you are responsible, who are rushing to their destruction? That doesn't seem to bother you too much."

To this the priest responded, "Our Holy Mother Church has been open for all men for almost 2000 years, and our Virgin Mary is still ready, besides all other Saints, to intercede for all sinners who repent and come to her."

Out host answered, "I did all that for many years, and have found no peace. Then in my despair I turned directly to the Lord Jesus Christ and He gave me complete forgiveness of my sins and peace for my soul."

After that the two *dominies* said, short and to the point, "We do our duty in the office that is ours every Sunday, behind the pulpit, as it should be. Whoever wants to hear will have to come to church. We certainly can't run after people out on the streets to ask them to come to church. They would look at us as though there was something wrong and would say, 'We know, don't we, that the church is open and when we want to, we will come. Don't bother about us any further.' And thus they would leave us standing on the street."

It had become late by this time and we had to take the last streetcar to get home. Later our brother told us that the clergymen had tried real hard to convince the group and that he as a layman didn't always know the right answer. But his peace with God they could not take from him, for which he was thankful. Shortly thereafter I had to come to his home again. He had bought a Bible, but as a Catholic he could not find his way very well in it. As he read it he had many questions which he wanted explained.

We spent many hours of discussion on many points that he wanted cleared up. Then he asked what his attitude toward an NSB (Dutch Nazi) should be. One of them was living across the street from him and was persecuted because he was considered a traitor to his country. As a person, he was a good man. Again and again he felt the inner urge to go to him and tell him how happy the Lord Jesus had made him. One could have this happiness without the need for any kind of political party. So he obeyed the inner voice and went to talk to this man. As a result, he suffered persecution and people called him a NSB and therefore a dangerous citizen. "And so, Father Jantzen, tell me, can't I speak to the man about Jesus anymore? Must I just let him go his way and not warn him?"

I answered him, "My dear friend, the Lord Jesus always went in to the despised tax collectors who served the Roman state and were therefore considered by the Jews to be traitors to their own people. For this they persecuted Jesus and called Him a 'friend of publicans and sinners.' They considered Him to be a collaborator and finally brought Him to the cross. He didn't stop seeing publicans and sinners, because their souls were at stake. Therefore, it is my advice to you that if the love of God drives you, go to the man and speak to him about his soul's salvation. You must do that even in the face of threatened dangers."

This made him very happy and he continued to visit the man. But the loving, simple brother suffered much abuse from the clergy as well as from other citizens.

He experienced what people usually go through in such a case. Whenever a person has had a real experience with God, so that the Holy Spirit has made him a member of the family of God, then he cannot remain silent, but he must witness. And that brings persecution.

One Wednesday evening we were together again at the home of Mr. W.—perhaps 25 or 30 persons. We were waiting for him, as he had not yet come home. His company was stationed some 15 kilometers from Arnheim on Grebbe Hill, where later the fierce battles between the Dutch and the Germans took place. Suddenly he entered the room in his robust manner and greeted all of us with his strong handshake and welcomed us. Then he stepped up to me, grabbed me with his strong hand and embraced me. He said, "Notice, ladies and gentlemen: Captain W., Dutch patriot and militarist, and in his arms Father Jantzen, an anti-militant and yet one in Christ! Is that so, Father Jantzen, yes or no?" "Yes," I answered with a strong voice. Many of those present wondered about that and asked, "How is that possible?" My answer follows:

"I am a witness and was present when the Holy Spirit made our dear friend Captain W. into a new creature. Since then he has been a joyous Christian, just like I am. Therefore, we are one in Christ, who, despite his militarism has accepted Him through the new birth. Who am I that I should now reject him? Paul teaches us in Romans, 'Accept one another, even as Christ accepted you to the glory of God.' As far as his militarism is concerned, I know that he has the Holy Spirit in him, who will guide him into all truth in His own time."

Soon after that evening, Captain W. came in his car to our house and asked me to go to Grebbe Hill with him to spend two or three days there and speak to his and other companies of soldiers, as well as to the officers in the casino. I agreed to that and went with him. There I lived with him in his quarters and ate my meals with him, which were served in his room. Only the noon meal we ate in a large hall together with his company. Before the meal he and the company stood up and he gave thanks aloud and asked a blessing on the meal. Then all were seated and everyone ate without much talking.

After the meal the soldiers took their Bibles, which the Captain had bought for them. He stood up, opened the Bible to an announced text, made a few remarks and concluded with prayer. Then he gave necessary orders, assigned the men their tasks and each man went to his duty. When I addressed the company they were always very attentive. Among them were many Catholics to whom the Bible was an unknown book. In the evenings, after I had spoken in the casino, many soldiers came to me, especially Catholics, and asked personal questions concerning their own salvation.

Since Grebbe Hill was an important strategic position, thousands of men worked day and night, digging trenches and building bunkers. This was early in 1940 and Hitler's troops were coming nearer to the Dutch border. No one trusted the assurances of Hitler on the radio that his troops would never march into Holland.

Captain W. was in charge of carrying out these defense preparations according to a plan given him. In doing this he was continually traveling about. He took me along and showed me everything that was being done. I was surprised at all that was done and asked him whether this would hold the Germans back. He shook his head and said, "No, they will fly over us to Rotterdam, The Hague, and the North Sea. In the meantime, they will mop us up here, which will cost many lives."

CHAPTER 28

▼

WAR IN HOLLAND

I planned to be in Alphen on the eighth of May, so he brought me home the evening of the seventh. Alphen is about 100 kilometers from Arnheim. In A. I stayed with the dear brother L. de L., whom I have mentioned earlier. At two o'clock in the morning we were awakened by the flight of hundreds of aircraft that flew over us, as well as by the roar of bombs and cannons. So we realized that we were at war. After daybreak we saw thousands of soldiers riding their motorcycles through Alphen, while in the direction of Leiden, about 20 kilometers away, cannons thundered incessantly. Soon we saw the black smoke of the burning seaport city of Rotterdam, rising into the air.

I rushed to the station to take a train to Arnheim, but was told that there were no trains running. The next day I tried to send a telegram to my wife, but couldn't get through. Alphen is not a large city, so there was no military installation there and it was not bombed so heavily. Only a few houses had been destroyed by bombs. The city was occupied by soldiers and tanks for three days. On the 14th of May Holland surrendered to the German super power.

After spending twelve days in Alphen I was finally able to get home and was greeted with great joy by my dear ones. In Arnheim nothing had been destroyed, but the entire city of 100,000 inhabitants was occupied by the Germans. As was the case in Russia, so here; the Gestapo was soon active and one had to be very careful what one said.

I made every effort to get in contact with my friend Captain W., as I had heard that Grebbe Hill had held out for four days and nights. I did learn that he survived the battle. A few weeks later I met him at his home, but how different, how aged he looked! He told me how his and other companies had fought; he lost half of his men. The most terrible was what happened after the Dutch had given up and met the terms of the armistice. The Germans locked 35 soldiers into a barn and set fire to the building, burning the men. This incident went to his head so badly that when his wife, after much effort, had found him two days later, she hardly recognized him.

When he and I were alone, sitting together on his sofa, I asked him, "Tell me, dear Brother W., is war from God?"

"No," he answered in his commander's voice.

"Of whom is it then?" I asked.

"From the devil," he answered, louder.

"Good, now tell me, may a Christian take part in it?"

"No," he said resolutely. So I felt that he was healed. A little later he resigned and moved to Haarlem, where I visited him some time later.

During this war period there were special experiences that need to be mentioned. It was in 1942. Arnheim was filled with the German military. Jews were required to wear a large yellow star on the chest and all citizens were strictly forbidden to have anything to do with them or to give them shelter. The secret state police (Gestapo) spied around in the city day and night. No one felt secure and the slightest accusation could lead to the firing squad.

Our prayer and Bible hour continued every Monday evening. Naturally the city was completely blacked out at night and not a glimmer of light dared be visible from any house. One Monday evening a young, handsome Jew, about 30 years old, came to our meeting. He was with another Jew who had been converted and baptized earlier and had been a member of our Free Church group for some years. Without the star, they sneaked through the streets to our home. We lived on the second floor. Below us lived a Jewish family who were friendly toward us. Often, during the late evening, we went down to them and visited with them about the Messiah, Jesus Christ, on the basis of Isaiah 55. Evenings their daughter opened the door to visitors who wanted to come and see us. Every Monday she volunteered to stand watch at the outer door to warn us if danger threatened. However, we were never molested.

This young Jew came regularly from then on, and finally experienced God in his heart and became a new creature. He had the assurance of being a child of God and witnessed of it with joy. He desired more Bible instruction and that as often as possible, for as he said, "I know that we Jews here in Holland will be doomed one of these days. Now I feel responsible to witness to my people about the Messiah Jesus Christ, by whose Spirit I became a Christian. I want to do this until I am destroyed." My reminder that it was very dangerous to be out on the street in the evening didn't deter him. I do not now recall for how many weeks he came, but it would be three or four times per week. He was a printer by trade. His father owned a large printing and bookbinding plant in Arnheim. The anti-Jewish movement continued to increase. Many were snatched away at night and disappeared. Their homes and contents were confiscated.

In the meantime, my dear Jewish brother was baptized and with great joy he witnessed to his parents and his people of what Jesus Christ the Messiah had done for him. In normal times his parents and his Jewish community would undoubtedly have sent him out of the house and from their relationship. But now, when all their lives were in constant danger, no one risked taking action against him, but rather they heard of his good fortune and happiness. Then finally it happened. One evening the entire family—parents, children, grandchildren, among them also this young man—were taken away. The printery, with the entire inventory, was confiscated. About a year later, and in a round-about way, we had a letter from our Jewish brother. It came from southern Poland. That was the last report we had from him. We can only imagine what might have become of him and his family. After the war it was determined that 110,000 Jews had been dragged out of Holland, never to return.

From the beginning of the war in 1940, Holland was under German occupation for five years. What we suffered during that time need not be reported here.

Some of it was so terrible that I do not even care to describe it. Let God be the Judge. Because of the war, my trips to Germany and other countries terminated completely. Even in Holland I could travel very little. Until September 1944, we in Arnheim continued with our prayer and Bible study meetings each week. Then began round the clock bombing of Arnheim by the Allies. This was perfectly horrible. We lived in the middle of town and expected momentarily that our house would be destroyed and we with it.

During a pause in the bombing, the Germans ordered all inhabitants to evacuate the city. Only 5 kilos of baggage could be taken. All doors were to be left open, and within four hours everyone was to be gone. My wife and I fled to Welp, a village about 6 kilometers from Arnheim. The highways were crowded with people. Since the German tanks, which were continually bombed by the enemy, kept meeting us out of Welp, many people lost their lives here too. From our friends in Welp, who took us in, we heard of the birth of four premature children. The number of deaths was never made known. After eight days we had to flee again, this time to a small village, Doestingham, about 25 kilometers further on. On this flight I had a heart attack and had to stay in bed much of the time. Dr. Bl. treated me so effectively that I was soon up again. We stayed in this village until the 26th of February.

It was a cold winter with much snow. Wood and coal weren't available and food supplies were very low. In deep snow my wife and our hostess, who was a school teacher, went to the woods outside the village and gathered a little wood. They had to beg the Germans to let them take it home. Doestingham was occupied too, and everything was under German command. All the citizens had to dig trenches and fortifications. Day and night the bombs of the Allies could be heard, and our home often shook as a result. No doubt we would have starved to death during that winter if it had not been for farmers who secretly brought us bread, milk, butter and other produce. I had learned to know them in my earlier services in the many churches in the area. In the large cities hundreds of thousands died of hunger during that winter.

But even here in the village, the bombardment became ever worse. Houses collapsed, burying those who were inside. On the night of the 26th of February we were forced to flee once more, this time to the northern province of Friesland. Through much effort, my wife succeeded in getting us into an enclosed truck, because I was ill. The following morning we arrived in Heereveen and could breathe more easily because it was so calm and quiet. No shooting could be heard. Here too I was known to many because of my earlier visits and so we finally found shelter in the village of Echten, by a dear Christian farmer. He shared everything he had with us so that we were never really hungry. Then too, the Lord arranged so that each Sunday morning we could have worship services in which 20 to 25 took part.

Soon I had regained my strength to the point where I could accept the invitation of a *dominie* to speak in his church one evening. The Lord's power was manifest in the meeting, so that one soul came to true faith. People wondered at this, since such happenings were unknown in this church. Their astonishment was heightened by a dramatic incident. After my closing prayer a person called out loudly, "I am lost; I am lost! O that I could speak with you!" We did visit together and she came to full peace, based on Romans 8:16.

We lived in Echten about six months. The war had ended and we received news from Arnheim that our home was restored so that we could move in and live there. So we traveled back home. But what a sight!! We were shocked to see our house again. All the doors and windows were shattered and the ceiling had holes so the sun could be seen through them. Only one room was somewhat watertight. Closets, buffets, desks, anything that could be locked had been broken into and were empty. All bedding was gone; just a few empty bedsteads remained, as did two tables and a few chairs. There was no running water or electricity. Seeing this near total destruction, robbed of all clothing and washables, made me sick again. During this time, our dear rescuers from Canada, C.F. Claassen and P. Dyck, visited us, but they were in a great hurry and couldn't stay long.

I was very sorry to discover that my beloved zither, with all its extras, had disappeared. My old zither, with its quality sound, that had been with me in all my travels through Europe. During many a twilight, its beautiful, soothing tone helped restore my look to God, and often healed my bleeding heart. For any reader who lacks appreciation of music this will seem over-sentimental. But that doesn't matter.

When I saw all the chaos, and feeling the loss of so many things, I wrote to a dear friend, D de V., who had often asked us to come to him, asking whether we could move to their place. He lived about 100 kilometers from Arnheim, near

Wilms. The dear friend took us, with a few items we still had, to his home. Here we lived for three years and three months. We finally found a suitable dwelling there in H.R.—E.G. near Hilversum. It was there that I wrote the greatest part of my memoirs. It was a little lonely there, but we lived in a nice forest. It was located about 45 kilometers from our friends D. de V., but they visited us often and the spiritual contact was most enjoyable.

CHAPTER 29

▼

SERVICE DURING THE POST-WAR YEARS

About a twenty minute walk from our home was a nice village with train service, by which we had access to the outside world. By this means our friends could still visit us. As I was invited to various places, people could get me and I could be of some spiritual help. This gave me the possibility to continue in my witnessing ministry.

One day Dominie Ter L., the local pastor, sent his car to me with the wish that I should come to see him immediately, if possible. He had had a heart attack and his doctor told him that he could die at any moment. We had known each other for several years and I had often spoken in his church. It surprised me that he should call for me in his critical moment, since he knew that I was not a church-man but a "freebooter," as they say here in Holland. I got right into the car and went there. His wife received me and took me to his bedside where he lay quite without pain. He was glad that I had come so quickly. I sat down by his bed and he told me what had happened and what the doctor had said. This made him think seriously, especially concerning his spiritual needs. Since he knew me well he had had the desire to have me come to him.

Then I asked him, "How can I be of service to you? I assume that as a *dominie* you have preached the Word of God for forty years or so."

"That is all well and good, but I can see that I am not in contact with God as you are. I must confess that after forty years of preaching I have drained myself dry, while this is not the case with you. This I can see clearly and yet you have been a clergyman for over forty years too."

"*Dominie*, it is difficult for me to explain, because I fear you will not understand me. The growth process or development in each of our lives has been so fundamentally different. You studied in the theological schools and learned a man-made theory of theology. Theology means 'knowledge of God,' which to me means a knowledge of Him, derived directly from Him. From the very beginning, after I had become a new creation by God's grace, I have obtained by prayer everything I have received as far as my spiritual life is concerned. And He taught me everything that was, and still is, necessary for me. This kind of school of theology has been very difficult for me throughout my lifetime. For you see, the difference in degree between the pupil, or if you will, the student and this all-highest teacher, God, is too great. How can such an insignificant, finite creature, man, understand the eternal God and Creator? That is completely impossible. When I run into this dilemma, I quickly go to my old textbook, the Bible, God's Word. There I find in John 16:13 what the Lord Jesus Himself said, that the Holy Spirit will guide us into all Truth.

"However, there were times in my life when I did not understand this Spirit of Truth. Then I searched in the Bible again. I read in the Epistle of James 1:5: 'If any of you lack wisdom, let him ask of God, that gives to all men liberally and without holding back.' This advice I have followed and still do, in all matters, especially the spiritual.

"For example, if I am asked to speak in a church, I realize that I do not know the church or the people. Quietly, in my heart, I say to my great Teacher, 'Lord, you know what is now before me. I stand before a congregation, which I cannot refuse. You also know how dry and empty I am. Therefore, I pray You, fill me with Your Spirit. Speak to this congregation Yourself, and bring honor to Your Name through the influence of Your Holy Spirit upon the audience, even though it all becomes audible through my mouth.'

"Trusting Him, I do not speak as a *dominie* educated here on earth, but as a witness for Jesus Christ, as I have experienced Him all my life on the mission field as well as here in Western Europe. My dear *dominie*, in this manner I have experienced the glory of the Lord wherever I have been asked to speak. This has been proven by the influence of the Holy Spirit upon my hearers, as well as upon me. For I experience Him personally every time; otherwise I am only a dry stick and without any worth. So I find that God hears the prayer I make before the meeting and He becomes ever more wonderful to me. I cannot understand that God should so reveal Himself to me. But my master Teacher becomes greater the longer I know Him, and I realize more and more how carnal I am. In spite of this, He hears my prayers and leads me in all aspects of life in a wonderful way."

Here the *dominie* sighed deeply and said, "Unfortunately, I am not acquainted with such matters; yet I would gladly learn it."

"My dear *dominie*, I would like to tell you of a very unusual experience which may shed some light on all this. As you know, my wife and I are still war evacuees from Arnheim. Because of this, we still get our ration cards from there, since our citizenship is registered there. I have a friend there who is authorized to get our cards for us and then mail them to us. The incident happened in 1947 when we lived with friend D. v de V. One day my wife said that she would like to visit for a week our married son who lives in The Hague. She did this and left our home on a Wednesday. The next day, Thursday, I received a special delivery letter from my friend in Arnheim in which he wrote: 'Dear friend Jantzen, I am writing about your ration cards. A new regulation has been made which requires of every cardholder to turn in the top coupons of the used cards in order to receive the next issue. If this is not done he will not receive any new cards for two months and he must be able to get along without cards or go hungry. Therefore, please send me immediately the top rows from your two ration cards.'

"After reading this I asked our landlady whether our cards were at home or whether my wife had taken them with her to use them when necessary. It turned out that she had taken them with her. This worried me greatly. Our dear landlord or host went to his office to telephone our son Hermannn, to tell Mother to bring the cards home immediately. But he came back saying he could not get Hermannn on the telephone. It was now evening and this made me even more concerned, so that I couldn't even sleep. After all, if I didn't get those coupons in the mail the next morning at ten o'clock, we would have no cards for two months and we knew what that meant.

"In this seemingly hopeless situation, I turned to the Lord, as I so often have done, and said, 'Lord Jesus, You say in John 14:16 that You are the Way and Truth, and in verses 13 and 14 You say, 'What you shall ask in my name, that I will do.' You say this twice without qualification. So I pray You now, in Your Name, send my wife here with the ration cards tomorrow morning before ten o'clock, because You know, Lord, that we cannot live without these cards.'

"I then went to sleep. Suddenly some one punched me in the side and said, 'Are you still sleeping?' I opened my sleepy eyes and saw my wife standing there before me. I sat up and asked, 'Why have you come home already?' She answered that she really didn't know herself why she had come. The evening before she had suddenly become very restless and again and again something told her, 'Tomorrow morning you must take the first train home.' Therefore she had come home, not really knowing the reason for it.

"I looked at my alarm clock and it was 9:30. I got up and hurriedly dressed, while telling my wife the reason for her coming home. Then I got the papers ready and at ten o'clock, when the mailman came he took them with him. That is living with God, and I must witness to it because I experienced it myself."

In great surprise the *dominie* called out, "That is really great. My wife and her sister, who are in the next room, must hear this too. Please call them in." Then I had to repeat the whole story, and both women exclaimed, "That is really astounding!"

I then replied, "All this happened in the presence of my friend Dirk and his wife Nels, as well as my wife. They often come here, so you can verify the story with them." After prayer with them, they thanked me for the visit and the testimony and I was brought home in their car.

In 1947 the first secretary of the one-time Russian relief committee, Mr. St., paid me a visit. He is a *Gereformeerde*, a dear man of very strict faith. He was just ready to take a trip, so he came to me and said, "Dear Vader Jantzen, I have a very serious question to ask you. We fanatical *Gereformeerde* have come today to a very serious problem for us patriotic people. What must be the attitude for us

Christians toward those politically guilty, who really were traitors, who now after several years of imprisonment are being released? There are many thousands of them."

I gave him my answer: "My dear G., that is really quite simple. We must first determine who and what a Christian is. A Christian is one who celebrates two birthdays every year. That is, one who is truly born again, as the Gospel of John requires. The importance of the new birth is emphasized by the 'Verily, verily' of the Lord Jesus. When a person has become a child of God in this manner, then he has eternal life and has a kinship with God. Through the new birth one receives the Father's nature and spirit which is love, for God is love.

"This attitude or disposition was demonstrated by Jesus Christ as he lived in Palestine. He loved to associate with the politically burdened and with collabora- tors, these publicans who were in the service of Rome. They, too, were consid- ered traitors. Of course the Lord Jesus was not a politician. He was concerned only for the souls of the publicans and sinners. The *dominies* of that day, the theologians and the scribes, the self-satisfied pastors, did not understand this, but rather brought Him, who did only good, to the cross of Calvary; and that because of jealousy. They mocked and blasphemed Him even as He hung on the cross in indescribable agony and suffering. And what did He say? 'Father, forgive them, for they know not what they are doing.' That is the nature of God, which is above man's nature. This is the nature of Jesus Christ. His mind, of which we read in Philippians: 'Let this mind be in you, which was also in Christ Jesus.' One who has the 'mind of Christ' knows what His attitude toward the politically bur- dened must be, and how to meet them, my dear E."

In deep thought, my guest walked back and forth in the room. Finally he stood before me and said, "If I were to send my car to you in a week or so, would you be ready to come with me and address the *Gereformeerden* on this theme for several evenings? I would arrange it so that you would have a different audience each evening. It seems to me that this is an important and a serious subject."

This request I agreed to fill and so, on a day agreed upon, he came to pick me up. I spoke for four evenings to the *Gereformeerden* (Christian Reformed) and the four following evenings to the *Herformeerden* (Reformed). But that wasn't enough, so I was asked to speak four evenings to the Lutherans. By pre-arrange- ment Mr. St. began each session with the question: "How must a Christian accept the politically burdened who are now being released from prison?" After my presentation, the essential contents of which are given above, there followed comments and debates by those present, so that some meetings lasted until 11:00. We started all meetings at 8:00. The debate after the first meeting was introduced by a high officer, with the following comments:

"Menheer Jantzen, judging by your answer, you are an anti-militarist, maybe even a Mennonite. However, I am also a Christian, and, as such, subjected to the higher power as admonished in Romans 13:1. As a Dutch patriot I fought at Grebbe Hill against the *Moffen* (derogatory for Germans) until the bitter end. With King David, a man after the heart of God, but who killed many people, I say 'I hate those, Lord, who hate You and it grieves me that they oppose You. I hate them in righteous earnest; they have become my enemies.' And that is my stand toward the traitors and criminals."

My answer: "Then you are not a Christian. Because Christ, the only begotten of the Father, who lived many centuries after David, brought a new Gospel from the Father, and forbade His disciples to take the sword. He said to one of them: 'Put up your sword in its place, for they that take the sword, will perish by the sword.' He also said in Matthew 5:44: 'Love your enemies, bless them that curse you, do good to them that hurt you, and pray for them who shall despitefully use you and persecute you, that you may be children of your Father who is in heaven.'"

The officer answered, "How can one understand then that a Gideon, a Saul, a David and others waged so many wars after the will of God, and now it should be different?"

"Israel was and is the nation of God and as such it received the order from God to carry out His sovereign will and destroy the heathen nations in the land of Canaan, according to His plan. But in the Sermon on the Mount the Son of God said, 'You have heard that it was said of them of old, Thou shalt love thy neighbor and hate thy enemy. But I say unto you, Love your enemy, etc ...' By that it is evident that the people of the Old Testament had a different commandment than the people of the New. Here it said, 'Put up your sword' and instead 'love your enemies.'"

The officer then said that he would take the viewpoint of David, as does their Christian government. To this I answered, "To call oneself Christian does not mean that one is a child of God, and if you place yourself on the side of David, that does not make you a Jew, because you have no Jewish blood in you. But if you wish to be a Christian and base it on the Old Testament, then for you, Christ died in vain, and your position with respect to the future is very dark." With this, our first evening ended. Within me I was very sad. I felt sorry for this man and the great darkness in this country.

The following eleven evenings went in a similar way. Each evening 30 or 35 upper class citizens were present and the debates followed much the same form, only the groups were different. Without question there were many pious and honest souls among them. But they were so steeped in the old traditions, and church dogmas and forms, that it was seldom that anyone could read the Bible without prejudice or bias. One *dominie*, Professor and Doctor of Theology, Dr. G., in A, said at one time, "Holland is a land of heresy, because everyone who has a different belief in theological questions than I do is a heretic. We should be very grateful that we have a government of free-thinkers, that calls itself Christian, that protects us from the burning stake, and that allows all faiths and religions. In our small country of ten million people we have more than a hundred different ways to heaven. One from the outside stands there and asks: 'Which of these many is the one that must be chosen in order to get to heaven, since everyone claims that his way is the right one?' But we do have in the country many who do not belong to any denomination, with strong spiritual evangelists. The Salvation Army is among these. And so, there are still some who are converted. But, so far as I know these people never go to church."

All of these denominations are based upon and organized under the name of Jesus Christ. All use the Bible as their norm and yet do not understand one another. Each one of these take a certain part of the Truth and make a sort of hobby-horse out of it, with which they ride through the land, so to speak, and judge all the others. And so each one rides forth against all the others, and yet each one finds Biblical grounds for doing so.

The beginning of this problem was already experienced by the Apostle Paul at Corinth. In I Corinthians 3:3–4 he calls it the carnal man's way or, as Luther calls it, "according to the flesh." People do not realize that the overemphasis of a part of the Truth is a poison fatal to the spirit. And the crown of it all is the self-satisfaction brought about by the training in the Christian-ethic, that one enjoys and that is so important for the family and the state. But this is not the eternal life that Christ speaks of to Nicodemus. Should one speak of an assurance of this eternal life, then he is accused of human conceit or boasting. Every church has its own Synod, which has its theological conferences in which the dogmas are discussed and determined and which do not permit any criticism or disagreement. These dogmas or doctrines then stand even above the Bible. Although these councils are opened with prayer, in which the guidance of the Spirit is invited, as I am told, I do not know just how to evaluate the whole process. Consider: More than one hundred denominations, with an equal number of Synods, all of which are conducted and led in "the name of Jesus Christ"—and still find no agreement or understanding among themselves, but rather a spirit of competition?

This has led me to the conviction that seemingly the Holy Spirit has been "placed in bondage," so to speak, by all these teachings and dogmas. As a result, He cannot lead because human interpretation and self-righteousness do not allow Him to express Himself. Therefore, the terrible divisiveness in Christendom! The God of love, revealed through his dear Son Jesus Christ, who died on the cross to make all one, has not been understood. If He were, such conditions could not exist.

I have now lived in this hospitable Holland for twenty years and have learned to love the land and its people. I have been invited to and participated in many theological and other religious conferences. In church circles I have been, and still am, a misunderstood stranger, but in the Free Church circles I feel at home. Here I am understood. Here the love of God stands at the apex, because everyone has experienced His creative power in his own heart. Here one doesn't find the veneer of self-satisfaction, since all children of God are conscious that they are all sinners saved by God's grace. Even where differences of opinion are found, they bear each other in love and get along with one another.

Often in the churches the real condition is not recognizable. The *dominie*, bound by the ordinances and rules of his Synod, takes his well organized written sermon and steps behind the pulpit. He delivers his sermon, which includes many foreign expressions, which his audience doesn't understand at all. In addition to this, he uses pathos and gestures to enliven his sermon. Much good singing, with organ accompaniment, is part of the service. Then the church members return to their homes without knowing how to make use of what they heard.

Finally there is the satisfaction of having the *dominie* address one as brother or sister and by this one can assume that this makes one a Christian. After all, the *dominie* is a learned man and he studied for this; his word counts.

During the last five years, since I fled from Arnheim and live in the country, I have often gone to church on Sunday with people of the community. On the way home then I asked them what they had personally received for their souls during the service. Then I received the oft-repeated, similar answer, "Oh, Meneer Jantzen, that I cannot tell you, because the *dominie* speaks with such difficult words, which we laymen cannot understand. We go to church every Sunday because that is proper and that is what our parents taught us to do. When we miss a Sunday, the week is not as complete as it should be. We are, after all, Christians and as such we must go to church."

I would then speak to them in simple words and emphasize the seriousness of life. From that I turned to the subject of the power of the Word of God through the Spirit to make us into new creatures. They loved to hear all this, but for the most part they could not seem to comprehend it all. The Dutch country folk— farmers—are an honorable, true-hearted people and very religious. In every home that we visited, there is a Bible. After the meal the father takes the Bible and reads a portion out loud. Then they fold their hands in silent prayer, after which each goes to his work. In some families the father prays out loud before and after the meal. The whole life style among the farmers tells me that our Mennonites descended from the people of this land.

The farmer folk are not involved in the church and denominational squabbles of the theologians, and the *dominies* are happy when the churches are filled on Sunday. I often remarked, "Yes, it is much better here than in Russia, where the churches are destroyed and worship is forbidden." In this country God is still considered an authority by most of the citizens. There are many Christian schools and theological institutes where the *dominies* are educated. They learn to know the Bible well and learn to speak well. In these fields most of the *dominies* are very successful. Yet I would wish that they would learn the art of witnessing of eternal life, as the Lord Jesus told Nicodemus. That, of course, is not learned in theological universities, but only from God Himself and His Holy Spirit.

It was before the war that an assistant pastor, who lived near us in Arnheim, invited me to visit him. A young theology student had come to him and he didn't quite know how to deal with him. I went to see him and found two well-dressed gentlemen there, dressed in the customary garb of the clergy. It soon became evident what it was about which they sought my advice. Both the men were about 30 years of age and had studied theology for several years. However they had not received an appointment. I could tell by the discussion that they were rather bitter and wished to know my opinion in the matter. I said, "Honored Sirs, before I can answer your question, I would like to ask one. Did you go to school because the Lord called you? Did the Holy Spirit lead you there because you are children of God?"

They didn't answer immediately, and both looked at me in surprise and asked what I meant. "We read in the Gospel of John how Nicodemus came to Jesus one night and how the Lord Jesus said to him, 'Except a man be born again, he cannot see the kingdom of God,' nor get into it. To the Lord Jesus this was so serious and important that he stressed it with the double, 'Verily, Verily.' So I ask you: Have you experienced this new birth through the Holy Spirit? If so, then He will be able to use you as His witnesses, for the Lord said to His disciples as He parted from them, 'You shall be my witnesses.' What the Lord Jesus thought of the *dominie* of His day, He made very clear to Nicodemus."

In response they asked me, in a note of great surprise, where I came from, since I belong to no church organization. It seemed obvious to them that I must belong to the clergy, though I am no *dominie*. So I explained to them in brief outline where I was born and where I lived and how I had personally communed with God. Then I continued:

"So God had mercy upon me for the sake of Jesus Christ and through the Holy Spirit He made me His child. By this I have become a witness to others to help them to the same experience. This change in me has cost me my complete ego. In other words, has cost myself. Because the Holy Spirit decides and leads me within, He also gives the power to do His will. But because I still am in this mortal, sinful flesh, I often miss the voice of the Spirit or do not hear Him clearly. This causes me to stumble and fall. Since to the Holy Spirit even the minutest sin is a foreign body within me, it must be destroyed immediately. This is done by confessing it to God and also to others, if I have wronged them. My heavenly Father forgives me for Christ's sake, who is my intermediary. Then my heart is filled anew with peace and joy. This, my dear sirs, is the transformation which the Lord calls for Nicodemus the new birth, which makes all things new

and leaves no room for sin. By this the love of God is poured into our hearts—
the love to God and to His Son Jesus Christ, our advocate.

"As far as I personally am concerned, I am a daily student in this school of theology and learn to experience that the flesh is incorrigible, but my whole effort
and desire is to please Him, my dear and precious Savior, and not to grieve Him.
For, if that happens, then the peace is gone and I sit there 'godless' in the dark
and that is terrible. In the course of my life I have learned to know myself better
and have seen how ungodly and powerless I am. This has caused me many bitter
experiences. So I try to practice what the Lord Jesus teaches us to do: 'pray without ceasing.'

"Then, too, I speak in my own way in the Spirit of God. Because as soon as I
quit reading, writing, or speaking to someone, and especially if I stop looking and
speaking toward heaven, then hell begins to speak from below. In that case I go
from one fear to another, so I strive to remain in contact with God. This does not
happen by our good works or pious living to earn us a place in heaven; no, but
only through our Savior Jesus Christ, who purchased me with His precious
blood. I do not want to grieve Him. That is why I strive to be near him who
through the years I have experienced in such wonderful ways. To tell you about
all this would take a long time. Because I have experienced him, I am a witness
for Him.

"Therefore, I should like to give you the following advice, my dear friends. Be
sure you really experience John 1:12–13 in your hearts. This will give you two
birthdays per year, the first your natural one when your mother gave you birth,
and the second when the Holy Spirit made you into a new creature. He will bear
witness to your spirit that you are the sons of God, Romans 8:16. Then to the
extent that you stay near the Lord Jesus, you will experience him daily, as a witness to yourself as well as to others.

"As far as your appointment as *dominie* is concerned, that you simply leave
with the Lord. He knows best where He can use you. The Lord, through His
Holy Spirit, always does things well, even though in our human limitations we
do not always understand Him. The more real and intimate our relations with
God are, the more we learn to understand that He is Light. In His Light we
become even smaller and He ever greater and more glorious, and He always gives
us light on our way. The abundance of His grace will be so great that we cannot

find words to thank Him. These have been my experiences and continue even to the present time."

Here I ended my discussion. Both my listeners had listened patiently, but the whole matter was strange to them. They rose and said, "We do not know or understand such a thing." We parted and, unfortunately, I have never heard from them again.

IN CONCLUSION

My dear reader, in all the years I lived in Western Europe, I attended many conferences and other meetings. Here I learned to know many high-ranking and highly regarded theologians, which finally led me to the discovery that people are not satisfied with the Lord Jesus Himself or His teachings. They turn to men like Luther, Calvin and others to discover their ideas. But they do not know the Spirit of Truth of whom the Lord Jesus speaks in John 16:13. It is true that the theologians and dominies often speak about the Holy Spirit, but they do not know Him!

When I consider the many divisions and groups, I can only conclude that just a few in this country read the Bible without preconceived ideas. I am not sure; am I understood? In view of these conditions, I suffer greatly, for I have learned to love these people.

That is not all that pains me. When I think of the East, of my children, grandchildren and many relatives, all of whom may have been killed; of the nations that live under the chaotic conditions of Bolshevism; when I consider the great political schisms among the nations, for which no one seems to have the answer, my heart all but breaks and my soul cries silently day and night in the words of the poet:

1. "Liebster Herr Jesu, wo bleibst du so lange?
   Komm doch, mir wird's hier of Erden so bange
   Komm doch, und wenn es Dir also gefällt,
   Nimm mich von dieser angstvollen Welt."

I assume that many Christians feel as I do in the light of these serious times. For 84 years now I have lived on this earth and weathered many a storm, so that at times

I didn't know which way to turn. But I agree with what the poet so aptly expressed concerning the final goal. He must have had experiences similar to mine.

2. "Durch manche Laenderstrecke trug ich den Wanderstab;
   Von mancher Felsenecke schaut ich ins Tal hinab;
   Doch über alle Berge, die ich auf Erden sah,
   Geht mir ein stiller Huegel—, der Huegel Golgatha!

3. Er ragt nicht in die Wolken mit eisgekroenter Stirn;
   Er hebt nicht in die Luefte die sonn'ge Alpenfirn;
   Doch so der Erd' entnommen und so dem Himmel nah',
   Bin ich noch nie gekommen, wie dort auf Golgotha!

4. Dort, O mein Erdenpilger, dort halte suesse Rest;
   Dort wirf dem Suendentilger zu Fuessen deine Last;
   Dann geh und ruehme selig, wie wohl dir dort geschah:
   Der Weg zum Paradiese geht ueber Golgatha!"

Translation:

1. "Dearest Lord Jesus, your coming so long is delayed!
   Do come! In this wicked world I am so afraid.
   Do come, and if it pleases you well,
   Take me from it, with you to dwell!

2. I've traveled through many a country, pilgrim staff in hand!
   From rocky crags, I've looked down on many a lovely land!
   But far above all the mountains that on this earth I see,
   My heart is touched by only one, the hill of Calvary!

3. It doesn't tower in the clouds, with ice-crowned brow!
   Nor lift sky-ward sunny Alps, capped with snow,
   But so out-of-this-world, and so near to heaven,
   As there on Calvary I have never ever been!

4. There, O my Pilgrim, halt for rest so sweet!
   There cast your sin-burden at the Redeemer's feet;
   Then saved and rejoicing, tell others so they too will see:
   The way to Heaven goes over the hill of Calvary!"

Thus I reach the termination of my pilgrimage. The long, often stormy journey has so bruised my body and made it so tired. As the last companions, many weaknesses and signs of old age set in. The feet are swollen and do not walk as they did; the hearing is lessened; the eyes are not as clear; the hands tend to shake or tremble. All this tells me that my time on earth will soon be run out. The older I get the more I feel like a stranger on earth, so that I have a great desire to go Home. Soon the Lord, my Savior, will come and take me home, into the Father's House, where no earthly sorrow can make the heart heavy. Neither will there be any sin there. But as long as I am here, my witness and the pastoral duties continue. While I still had my zither I loved to sing the "Song of Home" by Karl Gerok:

*

1. Ich móchte heim, mich zieht's dem Vaterhause,
   Dem Vater-herzen Gottes zu;
   Fort aus der Welt verworrenem Gebrauze
   Zur stillen, sanften tiefen Ruh'.
   Mit tauzend Wünschen bin ich ausgegangen,
   Heim kehr' ich mit bescheidenem Verlangen,
   Noch hegt mein Herz nur einer Hoffnung Keim:
   Ich móchte heim, Ich móchte heim!

2. Ich móchte heim, Ich sah in sel'gen Tráumen
   Ein bess'res, schón'res Vaterland,
   Dort ist mein Theil in ewig lichten Ráumen,
   Hier hab' ich keinen festen Stand:
   Der Lenz ist hin, die Schwalbe schwingt die Flügel
   Der Heimat zu, weit über Thal und Hügel,
   Sie halt kein Jágergarn, kein Vogel-leim:
   Ich moechte heim, ich moechte heim!

3. Ich móchte heim, das Schifflein sucht den Hafen,
   Das Báchlein láuft in's weite Merr;
   Das Kindlein legt im Mutterarm sich schlafen,
   Und ich, ich will jetz auch nicht mehr;
   Manch Lied hab' ich in Freud' und Leid gesungen,
   Wie ein Geschwátz ist Lust und Leid verklungen,
   Im Herzen bleibt mir noch der letzte Reim:
   Ich móchte heim, ich móchte heim.

*   Words by Karl Gerok   Music by Saur

"This world is not our home; we are looking forward to our city in heaven, which is yet to come."   Hebrews 13:14. NLT

*

Translation:

1. I long for Home! My Father's Home's up yonder!
   His loving heart will welcome me,
   Out of this weary win-warped world around me,
   Into His rest eternally.
   A thousand wishes once beguiled, enthralled me,
   Now coming Home, only one thing I long for—
   For in my heart one hope alone is growing:
   I long for Home, I long for Home!

2. I long for Home! I saw while I was dreaming,
   A better, fairer Father-land.
   There is my Home, my everlasting dwelling,
   And this old world' my home no more.
   Summer is o'er, the swallows all are flying,
   O'er hill and vale, to a South land far away!
   No fowler's snare, nor hunter's glue can keep them!
   I'm going Home, I'm going Home.

3. I long for Home! Little boat seeks safe harbor!
   Brooklet runs into wide, wide sea!
   Baby sleeps in Mother's arms securely!
   And I, I can't go on down here!
   Songs I have sung in joys and in sorrows—
   As empty babbling, they all fade away!
   In my heart, only one song is singing:
   I'm going Home, I'm going Home!

* From *Gesangbuch mit Notein* (Song Book with Notes, p. 559) 6th edition
   Mennonite Book Concern, Berne, Indiana, 1901
   Copywright 1890, Welty & Sprunger, Berne, Indiana

My dear reader, these are some of the reminiscences from my life. At first it was without God, which pains me to this day. Although He has forgiven all my erring ways, I can never forget my self-seeking ways. I have allowed you to take part with me in my life with God, how I experienced Him, how He wonderfully carried me along; how He guided me and often saved my life. For all this, I have realized that I can never thank Him enough. How inadequate are man's words of thanks as compared with His evidence of mercy! But because His mercy is much greater than all my sins and waywardness, and therefore I have an especially great Lord and Savior, I bring Him thanks and worship with a full heart, often silently. He sees and knows my heart. The perfect worship will only come from above, with eternal, holy lips, for which I am happy.

ADDENDUM

The above Memoirs or Autobiography were completed by Mr. Jantzen in the year 1950 or soon after, as indicated by him on page 146 of the translation. He continued with his lectures and personal witnessing as his strength allowed for another eight years or so. He died quietly in his rural home near Hilversum, The Netherlands, on November 13, 1959, and was buried there. He is survived by his second wife, now 90 years old, with whom he lived for 28 years.

As he reported in his Memoirs, he heard little or nothing about his children after leaving them in 1923, except for his eldest son, who was killed in prison. According to his obituary in the *Mennonitische Rundschau*, his other three sons were sent to Siberia.

In closing, a quote (in translation) from the obituary in the *Rundschau* of June 1, 1960, page 4:

> "And now he lies buried in Hilversum. A weary pilgrim has gone
> to his eternal rest with Jesus. On earth he was a man without a
> country, but his heart was filled with the warm desire and great
> homesickness for his heavenly fatherland."

April 1975

978-0-595-47658-9
0-595-47658-9

Printed in the United States
154525LV00003B/8/P

9 780595 476589